The Age of Foolishness:

A Doubter's Guide to Constitutionalism in a Modern Democracy

James Allan

The Age of Foolishness:

A Doubter's Guide to Constitutionalism in a Modern Democracy

James Allan

Academica Press
Washington~London

Library of Congress Cataloging-in-Publication Data

Names: Allan, James (author)
Title: The age of foolishness : a doubter's guide to constitutionalism in a modern democracy | Allan, James.
Description: Washington : Academica Press, 2022. | Includes references.
Identifiers: LCCN 2022939788 | ISBN 9781680537871 (hardcover) | 9781680537888 (paperback) | 9781680537895 (e-book)

Contents

Preface

As a conservative with a good many libertarian instincts, I have spent almost all of my working life in law schools around the common law world. (I practised law briefly in Toronto and London.) Today's law schools are all orthodox left institutions. The median law school academic in all of them (and this is true of virtually all today's law schools in the US, Canada, Britain, Australia and New Zealand, and true too of the wider universities as well) is noticeably to the left politically of the country's median voter. In some law schools that gap looks more like a chasm. I see myself as a moderate right-of-center voter who puts a high value on free speech, individual enterprise, small-not-big government, strong national defense, and democratic decision-making; who is firmly opposed to affirmative action or positive discrimination type programs by universities and employers; who detests cancel culture; and who thinks these five anglosphere countries are amongst the very best places on earth for anyone, ever, to have lived. That makes me patriotic. And all these views rest on what might be described as Hobbesian and Humean foundations, about human nature, about the sort of world we live in, about how to understand moral evaluations and the status of the claims they make, about the *prima facie* benefits of traditional structures and institutions, and so on. Accordingly, and as Boswell reports Johnson as saying of Hume, I am a Tory by Chance. That said, and despite my own self-perception as a moderate right-of-center voter, more than a few of the professoriate in these orthodox left academies consider those sorts of views of mine to fall a good way to the right on the political spectrum. Seriously. On occasion, I have even been described by those within legal academia as sitting at the hard or far right end of the political spectrum. Seriously. They think that says something about me. I think it says something about them, and about today's law schools and universities.

I do not know if it is those underlying views and attitudes of mine, or something else, but I am also an outlier when it comes to my views about constitutions, constitutional law, the proper role of judges and of how they should approach the task of interpretation of legal texts, the value of democratic decision-making, the worth of bills of rights, and more. My views are consistently opposed to today's legal orthodoxy, to the preponderant views and positions of those not just in legal academia but also of those in the wider lawyerly caste. As I have written recently in law review articles and in chapters in books in ways that touch on all those constitutional-related topics, it occurred to me that I might be able to take some of those pieces, revise them, add new parts, blend them all together into a coherent whole, and end up with a book. It would amount to a doubter's guide to constitutionalism (and its related aspects) in today's common law democratic world. So that is what I have done. Given the unorthodox' nature of my views – some in the lawyerly caste might well go so far as to describe them as Beyond the Pale – I thought this book's title might benefit from a phrase from Dickens, from the first paragraph of one of his great works.

Now as I am re-using bits and pieces of my past writings and blending them together with new bits into some sort of new whole, let me here acknowledge and thank the publishers of where these earlier pieces first appeared. My chapter in *The Political Approach to Human Rights* was published by Routledge; my chapter in *The Challenge of Originalism: Theories of Constitutional Interpretation* was published by Cambridge University Press; and my chapter in *The Legal Protection of Human Rights: Sceptical Essays* was published by Oxford University Press. Then there were twelve of my earlier law review articles of which I made use: 'Not in for a Pound – In for a Penny?' and 'Meagher's Mischaracterisation of Majoritarianism' appeared in the *King's Law Journal*; 'Why Politics Matters' in *Jurisprudence*; 'Against Written Constitutionalism' in the *Otago Law Review*; 'Judit Varga, Hungary and the Rule of Law' in the *Hungarian Review*; 'Informal Constitutionalism and the Role of Politics' in *E Publica Direito E Politica*; 'A Tribute to Australia's Killer of "Living Constitutionalism"' in *Public Law Review*; 'A Churchillian and Benthamite Defence of Democracy' in the *San Diego Law Review*; 'The

Special Kay Defence of Non-Originalist Judges' in the *University of Connecticut Law Review*; and 'In Honor of a Simple-Minded Originalist' in *Constitutional Commentary*. Thank you, again, to all those publications.

Lastly, thanks are due to my wife of more than three and half decades. She has put up with living with a professional heretic, iconoclast, apostate, skeptic, call it what you will. I was lucky. I married up.

I dedicate this book to my two kids, Cameron and Bronwyn. Great kids. One very lucky dad.

James Allan,
November 2021.

Introduction

This short book doubts much of the orthodoxy as regards constitutionalism in a modern democracy. Today's emerged consensus amongst the lawyerly caste in, say, the United States, Britain, Canada or Australia, as well as in many non-common law democracies, will be the target of my skepticism and doubt. At the risk of painting too broad a picture, there is amongst that caste too little love of democracy. Hand in hand with that disdain there also travels too great love for unelected judges adopting approaches to interpreting constitutions (and other laws) that leave those same judges effectively unconstrained. On this approach to interpretation the judges are not locked in by the intentions of those who were understood to have the legitimate authority to make the law in the first place, to create and craft the constitution. Indeed, it is hard to see anything that locks them in and binds the choices they can make, nothing external to the internal workings of their own brains – call that product their druthers, their policy preferences, their moral beliefs, their desire to achieve rights-based outcomes, their deep-seated commitment to discovering and implementing Kantian deontological duties, whatever. The point is that these sort of judges treat the constitution as 'living' and thereby become the Dr. Frankensteins who themselves create a newly-minted constitutional content for that jurisdiction. They transmogrify the constitutional text into substantive outcomes that look remarkably similar to what these judges would have produced were they legislators (with scope to choose their preferred policy) rather than judges (in theory supposed to be in search of the preferred policy of the law-maker). And these outcomes of interpreting in this 'living' constitution way are ones that sit above mere statutes produced by the legislature. They are inoculated against democratic gainsaying or over-riding by the voter because constitutional law is higher law. Yet the product of this new orthodoxy, its substantive constitutional content, is something that no present-day voter – or past-day constitution maker – has had any input into. Well, no input other than electing people who choose those judges. Welcoming that sort of approach to constitutional interpretation, with its seeming lack of mind-independent constraints on the point-of-application interpreter, is part of the new orthodoxy. It is something overwhelmingly taught in the law schools and taught in highly favourable terms. Likewise, it is something widely accepted in the large law firms and amongst much of the judiciary.

I am skeptical of this modern constitutional settlement or orthodoxy, both of its merits and its desirability. I am also skeptical of the generally unarticulated foundations on which this new orthodoxy sits, meaning of the view it implicitly (or occasionally explicitly) takes as regards the grounding of human rights. This book will give the reader the reasons for my various doubts. It will lay out why I am skeptical. In doing so I will not focus on any particular jurisdiction, though throughout it will be clear that I am thinking about the developed common law world. I think some of my doubts and skepticism apply as well to the non-common law world but will leave that for others to decide. Ultimately, then, my goal is to do as the title says and provide a doubter's guide to constitutionalism in a modern democracy.

My plan is to build from the bottom up. My doubter's guide will start in the foundations and consider human rights thinking and notions such as the rule of law. In any modern day democracy human rights thinking and concerns affect the whole panoply of law-making and law-interpreting that follows in its wake. Indeed the very notion of constitutionalism today carries with it, explicitly or implicitly, some sort of commitment to human rights. To a lesser extent one might assert something broadly similar as regards the commitment to the rule of law. So Part I of this book will set the stage. It will take a look at the main competing efforts to ground this notion of human rights and to give it a solid footing. Again, though, I will make plain that I have some pretty big doubts about how easy it is to give a solid foundation to human rights concepts and thinking. I will then look at the notion of the rule of law. Here too I will note my doubts and skepticism as far as the emerging orthodox view goes.

Then in Part II my doubter's guide will turn to democracy. Obviously in today's developed democratic world near on everyone will profess a commitment to 'democracy.' It is a potent rhetorical tool, placing yourself on the side of democracy. Still, it is not at all settled what is meant by the term, nor how morally fat or thin its proper remit. The emerging orthodoxy on this matter is again something about which I have serious doubts. The same goes for how the emerging orthodoxy seeks to balance liberal concerns against democratic ones. Or judges' last word power against legislators.' Or law against politics. In the course of raising my doubts I will look at all of these. And I will provide what I think is the best defense of democracy against the orthodox constitutional position of much of the lawyerly caste.

Part III of this short book then turns to constitutionalism itself. My doubts here will relate to various aspects of constitutional orthodoxy – the relative merits of written versus unwritten constitutionalism; of majoritarianism; of how best to understand this concept of constitutionalism; of the role of politics within it. Overwhelmingly I will be in the outsider's camp in these debates. So here again I will be expressing doubts.

In Part IV I will move from the big picture stuff of constitutionalism writ large down to the day-to-day world of constitutional interpretation. This is what really matters in jurisdictions such as my native Canada and in the United States and in the Australia where I have lived and worked the past decade and a half. How ought judges to interpret the words in the constitution? Why? Here I will side with the originalists, and indeed with the smaller of the two main camps of originalism, and set out my doubts as regards the more orthodox 'living constitution' subscribers. With written constitutionalism one is always locked in. That is its point. The choice, then, is between being locked in by constitution makers (however long ago they were doing that making) or by those doing the unconstrained interpreting today. The average voter will inevitably be locked in by one of those two groups. Today's constitutional orthodoxy amounts to a preference for being locked in by the beliefs, sentiments, judgements, druthers, and policy preferences of the lawyerly caste from which is taken the small handful of top judges in the country. Either they are locked in, and so are the rest of us. Or they are not locked in, but the rest of us are by these judges' views. Pick your poison. I pick the rather unfashionable choice of the views of those way back when who were given or acquired the legitimate authority to frame and ratify the constitution in play. If you don't like it, amend it.

And that will be that. By the end of that four part discussion – my promise to readers is to shun all uses of 'journey' and 'conversation' and 'discourse' and the like – the extent of my doubts about much of the orthodoxy as regards constitutionalism in a modern democracy will be clear. At least that is my goal in this book.

Part I

Setting the Stage

Chapter One

Doubts About Human Rights

In this initial Part of the book I will be voicing some doubts about some of the underpinnings of constitutional law thinking. If, since the end of World War II, we in the West might be said to be living through a time not inaptly described as 'the rebirth of natural law thinking era' or 'the dominance of its progeny human rights thinking era,' then any doubter's guide should start there, with those core foundations. Accordingly, I start with doubts about some of the usually offered foundations or underpinnings for human rights claims. There will be other doubts tied to both the political and the moral conceptions of human rights. Then there will be doubts about the ease with which any type of human rights dominated worldview and program for future action can co-exist with a worldview that puts democracy front and centre. Some of my doubts will be aimed at matters peripheral to the broader human rights worldview, some at core level strands. Some of the skepticism will be mild, some rather strong. I will here offer no over-arching theories, just some arguments to the effect that significant portions of what is claimed on behalf of the human rights worldview stand up rather poorly to scrutiny and that such a worldview has great difficulty co-existing with any vigorous understanding of democracy, and indeed in grounding various aspects of constitutional law orthodoxy and modern day interpretive practice.

1. Doubts about Foundations

When one claims that North Koreans have a right to free speech or that the homeless in New York City have a right to housing or that Shia Muslims or Christians or Bahai in Saudi Arabia have a right to freedom of conscience and religion what sort of claim is being made? What is the foundation or basis for these sort of human rights claims?

Most lawyers can tell you that rights are entitlements, or protections, or guarantees of a sort. Some will go on to note that analytically-speaking a right amounts to an 'others must' claim.[1] If I have a right to free speech then others must let me speak. Similarly, if you have a right to housing then someone or some agency must provide you with housing. Those rights, those 'others must' claims, are linked—they are correlated—to duties. A duty, then, is an 'I must' claim. My duty to care for my children is an 'I must' claim. So their right ('others must') is my duty ('I must').

One could go further with this analytical understanding of rights. One could continue by noting that rights and duties are themselves tied together by the concept of rules. Any right you care to mention I can transliterate into the form of a rule: 'She has the right to free speech' becomes 'There is a rule that allows her to speak her mind in the following circumstances.' Of course, the language of rules does not trigger the same frisson of self-entitled excitement as does the language of rights. But analytically-speaking, they are the same: A right is a rule.

Yet that sort of analytical understanding of rights only takes us so far. Yes, it provides insight into the sort of claim that is being advanced, and how it relates to other demands. But such Hohfeldian-type analyses of rights take us no closer to answering a more fundamental question about the source or origin of these rights. From where do these and other rights claims originate? What is the basis or source of these claims, these assertions of such things as a free speech right or a housing right?

Any answer will start by noting that once you see that a right can be transliterated into a rule, you can ask those questions I have just asked in blunter terms: Where does the rule come from that lays down what you are claiming? You can then notice, as well, that rights – broadly speaking – are of two sorts. First off, there are rights (or rules) where we all can see the basis of the claim. These are legal rights (or rules). They might be spelt

---

[1] See Wesley Newcomb Hohfeld, *Fundamental Legal Conceptions as Applied in Judicial Reasoning* (Yale University Press, 1919) for the best known analytical conception of rights.

out in a statute, emerge from a line of cases, be fleshed out of some amorphous constitutional provision by top judges using a best-fit Dworkinian Justice Hercules interpretive approach,[2] or maybe even traced back to custom. Yet whether you like the substance of these legal rights, or not, their source will be overwhelmingly patent and clear. You can say why these legal rights, these legal rules, exist, and none but a few anarchists will disagree that they do in fact exist.[3]

However, in other circumstances it is plain that we are not talking about legal rights, but instead about non-legal or moral rights. This is the second sort of rights claim that can be advanced. Indeed the examples above with which I began this Part, with my mooted rights to free speech in North Korea, to housing in New York City, and to freedom of religion in Saudi Arabia, might all be most laudable ones to fulfil. They are not, though, claims about the actual legal systems now in existence in those jurisdictions. Rather, they are moral claims; claims whose source must be traced back to theories or assertions about the moral world.

Hence notice this big – nay, huge – difference between the legal realm (including rights claims within that realm) and the moral realm (including rights claims within that realm). Claims about whether someone in fact even possesses certain rights, certain 'others must' entitlements, in the moral realm are often highly contestable and debatable. Smart, well-informed, nice people do not agree about whether a particular claimed moral right actually exists or not. There is reasonable disagreement[4]

---

[2] See Ronald Dworkin, *Taking Rights Seriously* (Harvard University Press, 1978), ch. 7.

[3] Of course the exact reach or parameters or scope of coverage of this legal right or that will still be unclear at the margins and so highly debatable at these peripheries. Or to make the point in Hartian terms, these legal rights/legal rules will inevitably have a 'penumbra of doubt' or 'open texture' where there are good reasons for thinking the right/rule applies as well as good reasons for thinking it does not. See H.L.A. Hart, *The Concept of Law* (Clarendon Press, 1961 – and I will make clear later why I cite the first edition of this magisterial book and not the later editions).

[4] In the context of bills of rights, and more particularly the undesirable nature of such instruments, Jeremy Waldron often puts weight on this notion of reasonable disagreement when it comes to rights-related issues. See Jeremy Waldron, *Law and Disagreement* (Oxford University Press, 1999); Jeremy Waldron, 'The Core of the Case Against Judicial Review,' (2006) 115 Yale Law Journal 1346. For my analysis

whether the moral rights being claimed in fact actually do exist in some mind-independent sense, whether they can persuasively be argued to rest on foundations that show the claims are good ones. On the plane of 'do these claimed rights even exist at all,' the doubts are many orders of magnitude greater in the moral realm than the legal realm. At this first step moral rights claims are vastly more open to doubt, and so to the same much greater extent more contestable, than legal rights claims.

Put differently, in the legal realm we overwhelmingly know if a claimed right or rule happens to exist in some particular jurisdiction. Disagreement there is focused on the desirability or otherwise of such a legal right, on whether to keep, amend or repeal it. In the moral realm, by contrast, disagreement occurs a step earlier. It occurs when one person makes a claim that some non-legal right X (a right to free speech in North Korea, perhaps, or one to freedom of religion in Saudi Arabia, maybe) in fact exists and another person disputes that claim. He says it exists; she says it does not.

That means that for non-legal rights claims the question of foundations—why it is you say some particular rights claim happens to exist—matters. There is no non-debatable, non-contentious answer as to the source or genealogy of these sort of rights.

Why does this distinction matter in a discussion on the topic of human rights? It matters because the modern day vocabulary of human rights is one that sits abreast the legal rights–non-legal rights divide. It finesses the distinction. It is a little bit of one and a little bit of the other. To varying extents, depending upon speaker and context, the language of human rights attempts to have it both ways at once–to offer something of the aspirational moral world of the 'ought' while at the same time giving you the concrete, enforceable, here-and-now legal world of the 'is.'

We can see this if we momentarily focus more narrowly on justiciable bills of rights, at least in the common law world. They sit partly in the legal realm, being entrenched in a constitution (and so giving top judges a power to strike down or invalidate statutes as one sees in the United States and Canada) or being enacted via a statute (and so giving

of Waldron's writings on bills of rights see James Allan, 'Jeremy Waldron and the Philosopher's Stone' (2008) 45 *San Diego Law Review* 133.

top judges a souped-up interpretive power to re-write legislation via a reading down provision as one sees in the United Kingdom and to a lesser extent in New Zealand). They also sit partly in the aspirational, moral realm to the extent that they fail to lock in answers as to how far the enumerated rights protections extend. Put differently, the more a bill of rights is treated as a 'living tree'[5] or 'living constitution' instrument whose meaning can change and alter and shift over time at the point-of-application – in part due to the interpreting judges' shifting moral judgements – the more such an instrument sits astride the legal/non-legal divide. Of course, the moral can even become the legal when 5 of 9 Supreme Court Justices extend what a right to a fair trial now means[6] or do the same with the right to vote.[7]

The point, though, is that the moral and the legal are intertwined with justiciable bills of rights. (Or, if you see this as a matter of degree because most law has a moral character, then these instruments are especially moralized.) And my broader claim here in this 'Setting the Stage' Part is that that same concatenation or commingling is at work with human rights more generally. The extent of this commingling will vary depending upon the grounds or foundations one offers for thinking some particular non-legal right actually exists. Let us turn next, therefore, to the various bases or foundations generally offered as underpinning human rights of the non-legal 'free speech in North Korea' variety. I will generalise here and note my doubts and skepticism as we go along.

i. Human rights as moral rights

If a human rights claim is being advanced, and it is clear that that claim is not being advanced on the 'as things actually are today in this jurisdiction' plane, then most often what you will be hearing is a moral

---

5 This phrase comes from Lord Sankey in *Edwards v Canada (Attorney General)* [1930] AC 124, the 'Persons Case.' This is the label one finds in Canada and much of the non-American common law world.

6 See the UK case of *Regina v A* [2001] UKHL 25.

7 See the Canadian case of *Sauvé v. Canada (Chief Electoral Officer)* 3 SCR 519 (2002), or even the Australian case of *Roach v Electoral Commissioner* 233 CLR 162 (2007), which did this without there even being a bill of rights in existence (as I set out in James Allan, 'The Three "R"s of Recent Australian Judicial Activism: Roach, Rowe and (no) 'Riginalism,' (2012) 36 *Melbourne University Law Review* 743.

claim. Its source or foundation will lie in morality. Accordingly, the plausibility of that rights claim will vary directly with the underlying plausibility of the moral theory on which it rests. Hence, if you are skeptical of the persuasiveness of some moral theory – or indeed skeptical of the meta-ethical position it takes – then you will to the same extent be skeptical of the non-legal rights claim which it underpins and supports.

Let me briefly run through some of the more obvious moral foundations said to provide a basis for thinking various claimed moral rights do in fact exist; that they have a plausible source or basis outside of a particular evaluator's own subjective moral sense or judgement or druthers.[8]

A. The most venerable, and historically influential, are all those moral theories related to or that draw on theism and a benevolent, theistic God who creates a world in which some conduct is wrong and some right. In that sort of world there will be non-legal rules that we humans can discover in two ways. They might be revealed to us by divine revelation. Alternatively, they might have been infused into the structure of the universe in such a way that we humans can reason to them; we can discover them on our own without recourse to any divine revelation. Yet what we are discovering or finding is only there because God put it there.

It is uncontroversial to say that thinking along those lines lies at the heart of the natural law tradition of Augustine and Aquinas. We can

---

[8] Jeremy Bentham described this as a person's 'sympathy and antipathy' sentiments – 'I like it' or 'I don't like it.' (See Jeremy Bentham, *An Introduction to the Principles of Morals and Legislation* (Clarendon Press, 1907, first published in 1789 and originally printed in 1780) chap. 16, p. 305). Certainly the attraction of utilitarianism, Bentham's preferred moral worldview, goes up considerably if all moral theories that make claims to having a mind-independent status are false or unpersuasive. Put differently, an inter-subjective standard of right and wrong (achieved by counting everyone equally to start and then going for what maximizes happiness or welfare or preferences) looks better than raw 'I happen to find that I like this' subjectivism. So if all moral theories that make less ephemeral, more mind-independent claims are for you ultimately unconvincing, then the sort of inter-subjective standard proposed by Bentham and by consequentialists more generally will be a least-bad option. At least I have argued as much. I have claimed that consequentialist moral theories are most attractive to those who find implausible and unpersuasive all the alternatives that offer standards of right and wrong that are not contingent on the way human sentiments happen to be. See James Allan, *Sympathy and Antipathy: Essays Legal and Philosophical* (Ashgate, 2002), especially the last chapter.

debate its influence on the sort of Jeffersonian claims about 'we hold these truths to be self-evident' in the American Declaration of Independence's second paragraph or in modern day natural law theory of the sort that John Finnis provides.[9] What cannot be denied is that the theistic worldview has driven much of the West's moral theorizing; that it has been extremely influential in historical terms. Likewise, it is clear that if its premises are correct – if a benevolent, theistic God created the world in such a way that humans can reason to right moral conduct, and hence to non-legal rules governing right action, and hence to non-legal rights – then the foundations of moral rights are secure. Individual humans may sometimes reason incorrectly and make incorrect claims, but the moral rights do exist. And they exist because they have a lineage going back to a benevolent, omnipotent God.

As it happens I am highly skeptical of this foundation for all the reasons that J.L. Mackie and indeed David Hume give.[10]

B. A related type of moral theory that provides the needed foundations for plausible, convincing moral rights claims are what I am categorizing as 'all natural law theories without God.' Clearly this is a big group, especially in our modern day more secular times. Just as clearly there will be reasonable disagreements about whether certain theories and thinkers fall into this category or the previous one. So we can debate not just about where to slot Finnis as noted above, but also about where to put a 'we are required to treat all people (or all rational agents) as ends not means' Kantian deontological theory, and no doubt plenty of others.

That said, there are also plenty of modern day moral theories that are indisputably secular (placing no reliance whatsoever on a theistic God in the background) while at the same time offering the same sort of end results as category **A** above. Let me nominate Ronald Dworkin as fitting clearly into this category. Dworkin builds a theory of law, and a theory of rights, out of a theory of how to interpret. We are to take, says the early Dworkin, all the jurisdiction's settled laws, its first 13 chapters in the chain

---

[9] See John Finnis, *Natural Law and Natural Rights* (Oxford University Press, 2011).

[10] See J.L. Mackie, *The Miracle of Theism: Arguments for and against the Existence of God* (Oxford: Oxford University Press, 1982) and see David Hume, *Dialogues Concerning Natural Religion* (published posthumously by his nephew after Hume's death in 1776; Kemp Smith edition, Bobbs-Merrill, 1947).

novel, and we are to build the best fitting background political morality that explains and justifies those inherited materials. So, for Dworkin, there can be no clear line between law and morality. Moreover, a super human Justice Hercules will be able to create this best background fit in such a way that in any dispute that reaches a top court – most obviously one involving rights-related disputes – one answer will be weightier and have more gravitational pull than any other. That will be the one right answer, the answer that gives the most integrity to the settled laws.[11]

Now it may well be that that sort of 'building a theory of law out of a theory of how to interpret' requires one to be a moral realist to make it work. Dworkin himself denies this at first, distinguishing between external and internal skepticism, but later says that he is a moral realist; that he rejects non-cognitivism.[12]Regardless of the exegetical disputes about Dworkin's theory, it is clear that Dworkin offers an account in which there are rights in a non-subjective (and indeed more than just inter-subjective) sense. He gives us a secular foundation for making such rights claims.

Again, it is a separate matter whether one finds Dworkin's theories persuasive. I do not. Many others do not as well, including A.W.B. Simpson, Larry Alexander, Brian Leiter, and more. But the take-away point here is that today's orthodox constitutional law edifice often rests on Dworkinian-type foundations, foundations that when made plain and subject to probing are hard to defend.

C. It is not clear where to put social contract or agreement theories that seek to provide a foundation for human rights. If the goal is to offer a theory of rights in pre-institutional terms, then these do so. We might put Locke here (though perhaps also in category **A** above). And Rawls. It seems true to me that by asking a conditional hypothetical question ('What would some reasonable or "behind the veil of ignorance" person prefer or

---

[11] See, for instance, Ronald Dworkin, *Taking Rights Seriously* (Harvard University Press, 1978) and Ronald Dworkin, *Law's Empire* (Harvard University Press, 1988).

[12] See Ronald Dworkin, 'Objectivity and Truth: You'd Better Believe It,' (1996) 25 *Philosophy & Public Affairs* 87, and see James Allan, 'Truth's Empire – A Reply to Ronald Dworkin's 'Objectivity and Truth: You'd Better Believe It'' (2001) 26 *Australian Journal of Legal Philosophy* 61. Notable non-cognitivists include Simon Blackburn (and his quasi-realism), Jeremy Waldron, J.L. Mackie and H.L.A. Hart.

pick if that person had this information or that?'), you are not creating a mind-independent standard. You are creating something akin to (but clearly not exactly the same as) an Adam Smith 'impartial spectator' or 'well informed person at the time' standard.[13] This sort of approach gives you a pre-institutional basis for your claims; but at the same time it does not seem to me to really rise up to being a mind-independent standard or basis for your claims.

Still, you do end up with a foundation for your non-legal rights claims; or rather you get one if you decide such social contract, agreement theories are persuasive. Again, I am skeptical. Imputing opinions and values and beliefs to a hypothetical (never actually having existed) being seems to me to be prone to collapsing into a thinly disguised 'this is what I, the maker of the theory, would have valued or believed had they asked me' game. You get out of the imagined agreement or contract what you put in. In Rawlsian terms, if you come to the task as a risk-averse person then the reasonable-seeming outcome of the 'veil of ignorance' imaginings will be a risk-averse one. But there are many real-life people in the world who are not risk averse. So, I have plenty of doubts that this social contract or agreement avenue will provide a solid foundation for non-legal rights claims.

Of course many readers will disagree with my broad doubts about the plausibility and persuasiveness of category **A**, **B** and **C** type attempts to provide a solid foundation for human rights. They will think one or more of these moral foundations is persuasive. If they are correct and I am not, then they have their basis – a moral basis – for making 'free speech in North Korea' type non-legal rights claims. Then they will be able to provide a more or less solid footing to the sort of human rights claims that

---

[13] As we will see later in this book, much of modern American originalism constitutional interpretation theory has forsworn the search for actual intended meaning ('intentionalism') in favour of original public meaning, which involves constructing a hypothetical well-informed person at the time and asking what he or she would take the legal provisions to mean. This is the Adam Smith game in a different guise. See, for example, Keith Whittington, 'On Pluralism within Originalism' in *The Challenges of Originalism*, edited by Grant Huscroft and Bradley Miller (Cambridge University Press, 2011). Justice Scalia of the US Supreme Court also more or less falls into this new originalism or public meaning originalism category.

permeate so much of the modern democracy's constitutional law edifice. If they are not correct, though, some other foundation will have to be sought.

ii. Human rights as tools to advance the general welfare

If you are a utilitarian, or more generally a consequentialist, then seeing human rights as tools to increase or advance the general welfare is a moral understanding of human rights. For non-consequentialists it is not. Put differently, if you give human rights a utilitarian foundation, some people (most obviously utilitarians, but other consequentialists as well) will consider that to be a moral foundation. Other people (non-utilitarians and non-consequentialists) predominantly will not. For my purposes this is just a classificatory dispute that I can side-step. I give this a separate sub-section solely to note the classificatory disagreement.

As I noted in a footnote above (see fn. 8), I think that the appeal of utilitarian-type theories depends in part upon one's answer to the meta-ethical question of the status of moral evaluations. If you are a moral realist or moral objectivist, for whom moral claims are supposed to have mind-independent status (so your Kantians and deontologists and theologically-driven theorists and more), then the appeal of an inter-subjective utilitarian standard of right and wrong is not obvious, and perhaps close to zero. Why go for the half-hearted, comparatively ethereal option when you believe you have the real thing? By contrast, if you are a non-cognitivist or moral skeptic (so your Humeans and Blackburns and Mackies and more),[14] it seems to me that the appeal will be greater. If moral evaluations have no higher mind-independent status, if they are a function at core of the sentiments and feelings that humans happen to have, then utilitarianism (and consequentialism more generally) can offer you a way out of raw subjectivism, a way to avoid what Bentham scathingly deemed 'sympathy and antipathy' or 'I happen to like it' and 'I don't happen to like it'

[14] As it happens, I find this non-cognitivist camp the more plausible one myself. See James Allan, *A Sceptical Theory of Morality and Law* (Peter Lang, 1998). But that is independent of the claim that consequentialist theories are more attractive the more you find implausible and unpersuasive all the alternatives that offer standards of right and wrong that are not contingent on the way human sentiments happen to be.

pontificating.[15] You can at least achieve an inter-subjective standard of right and wrong that escapes raw subjectivism, albeit falling short of any mind-independent status.

Whether you agree with me that non-cognitivists are more likely to find utilitarianism attractive, or not, let me briefly run through the basic way in which a utilitarian would understand non-legal rights claims.

The right thing to do for utilitarians is to aim for conduct and actions that will increase the general welfare (everyone in the specified group being counted equally to start, with Bentham advocating a 'greatest happiness of the greatest number' test).[16] Make human happiness or welfare the sole 'good-in-itself' and then aim for those likely future good consequences that will maximize that happiness (or that will keep to a minimum unhappiness or pain in situations when only bad things are on the menu).

But as modern day utilitarians realize we can often achieve better overall outcomes by the indirect pursuit of the good rather than by attempting to maximize the good on a case-by-case basis.[17] Put more bluntly, part of the modern day sophistication of utilitarianism involves the realization that sometimes best consequences are achieved by laying down clear rules, and always following them even though we know going in that all rules will at times produce sub-optimal results, will be over-inclusive and under-inclusive. In other words, we can accept the fact that no rule will ever have a 100 percent hit rate, a perfect record of producing good consequences every single time that it is honestly applied. Yet, despite that, and the less than 100 percent hit rate, it will nevertheless be the case that in some situations opting for a rule will deliver better overall consequences (all things considered, on average, over time) than case-by-case decision-making aimed at good consequences in each individual case.

---

15 J.L. Mackie offers a sort of hybrid possibility; he offers an error theory. Mackie argues that most people believe they are making mind-independent moral claims when they make them; it is just that they are wrong. So for Mackie we in fact live in a non-cognitivist world but many people think, and feel as though, they are living in a moral realist one. See J.L. Mackie, *Ethics: Inventing Right and Wrong* (Penguin, 1977).

16 See Bentham, *An Introduction to the Principles of Morals and Legislation* and Jeremy Bentham, *A Fragment on Government* (first published 1776, 2001), p. 93.

17 See, for example, how the non-utilitarian Larry Alexander makes the point in, Larry Alexander, 'Pursuing the Good – Indirectly' (1985) 95 *Ethics* 315.

One example sometimes given of this is a 'who can vote?' rule. Let us say a rule lays down something along the lines that 'any citizen 18 years of age and older, not declared mentally unfit by a doctor' can vote. That sort of rule clearly is sub-optimal; it clearly has a less than 100 percent hit rate. There will be 17 year olds well-versed in civic education who look far more qualified to vote than scores of 19 or 50 or 60 year olds. Yet such 17 year olds will, sub-optimally, be barred. Obversely, there will be know-nothing, alcoholic 45 year olds who have not read a newspaper in 20 years; under the rule they can vote.

Yet the point is that such a rule delivers better consequences than any non-rule alternative. To see this, imagine that you tried to decide who can vote by striking committees of people who would interview potential voters and then make decisions on a case-by-case basis. Not only would the costs of such a scheme be huge, the overall hit rate would be lower than that achieved with the rule. No real life human being, or group of human beings, will ever have a 100 percent hit rate of opting for the better consequences choice any more than any rule would. (Remember that fact because it is often forgotten or overlooked, especially by judges inclined to find a way around a legal rule on the erroneous assumption that they, personally, do have a 100 percent decision-making hit rate.) Plus there are the various frailties that flow from being a limited biological creature; there is the possibility of succumbing to corruption (say, excluding from voting bunches of those obviously on the other side of politics to you); there is the chance of moral failures (say, opting to exclude blacks from voting); and more.

So Rule Utilitarianism says that sometimes (as with who can vote) you do better by having rules and just applying them without exception. This is not true in all situations, of course. To see this just consider how we decide who can drive – here we go for case-by-case decision-making, despite knowing that that, too, is far from perfect (as you can see by noting all the teenage boys who manage to pass their driving tests).

But the point is that rules are sometimes the best way to achieve the optimal outcome or greatest happiness, which for utilitarians just is, by definition, the moral outcome. And as rules are just the obverse of rights, we can see that a utilitarian need not be restricted to the legal world of 'is';

she can make a calculation that there ought to be a rule to further free speech or freedom of religion in North Korea or Saudi Arabia, despite such rules being lacking there at present. The utilitarian is not conflating the 'is' and the 'ought.'[18]She is saying, in effect, that good consequences would go up if there were such a rule, such an enforceable rule, and so there should be one. We ought to work towards enacting one, towards creating such a legal rule.

As a non-cognitivist myself, I see the appeal of utilitarian and consequentialist moral theories, in least-bad terms if nothing else. That said, utilitarianism has well-known weaknesses[19] such as being incredibly perfectionist (treat the poor in Africa as counting equally to your own children) and being open to sacrificing the individual in certain extreme situations. So I am mildly skeptical here too about whether most people will find a consequentialist/utilitarian foundation for human rights all that attractive.

iii. Human rights where no foundations given – just assume they exist

Another approach to understanding human rights can be put quite frankly and simply. On this approach you just ignore the issue of foundations as far as possible. You sweep the question under the carpet and pass along in silence. The thinking here goes something as follows: If a commitment to fundamental human rights is the foundation of political legitimacy, then we just have to assume such human rights (whenever we stray into the non-legal realm) actually exist. Or as Stephen Smith puts it, without in any way endorsing such an approach, and in regards to the related issue of equality:

[18] Indeed Bentham was adamant that 'wants are not means – hunger is not bread': Jeremy Bentham, 'Anarchical Fallacies' in *The Works of Jeremy Bentham Vol 2*, edited by John Bowring (William Tate, 1843) 501. Bentham was well aware of the dangers of the naturalistic fallacy, of breaching Hume's Law. Hume makes his famous 'you can't derive an "is" from an "ought"' point in David Hume, *A Treatise of Human Nature* (L.A. Selby-Bigge ed, Oxford University Press, 1978), p. 469.

[19] Well known critics of utilitarianism include Ronald Dworkin, *Taking Rights Seriously*, (Harvard University Press, 1978), pp. 232–238, 269, 275-276, chaps. 9 and 12, *inter alia* and John Rawls, *A Theory of Justice*, (Harvard University Press, 1971).

> Just as in one kind of philosophy elusive but indispensable things like causation, time, space and continuity of personal identity are not so much observable facts in the world as commitments or categories we bring to and impose on the world, so equal moral worth is a starting point or necessary presupposition that we assume in order to deal with the normative and political world as it is. That presupposition need not be justified …on any other grounds.[20]

A basically related point is more commonly heard these days along the lines that one can view human rights in light of their function or role in international politics and law. Travelling down that road allows one to claim that the justification for human rights need not be based on some moral or philosophical account of human nature or of the world but instead can be cashed out more narrowly in instrumental terms, in terms of the role of rights in international affairs and interactions. But of course that is just a backhanded way of saying that core issues related to foundations can be ignored or assumed away. It is not unlike saying, 'these things are a force for good in the world, so don't ask too many questions about them.'

If you want the same basic attitude to foundations in terms that amount to caricature, then you can think of this school of thought as the one that just begins by looking at what Eleanor Roosevelt did with the Universal Declaration back in 1948 and moves on from there, as though that is all the foundation you will ever need. You ignore all deeper questions and doubts about foundations; you assume them away.

Of course you can give a consequentialist defence to this 'ignore or assume away foundations' approach. You will just need to make arguments for why best consequences flow from simply assuming certain human rights exist, and from ignoring any further questions about how to provide them with solid foundations. You will focus on their most desirable scope of application, or on how best to make them enforceable, and waste little time on more fundamental queries. To be blunt, my suspicion is that more than a few lawyers adopt precisely this attitude, or make this consequentialist calculation. In some situations it may well be the sensible route to take.

---

[20] Steven Smith, 'Equality, Religion, and Nihilism' *San Diego Legal Studies Paper*, 14-169 (2014): 9–10.

That said, offering no reasons for why you are so intensely committed to something, to the human rights worldview or to the existence of particular human rights, is far from satisfying for others, and possibly even for you too. Speaking for myself, I am more than a little skeptical of this attitude, and of the apotheosis of things that are put beyond questioning and seldom, if ever, justified. I think that sort of attitude and approach to foundations in fact has bad long-term consequences. I accept, though, that this 'just ignore foundational issues' strategem is not an uncommon approach or attitude, not least when it comes to matters related to constitutional law.

2. Doubts about Finessing Foundations

An alternative to simply assuming away the question of what are the plausible foundations of human rights is to assert that people do not need to agree on foundations in order to discuss and debate, say, their proper reach. In other words, we might be able to finesse this question of foundations.

This is most plausible where all the disputants agree that some set of human rights have a non-conventional, perhaps even a mind-independent, existence; it is just that none of them can agree on what the foundation actually is. So as regards some particular human rights claim the Kantian says the foundation for the claim flows from the fact that we are all required to treat people as ends, not means. The Christian says it flows from God's edict to love everyone, even one's enemies. The liberal egalitarian traces it to the obligation to treat all people with equal respect, or perhaps to the human dignity of everyone. And so on and so on. The idea is that you do not need agreement on foundations in order to move the debate to the next level, and indeed to settle a good many questions at that next level.

Again, I confess to having more than a few doubts – to being somewhat sceptical – about how far this attempt to finesse the issue of foundations can take us. Clearly there can be meaningful human rights discussions and moral resolutions within groups of like-minded people – the utilitarians can talk to the utilitarians, the Kantians to the Kantians, the egalitarians to the egalitarians, the Dworkinians to the Dworkinians, and so on. But when there are no shared premises and first principles the danger is of the sort of incommensurability described by Alisdair McIntyre.[21]This is the world in which rights-related arguments (on the justness of some war or anti-terrorism provisions, say, or the acceptability of abortion, or on some equality-related issue) seem completely cogent and persuasive on their own premises and presuppositions, but in which polar opposite conclusions can be reached when founded on differing premises. Disputes cannot be cabined sufficiently to narrow the plausible outcomes; the disputants talk past, not to, one another. As McIntyre puts it:

> Every one of the arguments is logically valid or can easily be expanded so as to be made so; the conclusions do indeed follow from the premises. But the rival premises are such that we possess no rational way of weighing the claims of one as against another. For each premise employs some quite different normative or evaluative concept from the others, so that the claims made upon us are quite of different kinds.[22]

In other words, this is the possibility that the attempt to finesse foundations leaves us with a world in which those who disagree with one another on rights-related issues (and who do not share foundational premises) will talk at each other, yes, but not so much with each other. They will lack any agreed arbiter or final appeal mechanism or rules of the game for resolving and ending disagreements. When you begin from different starting points, in fact from different core conceptions of what grounds and gives life to human rights, you simply will not get the sort of winnowing and narrowing and agreeing that is desired and hoped for by proponents of the 'let us just put to one side our disagreement about foundations and see if we cannot get agreement further up the food chain' gambit.

And that McIntyre view sounds right to me. I have a good deal of skepticism about any likely prospects for success when the strategy is to finesse the question of the foundations of human rights. Take away the shared premises and the Finnisian natural law adherent will differ from the

---

[21] See Alisdair McIntyre, *After Virtue*, 2nd edn (University of Notre Dame Press, 1985).

[22] *Ibid.*, p. 8.

liberal egalitarian on the correct reach and force of the right to freedom of religion; the Kantian will differ from the utilitarian on the effect of a right to equality; the list goes on and on, even as to whether certain rights do or do not exist in the first place. Hence, any move to descend from the Olympian heights of disagreement-finessing moral abstractions down to the quagmire of the day-to-day charting of the exact scope and specific requirements of human rights looks unlikely to bring much agreement, at least to me. Foundations matter; they matter when it comes to mapping how human rights ought to play out. So I have my doubts that this variant of the finessing option can take us very far.

There is a different variant, though, of the finessing gambit. Here what you finesse is not the widespread disagreement about the core foundations for non-legal human rights. Instead, on this second variant, what you finesse is the divide between legal and non-legal human rights. I mentioned above just before section ***1.i***, briefly, how justiciable bills of rights can be understood in this way – how they sit in the legal world and yet, when top judges appeal to morality to decide cases in the Hartian penumbra of doubt, how they also can be seen as sitting partly in the aspirational, moral realm. The moral understanding of 5 of 9 judges on a Supreme Court can become law; their moral judgements can move the coverage provided by some right from the purely moral to become part of the here and now legal. (As we shall see later in this book, constitutional rights can also be understood as having a largely agreed content by their adopters. But this pre-supposes a particular approach to constitutional interpretation.)

That same second variant of the finessing gambit can arguably be seen in the international law realm as well. Indeed this might be a better way to understand the view of those who try to see and explain human rights in light of their function or role in international politics and law. It depends upon the extent to which one thinks that international law rules are in a sense, or when first laid down, non-legal rules at the domestic level, and yet over time can become legal rules on that same level or plane.

So take an international, multilateral rights-related convention or treaty. Pick one of the many whose substantive provisions are articulated in vague, amorphous moral abstractions pitched up in the Olympian heights of disagreement finessing terminology. As far as the municipal law of some Western liberal democracies are concerned – those that do not treat international law as immediately part of national law, such as Canada, Australia and the UK – these rights-related international law conventions, these amorphously articulated human rights, are not enforceable in the domestic legal system. Well, not directly at first in any straightforward way. (And this is even clearer if you pick, instead, any non-democracy in the world you care to choose, an authoritarian one-party state, a theocracy, take your pick. The laid down international law right will have next to no effect or bearing on the domestic legal system in such non-democracies.) But in those above Western liberal democracies we may see that over time judges appeal to these international law rights (and so rules), first perhaps when deciding administrative law matters; then as defeasible presumptions when interpreting statutes; maybe even ultimately when interpreting constitutions. Over time the non-legal becomes, to varying extents, the legal. That is the finesse.

Notice, in addition, that with this second variant of the finesse the source of your human rights is plain; the source is evidently some man-made, laid down rule/right/treaty. You need go no further back than that. Put differently, if you have some multilateral convention or bill of rights to point to then you can ignore the issue of foundations; you can justify all you need to justify based on the role that rights happen to be playing, right now, in international affairs or in the day-to-day practices of judicial life. Or something like that, at any rate, is the general approach at the heart of this second variant of the finessing gambit.

For those, like me, who generally have significant doubts about the success and persuasiveness of providing solid underpinnings or foundations for non-legal human rights claims, this second finessing approach is not without attraction. That said, it carries with it notable disadvantages as well as advantages. The former are almost all related to the undemocratic nature of having unelected judges and an international elite of unelected committee members monitoring rights-related treaties and indeed a swathe of other unelected participants being the people who are giving specific content to these vague, amorphous human rights provisions as they move, here and there, from the non-legal realm to the legal one.

Having sketched out my doubts as regards the usually offered foundations or underpinnings for human rights and claims based on human rights, let us in the next chapter turn to some related foundational doubts. There we will look briefly at how well the human rights worldview does or does not mesh with a preference for democracy and democratic decision-making as well taking a look at the core constitutional concept of the rule of law.

Chapter Two

Other Doubts Related to Human Rights

I now leave behind direct consideration of how human rights might plausibly be underpinned and turn to two tangential issues. The first looks at the connection between human rights and democracy and how well, or not well, the two mesh together. Here I wish to raise some preliminary doubts about how easily a human rights worldview can co-exist with a commitment to democracy. After raising some doubts there, the second issue in this chapter takes us to some additional doubts I have about a commonly heard and commonly invoked human rights-related legal notion, namely the Rule of Law – about how it is generally understood and employed in the world of constitutional law.

Now readers should know that I will have more to say about democracy in Part II of this book. But here in the Setting the Stage portion of this book, where I am voicing some skepticism about how easily a human rights worldview might mesh with a strong commitment to democracy, I will need to lay out my basic understanding of the best way to grasp that concept. Leave that for just a moment, however, and go back to any of the chapter one full-blooded understandings of human rights as moral rights. For those who see human rights in those terms, there is clearly room to doubt how great the pull of democracy will be for them. If some human right enunciates a mind-independent standard of what is correct and proper moral treatment, then it is not obvious why that claim or moral obligation should lose out just because a majority of one's fellow citizens see things differently. In addition, the pull of a supposedly 'reason-based,' court-focused decision-making procedure[23] may well

---

[23] Steven Smith sets out this allure and then argues that judges, in fact, no more rely on reason than do legislators. See Steven Smith, 'Judicial Activism and "Reason"' in *Judicial Activism: An Interdisciplinary Approach to the American and European*

prove to be very great, its counter-majoritarian credentials notwithstanding. Indeed, democracy for such people is likely to be seen as just one good amongst many, and not one immune from the 'civilizing effects' either of a strong judiciary interpreting a potent bill of rights or of the demands of rights-related international law, or most probably of both.

Let me put it this way. If you see rights in non-consequentialist, 'strong rights' terms,[24] as setting out claims that have a basis or foundation over and above the way humans happen to feel about things, then being told that a majority of your fellow citizens feel otherwise is unlikely to be a knock-out argument for you.[25] It will have a prudential and procedural pull, yes. However, I have hefty doubts that it will for many such proponents have a substantive pull.

Of course one *can* make a strong rights, or deontological, argument on behalf of democracy. Jeremy Waldron does something along those lines with his 'you are not treating others as autonomous agents worthy of respect unless they have an equal say in decision-making, even over rights-related issues' type argument. This is how Waldron grounds his 'right to participate,' his 'right of rights.' Waldron does not rest it on consequential foundations.[26] So my doubts here are *not* that giving human rights a moral foundation (of the **A**, **B** or **C** sort outlined in chapter one above) must ineluctably undermine one's commitment to democracy; rather it is an empirical claim that for many it does.

Now, as advertised, let me sketch out my basic understanding of the best way to grasp the concept of democracy. You see in broad terms there are two main schools of thought here, one taking a fat, substantive approach and the other urging a thin, procedural sense. And I prefer the

---

Experiences, edited by Luis Pereira Cotinho, Massimo La Torre, and Steven Smith (Springer, 2015).

[24] For my distinction of 'strong rights theories' and 'weak rights theories' see James Allan, 'Bills of Rights and Judicial Power – A Liberal's Quandary' (1996) 16 *Oxford Journal of Legal Studies* 337. And see chapter one above.

[25] Larry Alexander makes this point in his Larry Alexander, 'What is the Problem of Judicial Review?' (2006) 31 *Australian Journal of Legal Philosophy* 1.

[26] See Jeremy Waldron, *Law and Disagreement* (OUP, 1999). I consider aspects of the Waldron view in James Allan, 'The Travails of Justice Waldron' in *Expounding the Constitution: Essays in Constitutional Theory*, edited by Grant Huscroft, (Cambridge University Press, 2008).

latter, the thin, procedural understanding of democracy.[27] On this thin, morally Spartan understanding when you think of democracy you are thinking of a procedure for making decisions in a world where smart, nice, well-informed people will and do regularly disagree. And this democracy procedure does not guarantee good outcomes. Yes, you might on average think those outcomes have a better likely batting average, or hit rate, than any other way of making society-wide decisions. But that assertion about what plays out best in the world of politics does not change the fact that democracy – on this procedural, majoritarian, letting-the-numbers-count understanding – just describes a way of making decisions. It is not a guarantee of the goodness or rightness or superior moral credentials of those decisions in any or all instances.

Issues can and do arise, in other words, where the majority speaks and you think it has spoken foolishly or wrongly or in a panic.

A quite different approach is to think of democracy in much fatter, more morally pregnant terms. Indeed, many people[28] do just that; they use the term 'democracy' to mean a great deal more than the process of majoritarian decision-making. For them, being a democracy and describing some country's system as 'democratic' carries with it an additional assertion that the decisions taken have reached a certain level of goodness or acceptability or rights-respectingness. In other words, for them, the noun 'democracy' and the adjective 'democratic' do not simply refer to how decisions are made, they also (to some extent or other) refer to the quality of those decisions.

People who use the word democracy in this fat, morally pregnant way want it to tell you two things, one about how a decision was made and another about the goodness or appropriateness of that decision. Democracy, on this view or understanding, means both a statement that

---

[27] I make this argument at length in James Allan, *Democracy in Decline: Steps in the Wrong Direction* (McGill-Queen's University Press, 2014) and take bits of the next couple pages from that earlier book of mine.

[28] For example, the Nobel Prize winning economist Amartya Sen. See Amaryta Sen, 'Democracy as a Universal Value,' (1999) 10 *Journal of Democracy* 8. See also Ronald Dworkin, *A Bill of Rights for Britain* (Chatto & Windus, 1990), p. 43: '[d]emocracy is not the same thing as majority rule, and that in a real democracy liberty and minorities have legal protection.'

decision-making is being done by some majoritarian process as well as a claim that the decisions pass some pre-established moral threshold.

This fat, substantive, morally-laden understanding of democracy is not, in my view, a desirable one. If decisions are made on a fair, open, majoritarian basis then it is better to be able to say 'country X is a democracy, but one that now ignores many individual rights and tramples on various economic freedoms' than to say it is not a democracy. I think it is important to keep separate the issue of how a country makes its key decisions, on the one hand, and on the other whether some or all of us think those decisions are generally or overwhelmingly rights-respecting or freedom-protecting or morally palatable.

Put bluntly, there are good grounds for leaving yourself room to be able to say 'that country over there is a democracy, but it is doing very wrong-headed, even wicked, things.' And that is true despite you, and I, also thinking that most of the time, overwhelmingly perhaps, democracies do not do wicked things or even that no other decision-making procedure would, on the whole, make better decisions.

To be clear, then, when I assert that it is those who see human rights as resting on strong rights, full-bloodedly moral foundations (of any of the **A**, **B** or **C** variants canvassed in chapter one) who may well find the pull of democracy less than determinative, it is to this thin, procedural sense of democracy that I refer. If, instead, you were to inflate your conception of democracy in a big way, and make it sufficiently expansive, morally-charged, and chock full of the need for liberal and rights-respecting outcomes to count as democratic, then quite plainly even the most robustly moral foundations for human rights could co-exist with the demands of democracy – because otherwise you would simply, by fiat, rule that any particular objected-to decision or outcome did not spring from a democracy.

Reject the fat, morally pregnant account of democracy, though, and co-existence becomes much more difficult to sustain. Hence my skepticism about the ease with which the grounded-in-morality human rights worldview and democracy are able to co-exist relates to my preferred thin, procedural understanding of democracy.

It gets worse. Even those who prefer to see human rights in consequentialist terms, or who seek to finesse the issue of foundations by making various human rights conventions and treaties their starting point, even for them the human rights worldview can be difficult to reconcile with a robust commitment to democracy. Take treaties. In the Westminster world these have highly diminished democratic credentials, being entered into under the prerogative power with no veto in the elected legislature. This contrasts with the United States where treaties are taken seriously, and hence where many fail to get through the US Senate – which may in part explain why fewer and fewer treaties there are approved under the old Art II procedure requiring two-thirds Senate approval, some now being effectively approved by mere majorities in both houses. Or take customary international law. A less democratic way to make law is hard to imagine. Or take the International Court of Justice. Many of the judges on this court come from jurisdictions that by no stretch of the imagination could be described as democratic, not in thin terms or thick terms. And the manner of appointment of these ICJ judges can look pretty awful too. The same, or worse, goes for the membership of the committees that monitor human rights conventions.

Put bluntly, there is a huge democratic deficiency in the making of this type of law. Or at least such was my claim in a previous book,[29] so here I content myself with this abbreviated listing of the areas or headings of democratic deficiency. If you accept these claims I make about the enervated nature of the democratic credentials of international rights-related law, notice that any attempt to finesse the foundations of human rights themselves (and that emphatically includes the second variant of the finesse outlined in chapter one) does not free you from this other deficiency, this undesirable emasculation of democracy. Yes, you avoid the highly contentious and debatable arguments encountered when seeking to provide a moral foundation for human rights, and you do so by simply making your starting point some laid down, constructed-by-humans, international treaty or convention or some customary international law ruling. You start with something that sits astride the legal/non-legal divide and you thereby side-step or finesse the question of foundations, at least

---

29 See Allan, *Democracy in Decline*, fn. 27 above, pp. 83-107.

in a way. But this finesse or side-step does not in any way at all reduce the democracy-enervated nature of your starting point.

Or for my purposes here let me put it in these terms: My strong suspicion is that the human rights worldview cannot easily co-exist with any full-blooded commitment to democracy in a thin, procedural sense. In fact I have a great many doubts indeed that they can easily co-exist. Of course, it is certainly also true that a good many people may well decide that that particular cost (in terms of the emasculation of democratic input) is outweighed by the benefits such a human rights worldview brings with it. But such costs there will be. And that, then, is why I have serious doubts about how easily a human rights worldview can co-exist with a commitment to democracy in my preferred procedural sense; why I doubt the two mesh well together.

I also noted at the start of this chapter that I have doubts about how the concept or notion of the 'Rule of Law' is often understood and employed in the world of constitutional law. These doubts are worth laying out in this Setting the Stage portion of the book because they will be relevant later on. Or at least the reader will see that the same sort of skepticism can be applied to various other constitutional law concepts. So let us consider this notion of 'the Rule of Law.' In broad terms, and allowing for a bit of generalising, there are again two competing senses in which this notion or concept or understanding of the Rule of Law is used – and readers who suspect the two competing senses mimic what we just saw with understandings of democracy would be correct. Hence there is what you can think of as morally thin or procedural sense. This is the more old-fashioned sense of the Rule of Law. Here the virtues we associate with this proceduralist or morally Spartan version of the Rule of Law include what flows from demanding that the law be created in terms of clear, general rules, applicable to all, known in advance, able to be complied with, and so easily able to be used and relied on to shape one's expectations. That sort of thing. Notice that the Rule of Law in this first sense, by asking that jurisdictions seek to employ legal rules that are prospective, consistent, clear, general, able to be complied with and the like, does not ensure that this, that or the other legal system will deliver heaven on earth. Nothing can do that. Instead it goes a considerable distance towards delivering the values of certainty, predictability and non-arbitrariness. These are in a sense procedural virtues – namely what follows from a set of procedural demands about how man-made laws ought overwhelmingly to be produced. But they are not assurances that each citizen or voter will think that all the laws that were enacted in this way ultimately end up delivering morally good substantive results, ones that each observer will consider always to be rights-respecting (or even, in extreme cases, ones that must be obeyed). On this thin understanding of the Rule of Law, then, there will remain plenty of room for reasonable disagreement about the rights and wrongs of enacted laws, say a Thatcher poll tax or an Obama Affordable Health Care provision or an Australian-style immigration law regime or a Canadian package of language laws, the list goes on and on and on. Put bluntly, the procedural understanding does not try to cram all possible good things into, or under the rubric of, this notion of the Rule of Law.

However, in the last four or five decades, at least in the developed Anglosphere common law world, there has grown up a competing concept or notion of the Rule of Law. This is a much fatter or thicker or morally impregnated and value-laden conception or understanding of the Rule of Law. On this second view, in addition to mandates as to how laws should be made, procedurally, you also build in demands about what those laws should ultimately look like once brought into being. They might need to pass, say, some threshold of rights-respectingness for this to be deemed a Rule of Law jurisdiction; or to be judged to further, say, human flourishing, equality, a chosen panoply of political goods (usually then translated into the language of human rights), whatever the assessor's preferred moral currency might happen to be. On this more morally laden understanding, therefore, whether jurisdiction X gets awarded the label of 'a Rule of Law regime' will in part depend upon whether you – the one doing the assessing – think its laws to be morally good ones. It is not enough that they were made according to the old-fashioned prospective, consistent, clear, general, able to be complied with procedural virtues. The end results have to meet some purity test; they have to overcome some moral threshold. Or rather you, the judge awarding the title 'Rule of Law Compliant,' you have to feel these laws so made have enough moral goodness in them. Otherwise you, the person assessing the substance of some law or legal regime, can withhold the label 'Rule of Law Compliant.'

In other words, we see the same sort of conceptual divide we saw when it came to understanding 'democracy.' Here too there is a basic divide between the thin, procedural conception of the Rule of Law and its newer offshoot the fat, thick, morally pregnant conception. Of course which understanding or notion of the Rule of Law (thin or thick) is preferable, or better, or right cannot be answered by opening up a dictionary and looking up a meaning. The morally Spartan and the morally pregnant understandings are competing accounts of a debatable or contestable concept, this notion of 'the Rule of Law.' There are strengths and weaknesses attaching to both of them and different people will weigh and choose differently. But be clear it is a choice you have to make on normative grounds. And I have clearly already tipped my hand as to my preferred understanding. Again, I favour the thinner, proceduralist account. So let me quickly run through three reasons why that is, why I prefer the proceduralist over the substantive understanding of the Rule of Law.

1. Reasonable Disagreement

Point one. The fat conception of the Rule of Law makes virtually no allowance for or mention at all of the fact that people disagree about best moral outcomes. Put differently, all of us voters disagree about how to promote human rights, human flourishing, equality what have you. Stuff all such substantive moral evaluations under the aegis of a morally overweight conception of the Rule of Law and you finesse all sorts of those disagreements. The morally pregnant understanding, concomitantly, virtually never concedes that all these sorts of disagreements are over morally contested social policy line-drawing disputes. They are disagreements best understood as being between smart, well-informed, reasonable and nice people[30] – people with whom you would be happy to have a drink regardless of whether they agree or disagree with you. It follows that if you alter your understanding of the Rule of Law to make it

---

[30] This is a point Jeremy Waldron makes throughout his writings, including in *Law & Disagreement* (OUP, 1999).

far more substantive and morally laden – to stuff in every morally good thing you can think of – then you will carry those moral disagreements with you. Now, though, the disagreement will not be directly about the specific moral issues concerned but instead it will be in terms of whether the Rule of Law does, or does not, apply. Or whether it should be invoked. Or whether it can be used in this or that instance to gainsay and second-guess some country's elected legislature. And somebody other than the voters – maybe judges, maybe some supranational elite representative – will have more power to make those calls. Accordingly, I think that the costs of that sort of move from a thin to a thick understanding would outweigh any and all benefits even if the move were made openly and in broad daylight. But often it is not.

This first point in favour of thin understandings of the Rule of Law boils down to the claim that it is better to leave moral disagreements in society, or between jurisdictions, focused on some specific actual law or policy (an immigration regime, say, or an argument about how much final say unelected judges ought to have or whatever), not to transmogrify them into broad, lofty abstractions about whether some morally obese understanding of 'the Rule of Law' has or has not been complied with. Put more bluntly, fat understandings can sometimes allow the language of 'Rule of Law Compliance' to become a political tool, platitudinously and unconstrainedly discharged with too great regularity. That is my reason one for having hefty doubts about the more modern understanding of the Rule of Law.

2. Democracy

This takes us to the place of democracy under any substantive, fat and clearly-intended-to-be-potent conception of the Rule of Law. This place for democracy and democratic decision-making, where all of us are counted equally and we vote for representatives who will decide key social issues such as immigration, can seem rather invisible under a morally laden, substantive Rule of Law conception. That, in a sentence, is a second rather big weakness. It leaves us with an insipid, desiccated reality as regards the actual scope for last-word democracy does this fat conception of the Rule of Law. (Whether such an impotent, emasculated reality is related to opting for a fat, morally pregnant conception of democracy is an interesting, if ancillary, question.)

Here is the danger. You see proponents of the fat understanding of the Rule of Law can sometimes appear to be wholly unconcerned and insouciant about the possibility that top judges, or supranational bureaucrats, might dress up their own social policy preferences in this fat, morally pregnant Rule of Law finery. And they might then invoke it to try to trump an elected legislature and have their way. After all, it is surely not inconceivable that a coterie of unelected officials might sometimes hold views different from those of the majority of a country's population. Or think of it this way. Under a thick understanding it can on occasion seem as though the Rule of Law is being made the cornerstone of democracy, rather than the other way around. Let me put my grievance here this way. As I suggested or hinted at earlier in this chapter, I have always rather thought that the gist of democracy was counting each citizen equally, be he or she plumber, teacher or high official of a supranational bureaucracy, and then letting the numbers count – without any overarching supervisory role for unelected judges or others on contentious, key issues of substance. That inevitably means that all of us will now and then be on the losing side of issues we care deeply about, even ones that can be translated into the language of rights or principles or – dare one say it – the Rule of Law.In a democracy, then, our remedies ought to be to work hard for a political party whose policies we like; it ought not to be to appeal to an almost undefinable, ineffable, morally obese conception of the Rule of Law to give us what the majority of our fellow citizens would not. I suppose then what I dislike most about these morally laden accounts of the Rule of Law is the implicit way that they leave us with an emasculated, enervated, Hong Kong-like version of democratic decision-making. So that is a second ground for having hefty doubts about the more modern understanding of the Rule of Law.

3. Attendant Costs of the Fat Understanding

My third and final point is this: Opting for a fat, morally laden, substantive conception of the Rule of Law has costs as well as benefits. In addition to the costs in terms of democratic decision-making and the masking of reasonable disagreement in society, there are particular costs related to the benefits that a procedural understanding of the Rule of Law would have delivered, but now will not. Think of the virtues we associate with this proceduralist version of the Rule of Law. These are the demands that law be in terms of general rules, known in advance, able to be used to shape expectations, clear, consistent, prospective. Opt for a thicker conception and much (or at least some) of the 'known in advance' benefits to the citizen will go because no one will know if law X or law Y is in keeping with that morally laden Rule of Law notion until some latter day officials or judges, perhaps long after the enactment of these laws, comes to town to tell us. Worse, if you admit that judge-made law – case law – is inherently retrospective, then more of the forward-looking benefits will go when it is judges dealing in the currency of a morally pregnant Rule of Law.

Now that might be a price worth paying if you thought a morally laden conception of the Rule of Law could do what a thin conception admittedly cannot do, which is to rid the world of all evil. Alas, I do not think I go out too far out on a limb in saying that fat conceptions cannot do this either. Handing some sort of overseeing power to a handful of top judges or unelected officials and telling them to exercise it on the basis of promiscuous assurances of the existence – or lack thereof – of substantive Rule of Law values guarantees no such thing. Put more bluntly, the main benefit that thick, substantive understandings of the Rule of Law seem to promise is one they can never deliver. Meantime, and despite what proponents of the thick conception sometimes suggest, there are tangible, down-to-earth benefits to the thin, proceduralist conception in terms of knowing what the laws are in advance, of their being laid down prospectively by the legislature and not shaped after-the-fact by non-democratic bodies or judicial decisions, of being able to decide how or whether you are going to shape your conduct and expectations to those general, clear, prospectively enacted laws. Heck, say this *sotto voce*, but there is even a sort of virtue and benefit in the scrupulous procedural observance of morally deficient laws if the alternative is, as it probably would be, their being applied arbitrarily, ruthlessly and on no easily predictable basis – which are the very sins the old-fashioned understanding of the Rule of Law aimed to enervate.

And of course those sorts of doubts about morally pregnant understandings of the Rule of Law can be applied to other big ticket workhorses in the world of constitutional law, ones such as the Separation of Powers.

As I made clear at the very start, the goal of this book is to voice some doubts about constitutional orthodoxy in much of today's democratic world, most notably the common law portions of that world. Put more bluntly, I am skeptical of a good deal of the emerged constitutional consensus amongst the lawyerly caste, a caste that I think has too little love of democracy and too great love for social policy-making by unelected judges and other unaccountable-to-the-voters elites. These first two chapters laid some of the groundwork for those doubts. To start we considered human rights, at the heart of much, if not virtually all, legal thinking in today's Western legal world. I aimed to show why there are grounds for being skeptical of attempts convincingly to ground human rights thinking and concepts in the way needed to make much of the orthodoxy plausible; then to doubt how easily a human rights worldview might mesh with a strong commitment to democracy; and after that to show that the modern trend to fatten up, and build lots of substantive moral content into, core constitutional precepts such as the Rule of Law is also open to doubts. This was done to set the stage for my next package of doubts, these ones related to the modern lawyerly caste's understanding of – and commitment to – democracy. I turn to those doubts now in Part II of this book.

Part II

Doubting Orthodoxy's Understanding of, and Commitment to, Democracy

Chapter Three

Why Politics Matters

I put this mildly when I say that there is a tendency amongst many judges, lawyers, and legal academics to downplay the merits of politics in favour of law and the legal resolution of social policy disagreements. At the start of this next Part of the book, therefore, I think it important to remind readers of the importance of politics. Think, in particular, of the issue of strong judicial review operating under a written constitution with an entrenched bill of rights, the more or less standard set of constitutional arrangements you would see in the United States, Canada, South Africa, Germany and elsewhere. I want briefly to argue why politics matters, and matters far more than many legal academics, judges and lawyers allow.

Now as I will elaborate on in the next chapter I am a Churchillian about democracy; it is the worst form of social decision-making going except for everything else so far tried, and that includes being preferable to decision-making by top judges (or as Waldron puts it, by committees of unelected ex-lawyers). For me 'who makes the call' matters because of what I see as the long-term benefits of counting everyone as equal and voting for elected representatives so that they can decide such rights-related issues as euthanasia, how to trade-off access to a lawyer against reducing drunk driving, who can marry. The list of what is now decided in the courts in Canada and the United States goes on and on and on.

Of course it is possible to make some sort of Kantian or non-consequentialist argument against strong judicial review of the enactments of the elected legislature. Jeremy Waldron gives perhaps the best known such argument, an argument that starts from autonomy and equality concerns and works its way up to a 'right to participate' or 'right of rights.' Or, one can make a consequentialist argument against strong judicial review, on the lines that on average, over time, in well-established democracies the elected legislatures have a better hit rate than the unelected courts. And to be clear the claim is that the legislature has a better hit rate when it comes to rights-respectingness. That would be my position in fact. You see I am a consequentialist; I much prefer Hume to Kant, on a host of fronts including Hume's account of human reason; I am a non-cognitivist, not a moral realist; the allure of deontology wholly eludes me, indeed at times it seems other-worldly to assert that consequences do not matter; as we will see next chapter I am very strongly in favour of democratic decision-making as a least bad option, and I certainly believe that the elected legislature is a far better bet than committees of unelected ex-lawyers; I am a critic of bills of rights; on democratic grounds I have doubts about the legitimacy of some aspects of international law; I think the unwritten constitutional set-up in New Zealand – where I lived and worked for eleven years – produces at least as much, no more, rights-respectingness as you find in those jurisdictions such as Canada and the United States with their written constitutions and their entrenched bills of rights with their extremely powerful unelected judges.

Still, for both Waldron and me 'who decides?' matters when it comes to resolving rights disputes and it matters in the sense that politics matters to us. Yet that desired emphasis on politics and last word power in the hands of the elected legislature sits outside of much of today's constitutional orthodoxy. Inside that orthodoxy, law matters more than politics when it comes to resolving rights-related matters.[31] Inside that orthodoxy, judges deciding after hearing reasoned arguments from lawyers for all sides is frequently a preferable process, and one that delivers outcomes that many exponents of orthodoxy think ought to be able – often, if not usually or always – to trump the compromise-laden products of the legislature.

I think otherwise. I think that when it comes to resolving rights disputes legitimacy concerns related to 'who decides?' matter and they matter a lot, which is why politics matter and ultimately matters more than law. Likewise voting and democracy. Take the example of a law school

---

[31] For an example near the far end of the spectrum see Alon Harel's *Why Law Matters* (Oxford University Press, 2014).

and the faculty having to resolve some heated debate (say, over some issue related to academic freedom) that is seen in terms of rights by at least some of the protaganists. I, personally, would prefer to have a vote within the faculty rather than a guaranteed hearing in front of the university president or law school dean. That preference of mine relates to long term consequences and my belief that the faculty will have a better hit rate in getting it right than will the university president or dean. But for the sake of argument put away all such consequentialist thinking and instead contrast Jeremy Waldron's 'right to participate' good-in-itself against Alon Harel's 'right to a hearing'[32] good-in-itself. In this sort of scenario does 'who gets to decide' matter for the non-instrumentalist? I cannot help thinking that for many it does. In other words, more than a few deontologists, in the law school scenario I have just mooted and especially if they themselves are law professors, would prefer a say in how their law school is run over, say, a guaranteed hearing with the university president (who will then make the call him or herself, having of course given you a fair hearing and with the duty to issue full reasons for the decision, etcetera etcetera). The odd Harel here and there would not agree, would think it better to have a hearing to having a vote. But many – I think most – would not.

It just seems to me that the 'how made' question, and the broader concern about legitimacy, is a much more important issue in social life

---

[32] See ibid. fn. 31 above. As I pointed out in my review of Harel's book in (2018) 9 *Jurisprudence* 132, if we assess or weigh up the pros and cons of last word decision making in terms of the 'right to a hearing' then at least for consequentialists like me one needs to factor in such considerations as: the various potential flaws in how hearings are conducted by top courts in the common law world; that test cases are often carefully selected by special interest groups to give them the best chance of winning; that government (the Executive) is sometimes not committed to winning in court, and thereby runs dead; that tactical concessions are sometimes made by counsel that may help the client in the case at hand but that assuredly disadvantage groups not before the courts; that a particular trial judge who happens to hear some case may be a long-time supporter of social change, meaning is predisposed to one side of the argument; that there is an asymmetry when it comes to *stare decisis* such that interpretively conservative judges will follow precedent with which they disagree while non-conservatives will follow their sense of justice; and the list goes on. Any right to a hearing before real life courts carry all these risks, and more. And all would need to be factored into any cost-benefit analysis of the merits of this sort of decision-making.

than the Harels of the world concede. Remember, if too many important decisions are made outside the realm of politics then democracy takes on a dessicated, enervated flavour. It becomes harder to see why people would bother to vote at all under too heavy an influence of these sort of court-centric preferred constitutional arrangements. What remains on the last word democratic table? Tax rates? Maybe, but only maybe. Meantime the panoply of social issues that people argue about and debate and care deeply about ultimately would get decided by a few ex-lawyers. It is a bleak prospect that chills me to the bone. Or let me put it this way. For me the way same-sex marriage was decided in Australia and Ireland (through direct democracy) or in New Zealand and the United Kingdom (in the elected legislature) is massively preferable to the way five unelected judges decided the matter in the United States and (in reality, if not in form) in Canada. And I say that leaving aside the plausibility or otherwise of the interpretive approaches employed by the judges in the cases in those countries. And I concede straight off that they gave the parties a hearing, and they reasoned, and they pondered and they issued a judgment, and they took rights seriously. But at the end of the day five people on the Supreme Court of the United States decided for 320 million. The nine Justices got a vote. No one else did. And this highlights my claim that 'who decides matters,' even if much of constitutional orthodoxy downplays the issue. So I am skeptical of those who downplay the importance of politics to constitutional law. And I remain skeptical even when those who do the downplaying rest or premise their core arguments on a certain view of human dignity, or on some right (including the right to a hearing) whose value is wholly independent of consequences, all in the service of defending some version or other of rights-related strong judicial review.

A variant of this argument against politics, and so another cause for skepticism, is what I will call the 'we don't want to be at the mercy of the legislature' gambit. There are two strands to this gambit. One is on my home turf of consequentialism, where you do a straight up reckoning of whether unelected judges or elected legislators do a better job (on average, over time, recognizing that no institutional body gets it correct each and every time) of protecting rights – though I suspect the more you met the judges in person the more you would like the legislature and the more you met the legislators in person the more you would like the judiciary. At any rate, if you think it is the judges who do better you will have grounds – based on a prediction of likely future consequences, themselves based on some sort of empirical analysis of past events – for wanting judges to have the last word on at least some rights-related questions. Sure, there might be wider consequences that push you towards wanting to limit the judges' last word input. These might include worries about judicial over-reach, ratcheting-up of the ambit of rights claims, enervating self-government, and more. Nevertheless, you will to some extent be swayed by this idea of 'not wanting to be at the mercy of the legislature' and that will be because of your calculation that citizens' rights are in some ways and to some extent better protected by courts.

The other strand of this gambit eschews consequences. Alon Harel is in this camp.[33] On this strand of the gambit you run the 'not being at the mercy of the legislature' argument even where and when you conclude that 'citizens' rights are not better ... protected by [a constitutionally entrenched and justiciable bill of rights because] citizens are freer under such a scheme, as they are not subject to the judgment or inclinations of the legislature.'[34] (p. 172) More bluntly, you explicitly rule out any and all arguments that look to see how citizens in fact fare with and without such strong judicial review. Harel himself does this, announcing his own skepticism that judges do in fact deliver more rights-respecting outcomes.[35] Instead, at least on the Harel version of this strand of the gambit, the argument for not wanting to be at the mercy of the elected legislature is based on an analogy or hypothetical under which B owes A $100 and A wants his money back.[36] For Harel, B's having a duty, or owing the money, is distinct from some sort of Billy Budd-like gift from B to A to help out in tough times. This analogy, that deciding rights disputes is somehow like being owed money and not some gift from the legislature, is in my opinion made to do a lot of work. Too much work.

---

33 See fns. 31 and 32 above.

34 Alon Harel, *Why Law Matters*, fn. 31 above, p. 172.

35 *Ibid.*, p. 186 *inter alia*.

36 *Ibid.*, p. 172, and in a similar form p. 141).

You see the Waldronian insight that goes missing with analogies such as these[37] is that virtually all rights-related disputes that wind their way up to a top court involve reasonable disagreement, where the purported scope of some right, how it does or does not play out against other rights, whether limits on it are reasonable, and so on are ones over which nice, smart, well-informed people differ. There is no self-evident answer. It is nothing at all like a situation where we know straight off 'that I owe John $100' or that 'B owes A $100' or even ones with Hartian penumbral doubts. So counting each of us as equal and giving us all a say on whether hate speech laws ought to be in existence or whether tobacco advertising ought to fall under the aegis of protected free speech is not at all equivalent to giving us a vote on whether B has to pay A what we already know (because we have been told upfront) is a valid debt owing by B, or even some less clear cut case of whether a debt exists or not.

Nor is it a persuasive characterisation to see such rights-related disputes as ones where those who disagree are at the mercy of the legislature, at least no more so than they are at the mercy of the top judges in the United States and Canada or at the mercy of anyone else – any human actors – who have the last-word power to decide these type of issues. Some set of human beings ultimately relying on their judgments and inclinations has to decide all such matters as these, be they judges in a German or Canadian or US set-up or be they legislators in New Zealand or (mostly in) Australia. So in one sense in a parliamentary sovereignty jurisdiction people are at the mercy of the legislature, if by that we mean the legislature has the last word. But, again, people are in that exact same sense at the mercy of nine unelected ex-lawyer judges in the US and Canada.

This non-consequentialist second strand of the 'we don't want to be at the mercy of the legislature' gambit therefore strikes me as pretty

---

[37] I made a similar point about choosing examples where 99.9 percent of readers' moral sentiments or moral judgments all point the same way, thereby finessing disagreement, in response to Larry Alexander and an analogy he used when arguing against 'letting the numbers count' decision-making. See James Allan, 'The Curious Concept of the 'Living Tree' (or Non-Locked-In) Constitution' in (eds. G. Huscroft and B. Miller) *The Challenge of Originalism: Theories of Constitutional Interpretation* (CUP, NY, 2011), 179 at p. 189 and fn. 22.

weak. It does next nothing to weaken my claim that politics matters and should matter. As for the first strand, its plausibility is directly related to the view you come to in weighing up the costs and benefits of handing important social policy-making decisions over to the unelected judiciary. Often in trying to make the case for preferring the judges to the legislature proponents will point to extreme cases, a legislature that is imagined to be mooting some truly egregious infringement on rights, rather than deciding some debatable rights-related line-drawing call. On this strand of the gambit consequentialist defenders of strong judicial review attempt to justify their position by imagining a Mugabe-like legislature run amok (the one in a ten million scenario), and then suggest the benefits of a panel of overseeing judges. Of course these attempted defences never keep the game going; they never carry on with the pretence that the legislature is now some Mugabe incarnate; instead they pretend that when the judges speak this imagined Mugabe legislature will meekly comply. It is patent nonsense. We can all have big doubts about whether such extreme cases have anything much to teach us. Likewise we can be skeptical of those versions of today's constitutional orthodoxy that downplay politics, and the importance of politics.

Chapter Four

A Churchillian and Benthamite Defence of Democracy

I now turn to my doubts about the orthodox understanding of democracy, or at least the understanding of it by significant chunks of those who comprise that constitutional orthodoxy. Within that orthodoxy there are significant worries about leaving core rights-related decision-making in the hands of the great unwashed majority. Filters, scope for gainsaying, restraints, dollops of what is in effect elements of aristocracy and more are all welcomed. My doubts about such orthodox thinking will be manifold. They will relate to my task this chapter of defending democracy against those Cassandras who are pessimistic, even in a comparative sense, about its capabilities and worth. This sort of pessimism, to make the point slightly differently, is common amongst those who defend strong judicial review under an entrenched bill of rights; it is a commonly heard refrain amongst the lawyerly caste in Canada and the United States and Britain and in many other democracies and supranational bodies. In broad brush strokes, one could be forgiven for concluding that amongst this caste there is little love of democracy and much love for unelected judges resolving a good many, for some most, social policy issues. And frequently it is part and parcel of that greater love for judicial decision-making to be quite down on democracy, to put it in colloquial terms. I am skeptical of that sort of gloominess. I doubt the Cassandra case.

That said, I expect that many of those pessimists about democracy will think me something of a Pollyanna, all too inclined to see the world through rose-colored spectacles that transmogrify what they perceive as the three-quarters empty glass into what I claim is a three-quarters full one.

So let me be blunt right from the start. Mine is a least-bad or Churchillian[38] defence of democracy, one that readily concedes that democratic decision-making has its flaws and faults (and a good deal more in some jurisdictions than in others) but that still insists that it beats any and all alternatives. In other words, my theme will be that democracy beats any alternative these Cassandras can suggest. It beats rule by unelected judges (which is an apt description the more judges appear to be unconstrained under their approach to interpreting laid down laws). It beats rule by a bureaucratic elite. It beats theocracies and military juntas. It beats rule by a far too unaccountable supranational body like the European Union ('EU').It beats rule by the smartest university academics, even if they all happen to be legal academics. It beats, as Mr. Churchill put it, any other alternative so far tried. Hence I am in no way claiming that democratic decision-making is perfect, or close to perfect. It is just better than anything its critics can suggest. At least that is my position and the standard against which my argument aims to be weighed or evaluated. Note, too, that my stance is wholly compatible with holding non-trivial worries about the future prospects for least-bad democratic decision-making. I am here simply defending comparatively best (or upper echelon) practice in today's democratic world against all constitutional orthodoxy's pessimists out there, not making predictions about its future resilience.

Now whether that be a Pollyannaesque position, or not, before I can set about trying to defend it I need to provide a clarification, make a distinction, and then suggest why we might, *prima facie*, expect democracy to be a least-bad decision-making system. I will turn to these preliminaries now and then later in this chapter consider and reject possible lines of rebuttal, thereby doing what space permits to make my Pollyanna case against the Cassandras.

---

[38] Winston Churchill's exact words were 'that democracy is the worst form of Government except all those other forms that have been tried from time to time.' 444 Parl Deb House of Commons (5th ser.) (1947) col. 207 (UK) (remarks of Mr. Churchill).

1. Preliminaries

First off, as I noted in chapter two I want to clarify again that I am here defending a thin conception of democracy rather than some morally pregnant or morally laden account. As I have defended just such a thin or morally Spartan account of democracy in the past,[39] at length, I will for present purposes be brief in setting out this clarification. If one imagines a spectrum ranging from accounts of democracy that are infused with moral substance all the way over to accounts that are almost wholly procedural and in terms of substance quite dessicated, then my defence will be of understandings of democracy that reside towards the latter part of that spectrum, the procedural end. What I want to rule out are accounts of democracy that assert something along the lines of 'jurisdiction X, in addition to anything else, only counts as a "democratic" one if it upholds the right to this, that and the other thing and in some moral sense or other must be a good, or at least an acceptable, jurisdiction.' Or put differently, I want to adopt a thin, morally enervated account of democracy – basically a procedural one – that just looks to 'how a government was selected' and overwhelmingly shuns adding on disqualifying conditions focused on substantive evaluations of whether what the government happens to be doing once in office (or promised to do during an election) passes some set of moral and political thresholds. I want to have room to say 'country Y is democratic but is doing morally bad things, even plenty of bad things.' I want any country to count as a democracy that chooses its government by counting each citizen or resident equally in terms of allowing almost all of them over a set age[40] a free and secret vote and then actually letting the numbers count in terms of picking that government (whether or not the

---

[39] See James Allan, *Democracy in Decline: Steps in the Wrong Direction* (McGill-Queen's U. Press, 2014) and 'Thin Beats Fat Yet Again – Conceptions of Democracy' (2006) 25 *Law & Philosophy* 533-571.

[40] We can put to one side such peripheries as whether convicted murderers or rapists ought, or ought not, to have a vote. In my view this falls into the Waldronian realm of reasonable disagreement and I side-step it (and variants of the prisoner voting debate) completely for the purposes of this overview discussion of democracy. I should also make explicit what is probably evident to everyone – that this chapter's defence of democracy is necessarily a brief one and hence focuses on replying to certain important claims against democracy, leaving numerous empirical, historical and other issues untouched.

result then be filtered through an Electoral College, or subject to the vagaries of a proportional voting system or bicameralism, or limited by a strong federalism of various sorts). I want there to be plenty of room to say 'that nation over there is a democracy but its government is doing some morally egregious things.' I do not want the largely procedural question of how a government has been selected to be irredeemably tangled up with substantive moral and political judgments regarding the choices it is making such that these substantive choices allow, or force, one to say 'country X does not count as a democracy since it is doing bad things or is denying all sorts of rights we (or I) judge essential to good government.' I do not want, in other words, the concept of democracy to have stuffed into it near-on every virtue the user of the term can imagine.

I think that on balance there are all sorts of good consequences in keeping separate the 'Is this a democracy?' and the 'Is it a morally good or at least tolerable government?' questions. Now as I said, I have argued that case in full elsewhere and so (as a clarification of the sort of understanding of democracy that I am defending in this chapter) will just assert it here[41] – that democracy is best understood in largely procedural terms only.

---

41 I think I could today add to the reasons I gave in the past for adopting a thin understanding of democracy. I would do so by taking up a core insight offered by Fred Schauer in his 'Rights, Constitutions, and the Perils of Panglossianism' (2018) 38 *Oxford Journal of Legal Studies* 635. In Schauer's piece he points to the frequently observed, however understandable, tendency many people (meaning also many academics) have of wanting to define away hard choices or zero sum conflicts of interest rather than having to choose between them in a way that requires tough choices and debatable evaluations. Schauer describes this unwillingness as the tendency to be 'Panglossian' and hence to want to paint a 'best of all possible worlds' where hard choices (be they between inconsistent factual presuppositions or competing value judgements) are simply assumed away. Those who insist on a morally laden or morally pregnant or morally fat understanding of democracy can be characterised in precisely similar terms, as Panglossians. They are in effect removing any possible conflict between democracy (and the democratic method for choosing a government) and a lack of tolerable rights-respectingness once an elected government is in office. To have the former, they say, you must avoid the latter, by definitional fiat as it were. And that means, for them, that all such conflicts between 'a good procedural way of picking governments, all things considered' and 'the possibility of bad, maybe really bad, choices being made by governments chosen thusly' simply cannot happen. The latter possibility is foreclosed under their more morally substantive definition of the former. In Schauerian terms, they are too Panglossian to

If that is the clarification I needed to provide, the distinction I will make can be stated quite briefly. I want readers to keep distinct in their minds the difference between two sorts of claims, roughly speaking between 1) 'democracy is not up to the job in today's world,[42] or is becoming ever less up to the job, or would be outperformed by a system with a much bigger role for unelected experts' and 2) 'democracy and democratic decision-making is today under attack from various unelected decision-makers.' The two claims are quite distinct and in this chapter I am taking issue with 1), not with 2) – the first not the second. So yes, I am defending democracy's credentials and track record against all comers. But no, I am not in any way whatsoever denying 2). Indeed, quite to the contrary, I have recently argued at book length that second is correct and that democracy and democratic decision-making are under attack.[43]

That brings me to my third preliminary point. Here, I want to set out why, without knowing more or if considering the issue at the dawn of the democratic age, one might nevertheless expect democracy and democratic decision-making to be the least-bad option on the table. Start with Jeremy Bentham, who in fact was writing at the dawn of the democratic age, and with his vigorous support for democracy. Readers will be aware that Bentham was one of the founders of utilitarian thinking.[44] And of course it is true that the early Bentham, not least in his *An Introduction to the Principles of Morals and Legislation* (IPML) and while focused on giving advice to the legislature, was naïve about power and

---

allow the possibility of such conflicts and hence the resulting hard choices and debatable value judgements that would ensue. They over-fill the concept of democracy with moral substance. They too readily define away Waldronian disagreement, if I can put it in terms Schauer himself did not.

[42] To focus the debate I will deliberately put to one side all questions of whether democracy works better in the developed world. For the purposes of this chapter I will be focused on the established democratic world, or even just on the main long-standing Anglosphere democracies.

[43] See fn. 39 above.

[44] See Jeremy Bentham, *An Introduction to the Principles of Morals and Legislation* (Batoche Books 2000), which although published in 1789 was in fact written a fair bit earlier, having been first printed in 1780. The gist of utilitarianism can certainly be found in pre-Bentham writers, including in David Hume's work, but Bentham was the first great systematiser of the utilitarian doctrine. See Geoffrey Scarre, (1996) *Utilitarianism* 57 at 72.

how it might need to be controlled. In IPML Bentham asks us to think in terms of sticks and carrots, of pain and pleasure, as the only tools at hand for a legislature to change people's behaviour. Sure, in any society there will be your Mother Theresas who if left all alone will act from their own inclinations so as to increase overall social happiness – 'the greatest happiness of the greatest number'[45] in Bentham's formulation. Conversely, there will be your potential or wannabe robbers, rapists and murderers whose natural inclinations have to be redirected by the legislature either by the prospect of reward, aka pleasure (for Bentham a good-in-itself), or failing that then with the threat and possibly the quite severe application of pain (for Bentham a bad-in-itself). Most of us will lie somewhere between these two poles.

But the early Bentham just took it for granted that if he pointed out to the legislature how to make laws that would be likely to increase social happiness (by their sticks and carrots application of incentives) the legislators would be inclined to travel down that path. The later Bentham saw his own early self as naïve. If, as Bentham thought, all of us want pleasure (broadly understood but in ways that vary from person to person) and do not want pain (also broadly understood), then he later realized that this must be true of legislators too, of those with power. In other words, if all of us, wherever our instinctive or inculcated proclivities may place us on the spectrum, want happiness and the avoidance of pain then this must be true of those with power, too. Hence, the obvious question that follows from that is what sort of incentives – what sort of application of the possibility of future pleasure and pain – might realign the behavior of legislators so that they did a better job of increasing overall social happiness in how they governed and enacted laws.

It is in answering that question, given his sticks and carrots view of human nature, that Bentham became one of the great supporters of

---

[45] See J.H. Burns, 'Happiness and Utility: Jeremy Bentham's Equation' (2005) 17 *Utilitas* 46 at p.46. See also IPML chapter I, paragraphs II-III, VII inter alia. Note that over his lifetime Bentham changed his mind on this, equivocating between 'greatest happiness of the greatest number' and 'greatest average happiness' – the latter building in a sort of 'strength of feeling' component. See Burns p. 46. But in the end, Bentham went back to the 'greatest happiness of the greatest number' measure as the other is too easy to game.

democracy and indeed was pushed from being an opponent of the new country of the United States to being one of its biggest supporters.[46] For him it was all about incentives to change behavior, just now with the focus on legislators rather than regular citizens. Sure, such a 19th century sticks and carrots view of human psychology is undoubtedly overly reductionist. But all the same, there is clearly a good deal to it. And so that is what Bentham did; he applied this sticks and carrots incentives worldview to those with law-making power. And what eventuated was a strong endorsement of democracy along the lines of the following sort of thinking.

To start, you give most everyone – over a certain age and who looks moderately sane – a vote on who gets to wield this power. Why? Because the goal is to increase the greatest happiness of the greatest number. And no one knows what will make the adult you happy better than you, at least so thinks the great anti-paternalist Bentham.[47] Notice again that this is no narrowly understood view of happiness. Some might get happiness from a higher income, some less so, a few Mother Theresas not at all. Some things might matter much more to you than having more money in your pocket and a lower tax rate. Bentham does not pre-judge. It is up to you to give an indication of what will increase your happiness – because you know this better than anyone else – by telling us with your vote, however blunt a tool that may be.

---

[46] See H.L.A. Hart, 'Bentham and the United States of America' (1976) 19 *Journal of Law & Economics* 547 at p.548.

[47] Bentham was nothing if not an anti-paternalist. This contrasts quite noticeably with one of his acolytes, also a utilitarian, the even more famous John Stuart Mill, who in comparison was a paternalist. See Robin West, 'Rationality, Hedonism, and the Case for Paternalistic Intervention' (1997) 3 *Legal Theory* 125. That said, one might be an anti-paternalist, broadly speaking, for two distinct reasons. Hence to the sort of 'I'm afraid that if left to pursue their own pleasure, many people would end up being beer-drinking, TV-watching couch potatoes' type retort one might reply A) 'If that's what they enjoy, that's what they should do' or B) 'That might happen; it would be unfortunate to be sure; but letting an elite decide what lives would be good for people is unlikely to produce any better results and would be extremely dangerous given the power such elites would have to have.' This B) reply might, or might not, be buttressed by challenging just how Philosopher King-like today's elites actually are. Thank you to Steven Smith for this distinction between these differing foundations for anti-paternalism.

On the other side of the equation, those with power need to win an awful lot of votes to stay in power.[48] If we assume that those running for office want to win[49] – that in some broad sense winning the election for this office will increase the candidate's happiness, or rather at the time of running the candidate thinks that it will – then letting-the-numbers-count democratic systems for choosing who will govern go some significant way towards realigning the interests of A) all of us voters and B) those who end up with power. It is by no means a perfect alignment of interests, and it will not play out that way all the time, but it is far better than what you have without asking people via voting and it creates a very real sort of accountability – certainly a more tangible sort than when some unelected judges or some 19th century aristocrats tell us that they have looked inside themselves and are truly doing what they think is of most benefit to others, that their decision has nothing much to do with what *they* want, believe, or prefer but rather is solely to do with what they believe *you* want – or should want. Bentham was scathingly dismissive of all such *de haut en bas* claims supposedly driven by altruism.[50]He wanted a tangible sort of accountability on those with power.

---

48 Just how many can vary with voting systems. But it will be a large percentage of the voting population's votes they will need to stay in office. To be sure of electoral victory they will need to aim to win noticeably more than half the votes of the electorate.

49 And notice that on this Benthamite understanding it is no coherent criticism at all to say of some politician 'She only wants to get re-elected.' That, for Benthamites, is what underlies the incentives in the system and what makes this politician accountable not to everyone in society but to as many as it is likely to take for her to have a good chance of being re-elected. Take away the desire to be re-elected and you remove the core incentive in the system until the next election when she is voted out. From now till then this politician becomes much, much more of a free agent and far less responsive to the views of the voting public.

50 Compare Bentham's brutal, yet immensely entertaining, description of what he thinks really lies behind moral claims that affect others but in fact do not look likely to increase overall social happiness (so are moral claims that do not align with what utility arguably dictates). See IPML chapter II, para. XIV nn. 1-9. Bentham says these are nothing more than 'I like it' or 'I don't like it' claims, but that to have any chance of swaying others they will be presented as being in keeping with such altruistic-sounding abstractions as 'the fitness of things' or 'the moral law' or 'God's will' or 'right reason' or in today's language with 'fundamental human rights.' See IPML chapter II, paras II, XVIII.

I might therefore sum up this third preliminary point of mine in this way. Those who downgrade, undersell, pooh-pooh, or attack the value or worth of democracy seem to me to be too insouciant about accountability concerns, too willing to ignore one of the core virtues of democracy and of democratic decision-making (understood as a procedural good). And this core virtue is a function of how democracy lets us 'throw the bums out' while, in a Benthamite way, going some worthwhile distance towards aligning the interests of the elected politicians – who, to keep their jobs and whatever attendant perks there may be, need to aim for the votes of more than half of those who go to the polls – with those of the voters.[51] So back at the dawn of the democratic age, having made accountability to as many citizens as possible a key goal, it seems highly plausible to me that one would have had strong, prima facie grounds for expecting democracy and democratic decision-making to be the least-bad option on the table, to outperform all those other forms of governing and decision-making that Churchill lumps together as 'having been tried from time to time.'

2. Considering and Rejecting Possible Lines of Rebuttal: Pollyanna prevails over Cassandra

That is a prima facie type case for thinking democracy is as good as it gets. Let me now consider some plausible rebuttals. I will lump these together in what some might consider to be an idiosyncratic way and one that has a bit of overlap between each heading or mooted rebuttal. But that is probably unavoidable.

i. Embrace Paternalism and Prefer Aristocracy

The above Benthamite-type defence of democracy is premised in part on an anti-paternalist view that the adult you is better placed than anyone else to indicate what is best for you – hence on average, over time, voters will beat experts (in a least-bad sense only, remember) when it

[51] An imperfect alignment, no doubt, but perhaps a least-bad one and better than just trusting judges – or anyone else – who cannot be removed from office anywhere nearly as easily, and certainly not by you and me the voters.

comes to increasing social welfare. One sort of rebuttal is just to reject that anti-paternalist premise. There are various bases for doing so.

1a) Here we focus on the voters' ignorance of facts. Many or most voters, goes this sort of rebuttal, are not well-informed on the facts. In that sense they are on the whole pretty ignorant. Combine that with an implicit or explicit belief that political disagreements turn overwhelmingly on getting the facts right, not on individuals' differing sentiments or value-judgements, and you have a potent attack on democracy – a further, often unspoken, premise of which is that a coterie of experts, of those who do happen to know the facts, be they top judges or bureaucrats or medical or corporate elites or whomever, would do better than majoritarian democracy. And that is precisely the book-length argument that several years ago Ilya Somin made[52] and that I then critiqued in a review in *Constitutional Commentary*.[53] As I said in that review, the picture Somin paints 'is one where social policy choices (outside of, perhaps, one's preferred abortion regime) would become largely self-evident provided all of the disputants knew (or agreed on) all of the facts.' (p. 488) Yet there are huge difficulties with that characterization, especially for those who follow the great Scottish philosopher David Hume in believing that reason is inert and, hence, that sentiments and feelings drive action not reason. (at p. 489) Further, they note that the naturalistic fallacy makes the move from 'is' to 'ought' fraught, that moral evaluations do not possess a mind-independent status, and so on. At the risk of a lengthy excerpt from my own previous work, here is how I put it in replying to Somin:

> Put differently, and leaving aside the philosophy, it is not just facts about the external, causal world that determine people's preferred social policy positions. We all bring different sentiments and preferences to the table. So we can know (or agree) all the costs of climate change and of a carbon tax and yet some will want to forego "5 units" of current consumption, some "20 units," and some will want to put money into coping

[52] Ilya Somin, *Democracy and Political Ignorance: Why Smaller Government is Smarter* (Stanford U. Press, 2nd ed, 2016). For a not terribly dissimilar sort of pessimism about voter ignorance see too Richard Kay's argument set out in chapter twelve below.

[53] James Allan, 'Do Judges Know Best?' (2017) 32 *Constitutional Commentary* 479. The next few paragraphs follow the critique of Somin-type arguments I made there.

with a changed world rather than foregoing any current consumption by cutting emissions. Or take the purely economic realm. Is it irrational or against reason to prefer to reduce relative inequality, even if (let us assume) such inequality-reducing-steps would lower a society's overall wealth levels, and indeed would even make the bottom quintile of the population poorer? I don't think so. Some people might simply prefer or value more relative equality to preferring more overall wealth in society, or even to preferring more absolute wealth for the bottom quintile than what they would have if inequality were not being reduced. Now that favoring of more equality over more absolute wealth (or more absolute wealth for those at the bottom) would not be my preference, nor would it be Somin's. But neither is the holding of that preference irrational, at least not on the Humean understanding of reason.

Somin seems to me to skate over these deep philosophical matters and just assume that most of the time "the facts" will do the work (or enough of the work) needed to resolve disagreement so that all that stands in the way of knowing what to do is political ignorance. Hence, for Somin, we just need to inject a bit of aristocracy (of the modern judicial variety rather than the older land-holding sort) into the political system and by doing that we will outperform the calls that would be made under a majoritarian set-up driven by the voters, such as you see most clearly in New Zealand (which, by the way, ranks higher in terms of economic freedom than does the United States, with its strong judicial review), or the United Kingdom before it entered the European Union.[54]

1b) And, of course, it is worse than that for Somin-style 'the voters are ignorant of facts so we can dispense with, or diminish the input from, democracy' arguments. After all, if each voter's sentiments and values and feelings do matter in achieving the optimal social policy position, then there is this further or related danger with expert-driven decision-making processes, namely that:

[S]ay, a lawyerly caste from which the top judges are chosen [might] tend, on average, to hold different political and social druthers than the majority of voters, [meaning that] on my [Humean] premises factual knowledge (or voters' ignorance of facts) would not be the only variable. The values being brought

[54] *Ibid.*, pp. 489-490 (footnote omitted).

> to the table by the ultimate decision-makers would matter too.[55]

This, in other words, is the danger of a non-majoritarian decision-making elite having values and preferences and druthers noticeably out of step with the majority's, and when afforded the power to do so of favouring their own side of the ledger. In today's world of an expert-imposed euro currency, Common Agricultural Policy, and mass immigration preference (to focus just on the European Union, and to choose from amongst a host of examples where the 'expert' preference in no way at all seems self-evidently better than the voters'), this hardly seems to be an insignificant worry or danger.

1c) Nor are those the only two weaknesses in the 'voters are ignorant' rebuttal to my least-bad defence of democracy. Another problem with Somin-type arguments that focus on voters' ignorance of facts is that proponents of that view are likely to frame hotly debated political issues in vague and amorphous terms ('crime reduction,' 'environmental protection,' 'security concerns,' etcetera) so that they can then (as I said in my review of his book):

> follow Somin and assert that "differences … turn primarily on disagreements over how to achieve widely agreed-upon goals" …. However, that seems to me to be because [they] have finessed disagreement by moving [their] focus up to the Olympian heights of "widely agreed-upon-goals." Make things sufficiently general, sweeping and generic and of course [they] are far more likely to find overwhelmingly shared human sentiments that then only require knowledge of likely facts to point [them] towards what to do. But descend down from those heights towards the quagmire of day-to-day detail and all those shared sentiments across the population start to dissipate. And then "knowing the facts" is not enough to make the decisions with the best long-term consequences. You need also to know what people's differing sentiments or preferences or values are, and no one knows those better than you do, the voter, and certainly not a committee of unelected ex-lawyers. Or so it seems to me…. [56]

---

[55] *Ibid.*, p. 490.

[56] *Ibid.*, p. 490 (quoting Somin, fn. 52 above, at p. 11).

2) The various permutations of the 'voters are ignorant of the facts' attempted rebuttal of my defence of democracy do not exhaust the options. Another possibility is far blunter. Given that paternalism amounts to the claim 'that I know better than you what is good for you,' this next possible rebuttal basically can be understood as forswearing paternalism – because at heart it doesn't much care about a big chunk of the voting population and those voters' professed happiness/welfare/preferences – in favour of a vigorous sort of aristocracy. Here, you just characterize a big proportion of the voters as 'deplorable' or in some other way unworthy of consideration. Of course, virtually any competent politician operating in one of today's long-established democracies would be adept enough not to admit to such views openly, publicly and on the record. Well, perhaps every once in a while such sentiments might slip out, by mistake, even from the mouth of a veteran politician. Meanwhile, I suspect that there are plenty of grounds for believing (not least as a result of my own personal experiences chatting with a good many others over drinks) that more than a few people do harbour such aristocratic sentiments – and here I am certainly not excluding from the ranks of such sentiment-harbourers those who happen to be top judges, law professors, law students, senior bureaucrats, people working for international agencies in top capacities (including United Nations personnel who pay no income tax), the list goes on. Sure, they may be careful not to reveal these views frequently or outside of a well-vetted coterie of friends. But something along the lines of this 'some of my fellow citizens are deplorable' outlook gives them grounds for thinking democratic decision-making can be improved upon. It is suboptimal.

My brief response to this sort of 'deplorables' rebuttal, of what amounts to demanding an aristocratic element in one's constitutional arrangements, is that such calls always look better – or so say I – when one is himself part of that aristocracy. Academics tend to see the value of academics having extra special input. Judges tend to see its value when it is other judges. And so on.

Worse, you could never sell it to people upfront and openly. If you tried, the 'deplorables' (and indeed others not as aristocratically inclined) would be likely to revolt. Hence, any such undisguised pleas for more aristocracy in any of today's long-established democracies would have bad net consequences, as well as quite possibly subverting the legitimacy of established democratic institutions even where those pleas were ultimately rejected. Of course, I concede that in theory best consequences can diverge from the path of honesty and of openness and of any realistic ability to sell the proposal to one's fellow citizens. But having conceded that, I also think most of us would be more than a little skeptical of the worth of preferred constitutional arrangements that can never honestly be revealed to one's countrymen. Accordingly, let me simply say that in my opinion there is just too much whiff of 'elitism piled on aristocracy' about any arrangements that attempt to enervate democracy due to the 'deplorables' critique – that they would smack too obviously of the arrangements of the European Union, and would be likely to unleash the sort of voter backlash we can occasionally see there, a backlash that flows from the paucity of the EU's democratic credentials. And all of that is without stating the obvious, namely that if you put such a call for more aristocracy to all of us voters in a referendum or at some sort of constitutional convention it would be defeated, and be defeated badly. So it has to be pursued in secret, or be heavily disguised.

That is a taste of one cluster of plausible lines of rebuttal to my least-bad defence of democracy, all the variants that in one way or another embrace paternalism and prefer aristocracy. I reject the core lines of attack of all such rebuttals. I do so for the reasons sketched above. Hence, in providing a Churchillian-style defence of democracy I think that Pollyanna has thus far warded off Cassandra.

ii. Reject Procedural Democracy on Wholly Moral Grounds

Another line of rebuttal focuses almost overwhelmingly on the moral realm and argues that in some way or another democratic decision-making – for proceduralists like me recall that that means decision-making rules that put majoritarianism and letting-the-numbers-count concerns front and centre – is less morally good than some preferred alternative. In other words, the claim here boils down to asserting that democracy fails on moral grounds, consequences be damned.

One of the most uncompromising versions of that sort of argument was mentioned in chapter three. This is Alon Harel's *Why Law Matters*.[57] Recall that Harel opts to make pre-eminent the 'right to a hearing,' though I can see no reason why one might not choose any sort of right to be what is claimed to trump democratic decision-making. What you end up with in the case of Harel's book is a wholly non-instrumentalist, 'morality trumps consequences' case for strong judicial review – to the extent that Harel himself concedes that the track record of unelected judges looks no better to him than that of the elected branches.[58]That said, my view is that this sort of Harelian argument requires one to prefer Kant to Hume (on a host of fronts, including their respective accounts of human reason), moral realism to non-cognitivism, deontology to consequentialism, not to mention one having to be quite sanguine about the legitimacy of international law, of unelected judges using a Bill of Rights to make veto-proof calls on a host of social policy issues, and of goods-in-themselves 'rights to a hearing' not being open to being gamed – not to mention having to overlook the sort of response Jeremy Waldron makes to Michael Moore.[59]

Worse for this sort of rebuttal is the fact that even from within a wholly deontological moral framework, one largely to Harel's liking, there is plenty of room to make a case in favour of democracy. After all, as I have noted in chapter three above, that is precisely what Jeremy Waldron has done. Waldron makes a strong rights, deontological argument on behalf of democracy – by starting with non-consequentialist equality concerns to get to his argument that people do not treat others as

---

[57] See fn. 31 above.

[58] Alon Harel, *Why Law Matters* (Oxford University Press, 2014), p. 186.

[59] The gist of that response is that it doesn't matter in practical terms whether the non-cognitivist or the deontologist (usually with Kantian meta-ethical and normative core principles) is correct about the status of moral evaluations. Humans are in the same position either way. Why? Because as Jeremy Waldron made clear in replying to Michael Moore, there is no universally accepted epistemic method for discerning what those 'true' moral principles are. Hence moral realist versus moral realist is in no different position from non-cognitivist versus non-cognitivist. See Jeremy Waldron, *Law and Disagreement* (Oxford University Press, 1999), chapter 8 and especially pp. 164-165. Accordingly there is no reason to believe judges, administrators, or anyone else will have superior insight about moral reality or rights than legislators, put to the side Somin's 'know more facts' thesis.

autonomous agents worthy of respect unless they have an equal say in decision-making, even over rights-related issues.And using that to ground his Waldronian 'right to participate,' his 'right of rights,' which lies at the heart of his deontological defence of democracy.[60]

All in all then, this class *B)* sort of rebuttal (or attack on a least-bad defence of democracy) will not convince anyone whose underlying starting positions are in the same solar system, or perhaps galaxy, as mine. And even in the Harelian part of the moral and metaphysical universe there remains plenty of room to doubt such rebuttals. Hence, I think Pollyanna has warded off Cassandra again. Of course Harel's is not the only sort of argument that prefers the unelected judges to the elected legislators and so we turn next in that broader direction.

iii. Assert that Strong Judicial Review (of the sort that cannot plausibly be characterized as a form of Constitutionalism) still Beats Democracy

Strong judicial review, the sort that empowers judges to strike down or invalidate statutes enacted by the democratically elected legislature (and in that sense the sort that can be distinguished from judicial review of administrative action – the weaker kind that does not involve a direct challenge to the elected legislature), can be supported on a host of grounds. Some of those grounds do not seem to me to involve anywhere near as direct challenges to democracy and democratic decision-making as others of those grounds. For present purposes only, I am therefore going to generalize and make a sweeping stipulation that divides the world of strong judicial review – at least in the common law world – into two camps. The first, I am going to dub 'strong judicial review that takes place as a form of constitutionalism' and the second, as 'strong judicial review outside the bounds of constitutionalism.' Defences of the former sort, judicial review as a form of constitutionalism, I am going to ignore. I am going to do so because in my view all such conceptions of strong judicial review are much easier to reconcile with democracy and I will sketch why in a moment. It is the latter sort only, strong judicial

---

[60] See Jeremy Waldron, *Law and Disagreement* (Oxford University Press, 1999), at p. 213.

review that is defended on grounds outside the aegis of a constitutionalism worldview, that I will here consider as a potential rebuttal to my least-bad Churchillian defence of democracy.

Let me therefore skip over all sorts of highly debateable value judgements as to whether any particular writer's defence of strong judicial review belongs in the first or second category, as well as what precisely might be needed to qualify for membership of one or the other. For present purposes (with more to follow later in this book) it will suffice if I speak in rough-and-ready terms and contend that the first occurs where a jurisdiction's top judges are upholding the locked-in meaning some authoritative and legitimate[61] lawmaker in the past laid down in a constitutional text. Put bluntly, the judges are not just making it up according to their own moral and political druthers; they are honestly seeking a mind-independent answer, however difficult to find that answer may be for limited biological creatures. As readers will see later in this book, I happen to believe, with Larry Alexander, Rick Kay, Richard Ekins,

---

61 Of course questions of legitimacy are themselves debatable and subject to reasonable disagreement. Plausible legitimacy-giving options might include: i) it was the result of a referendum where at least half the voters have to give it the nod (this basically being the Australian method of constitutional amendment); ii) it was the result of a democratically enacted statute (this being how the statutory bills of rights in New Zealand and the UK came into being); or iii) it was the result of the best form of widespread citizen input that was available at the time (this arguably being the case in the US for its written constitution). The 1982 Canadian method of entrenching a Charter of Rights was, in my view, a far less legitimate option compared to any of those given that in Canada there was never any referendum on the issue nor any election either, be it a federal or provincial one. See F.L. Morton, 'The Political Impact of the Canadian Charter of Rights and Freedoms' (1987) 20 *Canadian Journal of Political Science* 31 at 31-32. More generally, see Richard Kay, 'The Creation of Constitutions in Canada and the US' (1984) 7 *Canada – United States Law Journal* 111. A small coterie of the political class simply brought it in over the heads of the voters – which is not to say that the Charter of Rights is not popular today, because it is. But the legitimacy of how something came to be can be distinguished from its present day popularity. Perhaps even less legitimate, if that is possible in a modern day democracy, is how Australia, the last major democratic country with no national bill of rights, came to have a limited implied freedom of political communication. In my view the top judges outright made it up, for some because the voting population kept rejecting a bill of rights. See generally James Allan, 'The Three "R"s of Recent Australian Judicial Activism: Roach, Rowe and (no) 'Riginalism' (2012) 36 *Melbourne University Law Review* 743-782.

and others, that that requires some sort of intentionalist originalism, some search by judges for what the legitimate lawmakers intended. Yet whether you agree with me on that, or not, is not at issue here. Include within the first category any theory that plausibly asserts the judges are doing something other than legislating from the bench and there is then a sense that the answers they give can be understood as having been in some way or other locked-in – meaning, given our legitimacy stipulation, that earlier voters agreed to take certain things off the parliamentary sovereignty table. It will not have been an agreement to give the judges a blank cheque though. The list will not be ever-changing at the point-of-application and malleable in the hands of the judges. And as for issues not on that earlier agreed to 'these are off the table' list? Well, they will remain with the voters. Hence, strong judicial review as a form of constitutionalism seems to me to be a good deal more compatible with democracy.

But what happens if the world we live in does not happen to look much like one where our top judges are in fact doing what constitutionalism demands they do – perhaps they are treating the document as a 'living Constitution' or are affording it a moral reading or a Dworkinian best fit one? What then? Because as we shall see in more detail in chapter twelve this is precisely what Richard Kay happens to believe is the case, as a matter of empirical fact, as regards today's United States (and indeed Canada and elsewhere). '[A] fair examination of actual constitutional judgments is unlikely to convince many observers that those decisions closely match up with the rules in the constitutional text.'[62] And I agree with Kay, as I suspect do plenty of others.[63]Gaze around the common law world and, as he says, top judges look largely (nay, overwhelmingly) to be doing something that is very hard to categorise as 'strong judicial review as a form of constitutionalism.'

---

[62] Richard Kay, 'Democracy, Mixed Government, and Judicial Review' in (eds. Lisa Burton Crawford, Patrick Emerton and Dale Smith) *Law Under a Democratic Constitution: Essays in Honour of Jeffrey Goldsworthy* (Hart, 2019) 199 at pp. 212. See too pp. 223-224.

[63] For a particularly muscular and convincing expression of this theme see Robert F Nagel, *Constitutional Cultures: The Mentality and Consequences of Judicial Review* (University of California Press, 1989) and Robert F Nagel, *Unrestrained: Judicial Excess and the Mind of the American Lawyer* (Transaction Publishers, 2008).

And that gives us another type of rebuttal to my least-bad defence of democracy. Here you just say something along the lines that what such judges are doing under the second category above can be endorsed or reconceptualized as a sort of Super Senate, tricameralism-type check and balance; the top judiciary are often or largely discretionary decision-makers, true, but this is all to the good. Or such is claim.

Alas, this type of rebuttal suffers all of the weaknesses of the sort I set out in the *A) Embrace Paternalism and Prefer Aristocracy* section of this chapter above – it over-emphasizes voter ignorance; it implicitly requires an overblown trust in experts; it betrays an insouciance about accountability concerns of the sort that deeply worried Bentham; and, here too, it could never be sold to people upfront and openly.[64]

Cassandra has still not driven Pollyanna from the field. This rebuttal fails as well.

iv. Fret About Centralization and Growing Bureaucratic Power

I will be extremely brief with this mooted rebuttal to my least-bad defence of democracy. It will be the last rebuttal I will consider. Yes, there may well be a problem with growing administrative and bureaucratic power at the expense of democracy and democratic decision-making. And yes, too great creeping centralization may also be a legitimate worry. In neither case, though, is less democracy an answer. It will not be a bureaucratic supranational EU-like body that quite significantly deregulates, and removes numerous regulations for every new one adopted. It will be an elected administration. And no non-elected body is likely to fight growing centralization either, including university administrations.[65] Nor do the top judges in the common law federalist world have all that great a record (I put this kindly you understand) in

---

[64] As Richard Kay, a proponent of this sort of rebuttal to my least-bad defence of democracy, himself concedes. See Kay, fn. 62 above, at 221, 226. See too my discussion of this in chapter twelve below.

[65] This is a point I have made at more length in critiquing Australian universities. See generally James Allan, 'The Administration of Australian Universities: A National Scandal? Or Amiss in Funderland?' in (ed. W. Coleman) *Campus Meltdown: The Deepening Crisis in Australian Universities* (Connor Court, 2019), 23.

defending federalism and decentralization against the center, especially not in Australia.[66] Only the elected politicians, State or Federal, have any plausible hope of combatting this deleterious trend. Or so say I. Put differently, Pollyanna has little difficulty swatting away Cassandra's doubts about democracy on this score.

3. Concluding Remarks for this Chapter

In this chapter I have given readers my least-bad defence of democracy and then defended that defence against all those Cassandras who are pessimistic about its comparative capabilities and worth. I am a full-blooded Pollyanna when it comes to providing a Churchillian and Benthamite defence of democratic decision-making. That said, and as I made clear in the distinction I offered at the start of this chapter, there is a difference between attacks that assert 1) 'democracy is not up to the job in today's world and would be outperformed by a more elitist, more aristocratic, more expert driven system' and those that assert 2) 'democracy is today under attack from various unelected decision-makers.' As I there noted, I agree with type 2) claims.[67] In fact I even believe that elected politicians can themselves be part of such attacks (with the British Tory Party response to the Brexit referendum vote for some time – until Boris Johnson won the leadership – being an extremely plausible example of that). So category 2) can be expanded to include even the political class in a representative democracy.

I also made plain at the very start of this chapter that my least-bad defence of democracy is wholly compatible with my holding non-trivial worries about its future prospects. One significant cause for future worry might emanate from what could bluntly be described as 'tribal voting.' This is perhaps particularly so under Bentham's 'sticks and carrots,' 'put incentives on those with power,' 'inject some real accountability into the system' conception of democracy. Think about it. If people vote simply based on group or tribal identity (because she is a woman like me; because

---

[66] See James Allan and Nicholas Aroney, 'An Uncommon Court: How the High Court of Australia has Undermined Australian Federalism' (2008) 30 *Sydney Law Review* 245.

[67] Indeed, I have argued the point at book length in James Allan, *Democracy in Decline: Steps in the Wrong Direction* (McGill-Queen's University Press, 2014).

he is gay like me; because she is black like me; the list goes on) – if this trumps most all other considerations – then political parties and candidates are no longer disciplined by the Benthamite need to offer policies that they think will make you happy. Any policies will do, so long as they offer candidates that are in your tribe.[68] And the tribe with the most people in it will then be likely to win, or maybe the ones best able to form stable coalitions. Put differently, if most voters' biggest source of satisfaction/happiness/pleasure comes from seeing their own group (however defined) prevail, then the Benthamite defence of democracy looks a lot less persuasive. Or at least I think that most readers can sketch out for themselves the sort of possible future danger I mention here. I have called it 'tribal voting.' Those more polite and urbane than I might describe this cause for future worry about democracy in terms of 'the challenges associated with pluralism.' However you denominate it, it is a worry. Still, at least for the present, I happen to believe that even here Pollyanna is winning the race against this future challenge to democracy. But that is not to deny that Cassandra may be closing ground on this front.

[68] For a book length treatment on this wider problem, a very powerfully written one, see Douglas Murray, *The Madness of Crowds* (Regnery, 2019).

Chapter Five

A Reflection on Majoritarianism

My aim in this Part II of the book is to offer up some grounds for doubting orthodoxy's understanding of, and commitment to, democracy. As I said to start this Part, there is a tendency amongst many judges, lawyers, and legal academics to downplay the merits of majoritarian democracy in favour of what they would see as law and the legal resolution of social policy disagreements. So I spent time arguing why politics matters in chapter three and then in chapter four offered up a Churchillian and Benthamite defence of democracy, considering and rejecting various plausible attacks on that defence. To finish this Part II of the book I think a short reflection on majoritarianism itself is warranted before we move to considering constitutionalism itself, and my doubts on the orthodox view there.

So let us begin by thinking about the following hypothetical. Imagine that you are the parent of a thirteen- or fourteen-year-old teenage son. Your son is a good student at school, but in part that may be because you have until now taken an active part in directing him when to study and for how long. You now decide that the time has come for your son to gauge these things for himself. You tell him you will no longer instruct him when to study and for how long. But your son enjoys his good grades. He responds by informing you that he freely and of his own accord wishes you to continue advising him on how long and when (and even how and where) to study.

Let us say you refuse your son's entreaties to continue directing his study habits. And let us stipulate your motives, namely that you hope he will learn to do these things for himself. You want your son to make his own decisions. You believe this will have good long-term consequences as far as his life prospects are concerned.

As it happens in this hypothetical you have a next-door neighbour with a teenage son too. That neighbour's son is identical to yours in every way. And that neighbour, too, has been helping her son with his studies, in precisely the way you have. She too decides the time has come to stop. Her son, too, responds by saying he wishes her to continue. Unlike you, however, your neighbour accedes to her son's freely made decision — a decision, let us suppose, that he could at any time reverse in the future.

Here is an initial question. Who is better placed to be described as the 'anti-paternalist,' you or your neighbour? You want your son to make his own decisions, but to further that goal you are ignoring his initial decision to keep you heavily involved in his decision-making. Your neighbour, by contrast, respects her son's initial decision, but the cost of that is her continuing and ongoing oversight of all his other decisions.

Now it seems clear to me that both you and your neighbour have some basis for claiming the moniker 'anti-paternalist.' Your neighbour's claim rests on respecting her son's initial decision — the freely made and ongoing wish to have his mum overseeing and directing all later study-related decisions. Your claim rests on the fact that your son will end up having to decide all study-related issues for himself in future, that in terms of outcomes over time you will end up leaving study decisions to be made by your son while your neighbour will not. Of course to achieve that outcome you must first ignore or override your son's initial decision to have you continue as his overseer.

In all such situations where a person or group wishes others to decide things for them, there is the potential for the same dispute. Who is more deserving of the label 'anti-paternalist'? My view is that in this hypothetical you, not your neighbour, have the stronger case. Yes, your neighbour defers to her son on the initial question, but the effect of that is to leave her placed thereafter in the same position as any paternalistic, aristocratic, 'I know better than my son' parent would be. The most that could be said against you is that your ongoing and full-blooded anti-paternalism rests on an initial paternalism — your opting to ignore your son's decision to keep you overseeing his study habits.

Given that, in any direct comparison between you and your neighbour I think your claim to the label is the stronger one. In fact, if the criteria for judging between you and your neighbour are consequentialist ones — what ends up happening as regards the input into and final say over his studies that your son will have — then any attempt by your neighbour to cast herself as the anti-paternalist would be downright laughable.

Now put that hypothetical aside and consider instead, say, the question of a bill of rights. It might be either statutory (so in form less potent) or constitutionalized and entrenched (so in form more potent). Either way it will take at least some issues of social and moral and political policy-making and hand them to unelected judges to decide on a continuing basis, rather than their being decided by the voters on a majoritarian basis through their elected representatives. Assume, in addition, that a majority of voters freely opted for that statutory or constitutionalized bill of rights, and that such a majority could at any time in the future rescind, unentrench or repeal it with no greater difficulty than was encountered in adopting it. (Let me be clear, these are working suppositions or assumptions, nothing more.)

I set up this hypothetical, and translated it into the bill of rights scenario, because there is a fairly common position – perhaps not yet orthodoxy, but only perhaps – that anyone who condemns the majority's initial decision (freely made, *ex hypothesi*, and able at any time to be reversed etc, etc) to adopt a bill of rights does not today deserve the moniker 'majoritarian democrat.'[69] The focus of that fairly common position, in other words, is on the majoritarian credentials of the initial decision to bring in some sort of bill of rights. It matters not to this position that the effect of respecting that initial decision by the majority will be that it (the majority) disenfranchises itself and will continue to do so up until some unspecified point in the future when the majority grows up (or changes its mind if you prefer) and takes the power back from the unelected judiciary. None of the actual, ongoing consequences appear to matter much, or to be determinative. If the battle is over who gets to use

---

[69] See, for example, Dan Meagher, 'The Democratic Credentials of Statutory Bills of Rights (and Those of a Self-Styled Majoritarian Democrat)' (2008) 19 *King's Law Journal*. The self-styled majoritarian democrat under attack in that piece was I, and my reply was: James Allan, 'Meagher's Mischaracterisation of Majoritarianism' (2009) 20 *King's Law Journal* 115. Much of this chapter follows that reply of mine.

the label 'majoritarian democrat,' then the orthodox position – I will take the liberty now of assuming it has been promoted to orthodoxy – is that this label must be awarded solely on the basis of who respects the *initial decision* by voters to abdicate crucial, important rights-based social-policy issues to the judges.

In other words, orthodoxy sides with your neighbour and insinuates that those (like me) who side with you (remember, you opted to disregard your son's plea for regular, ongoing oversight of his studying) are not easily seen as being on the side of majoritarian democracy – more bluntly, it intimates that you and I are far from the majoritarian democrats that we might claim to be.

Well, I have some very big doubts here and think that orthodoxy gets this comparative question of who is more deserving of the label 'majoritarian democrat' wrong. On top of that, I have significant doubts about positions that appear to think that there is something illegitimate in the use of that label 'majoritarian democrat' by those who lament the initial bill of rights decision and look to the long-term undermining of majoritarian self-government that that initial decision will bring with it. For the moment put my claim no higher than this. The orthodox position is not a pluralist one as far as who can claim to be a 'majoritarian democrat' goes.

Or put slightly differently, the orthodox outlook or position wants to award the moniker in blind indifference to the ongoing consequences of abdication to the judiciary, so that were it to have its way the tag would only be applied to someone who — by respecting the initial decision of the majority — left us with a situation where important decisions about immigration, what criminal procedures are acceptable, who can receive certain benefits that flow from marriage, what jobs only judges can perform and much else besides were not made by the majority, but by committees of ex-lawyers (as Jeremy Waldron enjoys describing top courts). It would be a situation, save for that initial and ongoing decision by the majority to defer and abdicate, that would be largely indistinguishable from one desired by the most judge-loving, cynical-of-the-abilities-of-his-fellow-voters, aristocratic paternalist imaginable.

At the very least, therefore, this sort of orthodox (or on its way to becoming orthodox) position as to who can claim the label 'majoritarian democrat' is highly debatable. In no way is it self-evidently correct. In effect, orthodoxy argues as though your neighbour's response, not yours, is uncontestably the anti-paternalist one.

Remember all that and let me apply it in more detail to the comparatively new member of constitutional orthodoxy, the statutory bill of rights of the sort one today finds in New Zealand and Britain. You see two claims are frequently made as regards these instruments. The first is that statutory bills of rights have strong democratic credentials. The second is that critiques of statutory bills of rights premised on a preference for 'letting the numbers count' type majoritarianism over a preference for rule by unelected judges — and that would describe my views — run afoul of the very majoritarianism that motivates the critique.[70] This is a claim not just about who warrants what label or moniker or the tag 'majoritarian democrat,' but also (implicitly) one about the best basis for understanding and defending rights — and so sometimes about the merits of opposing bills of rights.

A core element of the dispute, then, revolves around just how strong the democratic credentials of statutory bills of rights are. Emerging orthodoxy asserts those credentials to be far more impressive than I would. Of course, that sort of claim is ambiguous in just the way my above hypothetical was ambiguous. More specifically, one can look for evidence of these democratic credentials at differing points of time, in particular before enactment or after. The *process* that led to a statutory bill of rights becoming law can be assessed to measure how fully it complied with majoritarianism, with its having been a decision of the majority of voters and having 'let the numbers count.' Alternatively, the *outcome* that that initial decision brings about can be measured or weighed to see how fully it leaves in place majoritarian decision-making or decision-making that 'lets the numbers count.'

Now it is true that more than a few defenders of statutory bills of rights – members of constitutional orthodoxy in Britain and New Zealand at a minimum, but probably also in Australia too now that attempts there

---

70 See Meagher, fn. 69 above for this very critique spelt out in detail.

to entrench a constitutionalized bill of rights look hopeless[71] – do genuflect in the direction of claiming that, once in place, a statutory bill of rights will leave majoritarian decision-making largely untrammelled, that the *outcome* is not to be feared by democrats. That is a common, or even the usual thrust or argument by defenders of statutory bills of rights. It will become plain later in this book that I think that usual line of defence is unconvincing — because of the scope that reading down provisions such as the Human Rights Act 1998 s. 3 afford to judges,[72] because of the way judges' decisions about rights are explicitly and implicitly treated as somehow the correct or right or indisputable and certainly authoritative ones, and because the accumulated evidence thus far is that elected politicians virtually always cave in to (or defer to) judges' declarations of inconsistency.[73] Indeed it is trite, and in no way original at all, to point out that a majority of people can freely vote to live henceforth under a dictatorship. The vote to do so can be on the basis of 'majority rules,' but what ensues — the *outcome* in that sense — is in no sense at all in keeping with my conception of democracy, or anyone else's for that matter. In fact, this would still be the case even if the vote to live under a dictatorship were somehow a revocable one. The fact that a majority of citizens — by majority vote — could disempower their dictator does not change the fact that until such time as that transpires it will be the dictator, not any majoritarian process, who decides and resolves all the many contentious and debatable social policy issues in society, including those raising issues of rights or articulated in the language of rights.

---

[71] See James Allan, 'Why Australian Does Not Have, and Does Not Need, a National Bill of Rights' (2012) 24 *Giornale di Storia Constituzionale* 35.

[72] See *Ghaidan v Mendoza* [2004] 2 AC 557. For my take on this case see James Allan, 'Statutory Bills of Rights: You Read Words In, You Read Words Out, You Take Parliament's Clear Intention and You Shake It All About – Doin' the Sankey Hanky Panky' in (eds. T. Campbell, K. Ewing and A. Tomkins) *The Legal Protection of Human Rights: Sceptical Essays* (Oxford University Press, 2011), 108-126.

[73] See Francesca Klug and Keir Starmer, 'Standing Back from the Human Rights Act: How Effective is it Five Years On?' [2005] *Public Law* 716, 721: '[i]n *every* case where remedial action had not been taken before the [judicial] declaration was made, the government responded by repealing, amending or committing to repeal or amend, the relevant provision' (emphasis mine). And note that these are authors who see this as a good thing, unlike me. Since Klug and Starmer wrote there is one instance of the government in Britain standing up to the judges, on the issue of prisoner voting.

That said, and regardless of the comparative plausibility of claims as to *outcome*, as to how much scope for democratic decision-making one believes is left after the enactment of a statutory bill of rights, this chapter is focused on the other side of the ledger – the *process* by which these instruments are enacted. So let us start with a few observations about how any bill of rights might come to be adopted. Firstly, some processes will be more in keeping with 'letting the numbers count' than others. This is obvious. For instance, a bill of rights might be adopted after a referendum, or after a general election in which it features centrally, or on a party-political basis, or without any referendum or election at all bearing on the question but simply by passage through the legislature without prior signalling to the electorate.[74] All of these could be described as majoritarian processes, though some are more desirable than others in my view. That said, I would certainly agree that as between a majoritarian process and a non-majoritarian process, where both resulted in similar bills of rights being enacted or entrenched, the majoritarian process — not the eventual outcome, note, but the method used to achieve that outcome — is more democratic and in that sense desirable. Accepting that, though, does not entail denying the obvious, that some decisions made by elected legislators are bad ones, sometimes immoral ones (just as the odd judicial decision under a bill of rights is a bad, even immoral one). As I tried to make clear in chapter four, I support democratic decision-making as the least-bad option going.

No, the interesting question here is whether a majoritarian can condemn the majority's initial decision to opt for a statutory bill of rights whose effect, or outcome, will be to abdicate decision-making to others. Can the majoritarian process used there – no matter how exemplary in majoritarian terms – be found wanting by the same majoritarian, because of what it delivers?

I will resist the temptation simply to assert that my opening hypothetical in this chapter makes it plain that the answer to this question is an unequivocal 'yes,' and hence that attempts (be they orthodoxy or otherwise) to claim that majoritarian democrats are somehow prohibited

---

[74] The last of these is arguably what happened when Canada entrenched its *Charter of Rights and Freedoms* in 1982.

from such condemnations by the logic of their own position are wrong. I will resist because, in fact, there might possibly be something to that sort of attack on the majoritarian. It is just that it does not apply to majoritarians like me. Let me explain.

The question to ask is what might prevent a majoritarian democrat from condemning a decision by the majority to abdicate rights decisions — most obviously those that have little realistic prospect of being gainsaid by the majority — to judges. And the answer to that, I think, is an unwillingness to look to consequences because you support majoritarianism on non-consequentialist grounds.

Or in terms of my above hypothetical, the reason I would suggest you give for refusing your son's entreaties is one that would be couched in consequentialist terms. The long-term effects of your son deciding these matters for himself, rather than you deciding them, will be good ones you would calculate. There may well be a few short-term costs. But over time the good consequences for your son will more than outweigh the bad. The reason for refusing your son would, I suspect, be much less plausible if grounded in non-consequentialist reasons, say in terms of autonomy or equality.

Similarly, there are both consequentialist and non-consequentialist bases for defending the view that society's moral and political line-drawing decisions ought to be made on a majoritarian, 'letting the numbers count' basis. As I have alluded to in earlier chapters, Jeremy Waldron gives a critique of bills of rights and the strong judicial review they give rise to that is explicitly premised on a non-consequentialist foundation. Recall the gist of Waldron's anti-bill of rights argument. He starts from a strong rights perspective, one that does not see rights as ultimately resting on some sort of consequentialist foundation. From that strong rights starting point — where rights are understood as goods in themselves and each individual seen as an autonomous agent — Waldron reminds us that each of us also has a right to participate in social decision-making. Indeed, this right to participate stands as a sort of right of rights. And it exists in the context of a world in which disagreement is a fact of social life — disagreement that takes place between reasonable, well-meaning, smart, even nice people and does so on questions over which the unelected judiciary has no obviously greater moral perspicacity than anyone else. In such circumstances, bills of rights, and the privileged position they afford the judiciary, are highly suspect because they fail to take seriously this right to participate in social decision-making. In other words, Waldron has turned the strong rights-based arguments grounded in autonomy and equality — arguments relied on by so many bills of rights supporters — back on to those same people who defend the unique role such instruments give to unelected judges.

So for Waldron and Co. we should all have a right to participate in social decision-making, even as regards decisions about rights — how rights ought to relate to one another, when they can justifiably be limited, what is their proper scope and range, and more. This right to participate, this Waldronian right of rights, should not be handed over to a small group of unelected judges.

Notice, however, that this sort of non-consequentialist attack on bills of rights might leave the Waldrons of the world finding it difficult to condemn a majoritarian decision to abdicate rights decisions to judges. Or rather, the fact that the majority could at any time in the future, using a simple majoritarian process, take that decision-making power back from the judges seems to me to cause severe difficulties for these Waldronians in a way it does not for a consequentialist like me. Here is how I put the difficulty facing them (when it comes to criticizing a majority that had opted to abdicate decision-making power to judges or some small group of others but could take it back anytime on the same basis) back in 2008.[75]

> At first glance, it appears as though at least some of the political illegitimacy attaching to unelected judges second-guessing the elected branches on rights issues has been dissipated. The elected branches can override or gainsay the second-guess; Parliament can do so on a 50 per cent plus one basis; it does not appear that an earlier generation (the one opting for judicial oversight) is locking in a later one.
>
> Concomitantly, someone like ... Waldron — unlike the consequentialist or utilitarian defender of rights and, in

[75] See James Allan, 'The Travails of Justice Waldron' in Grant Huscroft (ed), *Expounding the Constitution: Essays in Constitutional Theory* (CUP, 2008), 161 at 175-176 and 179-180.

> particular, of a right to participate in social decision-making — can hardly point to and castigate the fact that these autonomous voters and their elected representatives choose never (or virtually never) to use the override [or repeal the statutory bill of rights], that they are overawed by the language of rights, or that they need protecting from their own follies and have to be made less cavalier about excluding themselves from the decision-making process.
>
> As Jeffrey Goldsworthy argues,[76] a strong-rights, non-consequentialist defender of the right to participate, someone like … Waldron, might, in theory, think that a good deal of the illegitimacy of [this] has been abated by [a Canadian-style] override clause [or by the procedural ease with which a statutory bill of rights can be repealed].
>
> … That said, it strikes me that if [a situation where the Parliament could in fact respond on a majoritarian basis] were to materialise, [an imagined] Justice Waldron should find his task of rights-based adjudicating much less illegitimate, perhaps not illegitimate at all. Of course an imagined Justice Bentham would not think an acceptably worded notwithstanding clause [or a Parliament free to respond] did anything to improve the bad consequences of committees of ex-lawyers imposing their own moral views on the rest of us — whether we want them to or not — and so did nothing to ameliorate the political illegitimacy of his job. But [an imagined] Justice Waldron, who appears to forswear appeals to consequences, has different bases and justifications for upholding the right to participate than an imagined Justice Bentham.

Think back to my opening hypothetical. If the reason your neighbour has for wanting her son to make his own decisions is that she conceives of this in some sort of autonomy-grounded or Kantian or transcendent or deontological or any other non-consequentialist, strong rights basis,[77] then notice how few resources she has for objecting to his

---

[76] See Jeffrey Goldsworthy, 'Judicial Review, Legislative Override and Democracy' in J Campbell, T Goldsworthy and A Stone (eds), *Protecting Human Rights: Instruments and Institutions* (Oxford University Press, 2003) 263.

[77] For my distinction between strong rights foundations and weak rights foundations, see James Allan, 'Bills of Rights and Judicial Power—A Liberal's Quandary' (1996) 16 *Oxford Journal of Legal Studies* 337, 340–2.

freely-made decision to keep her as overseer. The same goes for strong rights-based objections to the majority opting to transfer important social policy decisions over to the judiciary. If your starting point there is a non-consequentialist right of rights or right to participate, then providing the transfer can at any time in the future be revoked or gainsaid on a simple majoritarian basis, you would seem to be foreclosed from pointing to bad consequences.

On the other hand, those, like me, who base their majoritarianism on a consequentialist foundation are in the same position as you are in my hypothetical. You and I can point to all the bad consequences that will flow from abdicating these decisions to the unelected judiciary — the voter apathy, the growing cynicism about politics, the temptation for politicians to take irresponsible positions (think of flag-burning in the US) knowing the judges are standing behind them to overrule them, the focus on how judges are chosen, the even more elevated position in society that lawyers (and for that matter legal academics) will win, all the various lost republican virtues associated with an involved citizenry, the plausible claim that on many issues there is wisdom in numbers, and more.

Your neighbour Waldron will struggle to raise these as relevant considerations.

That is why it is an error simply to split the world into those in favour of rights and those against. That sort of bifurcation is too simple and too pat. People support rights on different bases. More specifically, there are those who support rights on strong rights bases (be they Kantian, transcendent, deontological, natural law or some other non-consequentialist variant) and those who support them on weak or instrumental or consequentialist bases. That choice spills over into, and can affect, their views on myriad questions related to bills of rights. Indeed, and this is one of the points I'm trying to make in this chapter, that choice is not irrelevant to the ease with which a majoritarian democrat is able to object to the majority's decision to opt for a statutory bill of rights.

Nor is it irrelevant to one's ability to distinguish between different sorts of delegations by the majority to judges, to Reserve Bank governors or to anyone else. The consequentialist can look and see how circumscribed the receiver of these powers is, how broad or encompassing the delegated power is, and whether there is any practical likelihood of the majority being able to take that power back in the near-to-mid future. And he or she can then support or oppose it based on how the consequences are perceived likely to play out.

I noted above that Waldron's anti-bill of rights argument is structured so as to turn the strong rights-based arguments — non-consequentialist arguments — back on to the many bill of rights proponents who defend these instruments on that same basis. But in fact even Waldron himself once conceded the difficulty of defending rights on a non-consequentialist basis. As early as 1984 he wrote:[78]

> Non-utilitarian theories [of rights] … often contain little more than a bare assertion that certain rights are intuitively evident or at any rate are to be taken as first principles.

Of course that is a debate with a huge literature and one that remains unresolved. It may always be thus. That said, on this narrow point regarding the scope that any majoritarian democrat might have to condemn the majority's decision to have enacted a statutory bill of rights, the consequentialist defender of rights and of majoritarianism — and likewise the consequentialist opponent of bills of rights — is much better placed to make that condemnation. Like you, when it comes to your son in the above hypothetical, he or she can point to all the negative outcomes and consequences to which that initial decision will give rise.

For the consequentialist anti-paternalist, like you, ignoring your son's initial decision to keep you as overseer does not undermine the very anti-paternalism you seek to establish. At most it amounts to the claim that your full-blooded and ongoing anti-paternalism rests on an initial paternalism. Compared to your neighbour, however, there is no persuasive basis for thinking you are not an anti-paternalist.

Similarly for the majoritarian democrat, provided he be a consequentialist, there is nothing improper, inconsistent or against his own first principles in condemning the majority's decision to opt for a bill of rights — even a statutory one that can formally be revoked or repealed at

---

[78] Jeremy Waldron, introduction to J Waldron (ed), *Theories of Rights* (Oxford University Press, 1984) 19.

any time on that same majoritarian basis – and to note how difficult it will be, once in place, to remove.

Or to make the claim more broadly, there are different bases on which to support majoritarianism and the one chosen can matter. It can affect one's views about preferred constitutional structures. Here, as with the grounds on which one supports human rights, foundations are crucial. My doubts about constitutional orthodoxy flow in large part from my skepticism and doubts about orthodoxy's first principles and foundations (though admittedly these core aspects of orthodoxy are often never explicitly laid down, nor defended, and may sometimes not even be consciously held).

Part III

Constitutionalism in the Democratic World

Chapter Six

Start with Informal Constitutionalism

Here in Part III of this short book I now turn to the general theme of constitutionalism itself. My doubts here will relate to various aspects of constitutional orthodoxy – the relative merits of written versus unwritten constitutionalism; of majoritarianism; of how best to understand this concept of constitutionalism; of the role of politics within it. Overwhelmingly I will be in the outsider's camp in these debates. So here again I will be expressing doubts.

What I take my self-imposed brief to be in this chapter is to write on informal constitutionalism. This sort of task seems well-suited to a native born and educated Canadian like me who has been a law professor in Hong Kong before the 1997 handover (one task while there being to teach British constitutional law), then in New Zealand for eleven years (teaching constitutional law in the democratic world's last true unwritten constitution jurisdiction, a post-Brexit United Kingdom now returning to that fold[79]), and for the last seventeen years has been one in Australia (teaching constitutional law in a country which straight out copied the US Constitution, or at least the Madisonian pre-bill of rights version). If you are in the camp that thinks Kiwis and Brits have more experience than most with informal constitutionalism, and that the Aussies have an unusual sort of formal constitutionalism, then I am moderately well-placed to consider informal constitutionalism.

Let us start by considering how we should understand this self-imposed topic of mine. No doubt we will need some idea of what is captured by the notion of 'constitutionalism' before we can move on to

[79] Note, too, that some people put Israel in the unwritten constitution camp, though the claim is harder to sustain there than it is with New Zealand.

ponder what might fall within the aegis of 'informal constitutionalism.' Maybe there can even be different ways in which the tag 'informal constitutionalism' can apply to a country? Meanwhile, most of us probably suspect that all countries make use of informal constitutionalism to some extent. I start this chapter with those sort of questions before shifting to bring some of the insights of chapter three to bear, by looking at the role of politics in constitutionalism – of both the informal and formal sorts.

1. Constitutionalism

Over two decades ago Larry Alexander edited a perspicacious book length treatment of the topic of 'constitutionalism.' For the purposes of this first part of my chapter, I would like to highlight or poach some of the key insights from that book (at least by my way of thinking). Here is my precis.

Constitutionalism is about locking things in. It is about settlement. And the reason the people in a nation might opt to do that, to choose security over flexibility, is that they believe 'that there is far more danger of loss of political wisdom and morality or of political akrasia than there is danger that wide agreement on better rules will be thwarted.'[80]Outlining Richard Kay's understanding of constitutionalism, with which he overwhelmingly agrees, Alexander says that:

> For Kay, the purpose of a constitution is to lay down fixed rules that can affect human conduct and thereby keep government in good order. ... [Constitutionalism] brings about predictability and security ... by defining in advance the powers and limits of that government.
>
> The price of [constitutionalism] ... is rigidity, or put differently, suboptimal response to change.[81]

---

[80] See Larry Alexander (ed.), *Constitutionalism: Philosophical Foundations* (Cambridge University Press, 1998), p.2.

[81] *Ibid.*, p.4. Richard Kay makes these points himself in his own chapter in that book, 'American Constitutionalism' (pp. 16-63). For instance, Kay says that '[t]o embrace constitutionalism is to concede the costs of suboptimal public responses to change as an acceptable price to pay for the security obtained. Constitutionalism is risk-averse in the sense that it prefers the awkwardness of rigidly bound state action to the

Nor is it just Alexander and Kay who understand constitutionalism in these terms. So, too, does Michael Perry. As Alexander puts it, '[l]ike us, [Perry] answers the question of why norms should ever be entrenched against majority repeal by reference to distrust of our future politics.'[82]

Hence on these sort of views, and remembering that we are limited biological creatures (not Gods) who regularly have to make least-bad choices, opting for constitutionalism is opting for rigidity and comparative certainty over flexibility; for security over potential rights-infringing 'short-term considerations of collective welfare at the expense of the liberties of individuals and minorities';[83] for the specified, laid-down and known (though certainly also imperfect) over the uncertain and flexible (which will sometimes be better and sometimes worse); and for the locked-in and settled over the contingent and comparatively unconstrained.

Now going along with all that one needs also to suppose or believe that written rules can convey fixed meanings – that decisions made in the past by those considered to have the legitimate authority to do so have the capacity to lock us in today. Otherwise, while you might have thought you were buying certainty and security, there would in fact be nothing actually locking you in to the various choices and decisions made in the past. You would in fact have bought smoke and mirrors. In other words, to achieve those sort of locked-in outcomes may require the later-in-time interpreters to adopt a particular approach to constitutional interpretation. As it happens, and as will become clearer in later chapters, I believe that it does require that. So too do Larry Alexander, Stanley Fish[84] and others. However, for the purposes of this chapter I will simply point out that connection – between the claimed attractions of constitutionalism and the potential need to interpret a constitution in a particular manner – and move on. My focus here is on the formal and informal varieties of

---

possibility that government will overshoot the mark in dealing with new circumstances.' (p. 24)

[82] *Ibid.*, p.6. This is fleshed out by Perry in his chapter of the book, 'What Is "the Constitution"? (and Other Fundamental Questions),' from p. 99.

[83] Richard Kay, *ibid.*, p. 24.

[84] See both these authors' chapters in G. Huscroft and B. Miller (eds.), *The Challenge of Originalism* (CUP, 2011).

constitutionalism, ignoring or if you prefer pre-supposing or indeed postponing the concomitant interpretive issues that surround it.

Hence, let me turn back to the trade-off lying at the heart of choosing constitutionalism, the one between certainty and flexibility, between the locked-in and the contingent. I want for a moment to consider the nature of that trade-off (that understanding of constitutionalism) through the prism, firstly, of paternalism and secondly, of democracy. Start with the former, because it is plain that there is a potential connection between constitutionalism and paternalism. Go back to the time of the framers and ratifiers, the time of the making of a constitution. If a core motivating reason for my wanting to lock things in *now* is a distrust of *future* politics then it follows that I think the deal on offer (at least when it is one 'that most believe [is] good enough'[85]), with all its constraints on future decision-making, is all-things-considered and on-average-over-time better than what future generations would produce if left more unconstrained. That might look like arrogance, but provided it is combined with a desire for the on-balance best outcomes for future generations in one's country and a belief that that will eventuate then it is better seen as paternalism.[86]I, as part of the group drafting and ratifying the US Constitution (or far less plausibly in my view, but allowing me to make a European Union reference, the Lisbon Treaty), am doing this for you – my grandchildren, and great-grandchildren and great-great-grandchildren – because I believe it will deliver better overall outcomes than what you could deliver for yourselves if left more unconstrained. Now that is paternalism, and at first glance it is hard to see how it can be completely severed from the Alexander/Kay/Perry concerns that motivate constitutionalism.

---

[85] Larry Alexander (ed.), *Constitutionalism: Philosophical Foundations* (Cambridge University Press, 1998), p.2.

[86] Of course one might argue that the founders do not see themselves as better or more moral, just as having invested more time and thought in the matter. But that, if true, is still a form of paternalism. 'Trust us because we've put a lot of time into this' may be less distasteful than 'Trust us because we're better and more moral people than you are,' but both count as versions of 'we know better than you do.' Nor, in my view, does it become anti-paternalistic if the motivating desire is trying to protect later generations against wicked elites, say. A future majority can do that just fine in a parliamentary sovereignty set-up.

Before I say why I think that first glance conclusion can in some circumstances be wrong, let me just observe or note what happens as we move forward in time. It is this. The paternalism in the years 1787-1790 that motivated the drive for constitutionalism transmogrifies more than two centuries later into what some describe as 'ancestor worship.' The effect of constitutionalism later in time, years after the founding, is that citizens are locked in to (in the sense that change and amendment is hard, harder than what is needed to pass a statute) what people in the past designed and laid down. They were the ones we today accept as having had the legitimate authority to make the constitution, these metaphorical ancestors of ours. And provided the point-of-application interpreters of that document find its meaning in what those back then with the legitimate authority to do so wrote into the document and intended it to mean, then one side of constitutionalism – viewed from the present day looking back to its drafting and ratification – can be described as ancestor worship.[87]To sum that up in blunt terms, constitutionalism seems to carry with it traces of paternalism and ancestor worship.

In my view that is undoubtedly the case when we are focused on, say, the US Constitution or the Canadian Constitution. As I have noted earlier in this chapter, it is hard to see at first glance how traces of paternalism (and down the road of ancestor worship) can be completely severed from the Alexander/Kay/Perry understanding of constitutionalism. And yet that first glance conclusion is contingent, not necessary. That is what the Australian Constitution teaches us. And that is because Australia's Constitution is more or less the pre-Bill of Rights Madisonian US Constitution. So the Australians, albeit within the

[87] Of course if the sort of interpretive approaches to interpretation we will consider in later chapters (often lumped together under the label 'living constitution' approaches) are used by today's interpreting judges then (to the extent these approaches are unmoored from original intentions, say some, or from original public meaning, say others) the tie to the past is severed and ancestor worship evaporates. In its place grows up 'worship of today's top judges' because the rest of us are still locked in. True, we are no longer locked-in to what those in the past intended the Constitution to mean using words to effect those intentions. Instead, we are now locked in to what some collection of unelected judges in the present deems best, proportional, suitable, what have you. I return to this point in later chapters, and briefly towards the end of this chapter.

inherited British Westminster parliamentary model, copied and mimicked a US-style elected Upper House Senate rather than the Canadian or UK options; they also copied the American one-list model of federalism rather than the Canadian two-list model; they left the choosing of the top State court judges to the States, as in the US, not to the center, as in Canada; the Australians even mimicked the US in opting to create a national capital city not part of any State (and whose residents did not have a vote for the Senate or House until the 1970s).[88]However, after much debate and with a thorough understanding of the then US 1st Amendment jurisprudence, the Australian constitution-makers rejected a bill of rights of any sort. They chose to leave all such matters to the elected Parliament. Indeed, the Australian Constitution has references throughout to 'until the Parliament otherwise provides.'[89]

In other words, if you shun any sort of bill of rights and any sort of strong judicial review on rights-related grounds, what you lock in can look a lot like parliamentary sovereignty filtered through bicameralism and federalism – and that is hardly an overtly paternalistic choice. Sure, you will still have strong judicial review and the striking down of statutes on federalism grounds. But as we will consider in a later chapter, as far as leaving each generation to make choices for itself through the democratic process there is a big difference between rights-related review and federalism review.[90] With heads of powers federalism related judicial review the unelected judges are choosing between which of two democratically elected legislatures can do precisely what some statute is

---

[88] The High Court of Australia case that decided that Territorians could be given representation by Parliament, though they were not given the same number of Senators as a State, was *Western Australia v Commonwealth ('First Territory Senators Case')* (1975) 134 CLR 201.

[89] For example, in sections 7, 31, 34, 39, 46, 48 and a good deal more.

[90] This is not, of course, to deny that a judge inclined to do so would lack the tools to manipulate federalism review to achieve an outcome he or she actually wanted on rights-related grounds.Nor is it to deny that the attachment to one level of democracy over a bigger one might not lead to, say, an American Civil War (to the extent the South could be described as being democratic). Relatedly, it is harder to make that 'small democracy versus bigger democracy' claim in the context of the United Kingdom and Brexit because, in my view, the EU is simply not very democratic in its internal operations. So the structural contest there is not easily seen as between a more local democracy and a bigger democracy.

attempting to do – the judges are not putting this precise attempt beyond the reach of all democratic politics, state or national (as happens with rights-related judicial review). Hence, what you end up with under the locked-in Australian Constitution is a checks and balances, diffusion of power set-up. It is assuredly not the full-blooded New Zealand-style unwritten, unicameral, unitary constitution with its full embrace of parliamentary sovereignty, true. But in terms of being anti-paternalistic it is much closer to the Kiwis than it is to today's typical or orthodox written constitutions with their bills of rights authorising strong judicial review of virtually all imaginable social policy-making undertaken by the elected legislatures.[91] Of course the empirical truth is that virtually every democratic country in today's world has a national bill of rights – that is constitutional orthodoxy in a nutshell – while Australia does not. But that is a contingent truth, not a necessary one, with virtually no countries on earth, democratic or otherwise, having judicially enforceable bills of rights as recently as the end of World War II. The evident traces of paternalism and ancestor worship that come with constitutionalism do so because rights-related review happens also to have been widely locked in. Or put differently, the Alexander/Kay/Perry understanding of constitutionalism, centered as it persuasively is on locking things in and preferencing rigidity and security, does not *entail* hefty dollops of paternalism. That is just what we happen almost always to see. Nevertheless, the pre-bill of rights Madisonian Australian Constitution (admittedly a rarity) shows that (if we want) we can have our constitutionalism without the paternalism on the side. (Or rather, we can have it without very much paternalism as

[91] Just looking at the US and Canada we see that under rights-related strong judicial review the judges have the last word as regards such issues as abortion, euthanasia, whether there will be same-sex marriages, whether each and every refugee claimant must be given an oral hearing (at huge taxpayer expense and with security implications), whether democratically enacted restrictions on carrying handguns will be struck down, capital punishment, whether incarcerated prisoners must in all cases be allowed to vote and plenty more besides those. Either that is being done on the basis of moral entitlements articulated in the language of rights that were locked in by the framers and ratifiers – hence, with dollops of paternalism and ancestor worship evident – or today's judges are 'unlocked in' by past people's choices when they decide a bill of rights case but are nevertheless locking the rest of us citizens in to what amounts to the judges' own moral druthers and policy preferences. I have doubts about the desirability of either.

federalism adjudication and limits are certainly open, now and again, to being – and indeed have been – manipulated to achieve substantive results.)

If we turn now to the relationship between constitutionalism and democracy it is clear that some aspects of that were touched upon already when thinking about paternalism. So here, remembering that we have already fleshed out a Churchillian defence of democracy in chapter four, I want only to focus on one particular subset of that relationship, namely whether constitutionalism need be understood as antithetical to democracy. This is a question not usually asked. When it is, and when we do consider constitutionalism's relationship to democracy, odds are we will run into the above pointed-out (and likely to be true as a matter of empirical fact) assumption that constitutions will have bills of rights. For instance, in his introduction to his edited book, Alexander says of Jeremy Waldron's chapter, that 'Waldron quite correctly argues that constitutionalism is not democratic even if it is established democratically.'[92]Now I have no quibbles with the argument that X need not be democratic even if the process for choosing X is itself a democratic one. That is patently true. My quibble is that Waldron was actually discussing a particular sort of pre-commitment, namely whether Britain in 1998 ought to commit itself to a bill of rights. So yes, as I conceded in chapter four, a democratic majority of citizens can opt for one of those instruments and yet (here I agree with Waldron) once one is in place it does not deliver full-blooded democratic decision-making – at least not if it gives you a strong form of judicial review.[93] But that begs the question of whether constitutionalism itself needs to include a bill of rights

[92] Larry Alexander (ed.), *Constitutionalism: Philosophical Foundations* (Cambridge University Press, 1998), p. 10. The Waldron chapter in that book ('Precommitment and Disagreement') begins at p. 271.

[93] As for statutory bills of rights, well that is a matter of contingent fact. I say that the evidence is such that the British statutory bill of rights has in fact delivered what amounts to strong judicial review virtually up to US levels and hence non-democratic decision-making. See, inter alia, James Allan, 'Statutory Bills of Rights: You Read Words In, You Read Words Out, You Take Parliament's Clear Intention and You Shake It All About – Doin' the Sankey Hanky Panky' in (eds. T. Campbell, K. Ewing and A. Tomkins) *The Legal Protection of Human Rights: Sceptical Essays* (Oxford University Press, 2011), 108-126.

instrument. As I have argued earlier in this chapter, and as appears obvious both to me and to the pre-bill of rights Madison for that matter, constitutionalism does *not* need to include such an instrument. Move to Australia and see for yourself. What you will find Down Under, leave to one side a fairly minor recently 'discovered' (or in my view made-up by the judges themselves) judicial doctrine about a limited implied freedom of political communication,[94] is constitutionalism that delivers a strongish version of parliamentary sovereignty filtered through bicameralism and federalism. Those and a Swiss-style amending formula are at the heart of what is locked in – just non-judicial and non-rights-related procedures for checking and balancing power.

Accordingly, constitutionalism can be, preponderantly will be, but need not be, understood as antithetical to democracy in a full-blooded sense. Or put differently, any conflict between constitutionalism and democratic decision-making is contingent not necessary.

2. Formal and Informal Constitutionalism

It is tempting at this point simply to equate 'formal and informal' constitutionalism with written and unwritten constitutionalism. On that understanding New Zealand, the world's best example of a parliamentary sovereignty democracy that lacks a written constitution, would be the poster boy for informal constitutionalism. If we were to go down that road then it is easiest to understand an unwritten constitution in terms of what is missing. And what is missing in New Zealand is some over-arching single document – a written constitution – from which other laws obtain their legitimacy and which provides much (though not all) of a jurisdiction's Rule of Recognition.[95]Such a written constitution, in addition possibly to giving a federalist division of powers and opting for bicameralism or unicameralism, might also decide to entrench a bill of rights, which as we have seen is the overwhelming (but not required) choice in today's democratic world. Taking that as giving the main shape

---

94 See James Allan, 'The Three "R"s of Recent Australian Judicial Activism: Roach, Rowe and (no) 'Riginalism" (2012) 36 *Melbourne University Law Review* 743-782.

95 This term was coined by H.L.A. Hart in his magisterial *The Concept of Law* (Clarendon Press, 1961).

of a written constitution then affords us a basic idea of New Zealand's unwritten constitution – which is the absence of any sort of single over-arching document doing all or any of that.

Now I happen to think that succumbing to the 'informal equals unwritten' temptation would hardly be fatal. Do that and the upside is that you have room to describe New Zealand (and for that matter the Britain that existed before its entry into – and now after its exit from – today's European Union) as having a constitutional government. Yes, because of its unwritten and therefore informal nature it would not be a core case of constitutionalism, more like a penumbral instance. That said, surely it would be odd to be forced to describe today's New Zealand, as well as what was arguably the world's first democracy Britain, as lacking constitutional government. And to have to do so solely because the Kiwis and Brits (at least for the latter pre-1972 and post-2020) lacked a written constitution.

On the other hand, the temptation to concatenate *a)* the notion of informal constitutionalism with *b)* what you observe in democratic jurisdictions that happen to lack a written constitution is not cost free. Recall the Alexander/Kay/Perry notion of constitutionalism from above. This involved, to some degree at least, the preferencing of rigidity, security, the certain and the locked-in over flexibility, room to manoeuvre, the contingent and the non-locked-in. But if New Zealand counts as an example of constitutional government, because we opt to equate informal versions to unwritten ones, then we may have to qualify bits of the Alexander/Kay/Perry understanding. After all, a full-blooded parliamentary sovereignty set-up – one that has a Kiwi-style unwritten, unicameral, unitary constitution – goes as far as you can in preferencing flexibility and anti-paternalism and democratic decision-making. So succumb to the 'informal = unwritten' temptation and we would have to qualify our core level understanding of constitutionalism. It could still center on the desire to 'lock things in'[96] but now would expand to include

[96] Because of course there will be locked in norms even in pure parliamentary sovereignty jurisdictions such as New Zealand. For instance, even to have politics one must have rules that constitute the legislature – what the legislature will be; how it is selected; how it passes laws and so forth. This sort of procedural constitution will be locked in. It may not be procedurally hard to change or secured with too difficult a

more informal methods of limiting power and even ways of locking outcomes in. Sure, there would still be the archetypical formal route of a written constitution with a bill of rights, the guardians of which would be an independent judiciary with the power to invalidate statutes. But in the democratic world power can also be limited more informally, without a written constitution, and under our expanded understanding of constitutionalism we would include this as a penumbral case. Consider again New Zealand. Are there limits on power there? Of course there are. Can those limits largely or overwhelmingly be traced back to one over-arching document, as in Canada, Australia and the United States? No. Limits on power in New Zealand flow from a bunch of statutes, all of which can be altered in the normal way by Parliament. And they flow from conventions (in loose terms these are the real limits arising from history, traditions and prevailing attitudes), and more there perhaps than elsewhere. Most obviously they flow from elections and the democratic process. Yes, it is an incredibly democratic set-up, each generation being left to vote for Members of Parliament ("MPs") who, through Parliament, can do what they think is best. Hence more than a few might wonder, "But where are the legal limits on what the elected parliament can do?." And the answer is, the limits on parliament are not legal. They are moral and political. New Zealanders vote for MPs who more-or-less share their moral worldview. And if shared morality is too ephemeral for your likings as a power-constraint, well the limits put on MPs by the desire to get re-elected are powerful limits indeed. Democracy is a potent check on power, indeed as we saw in chapter four it was for Jeremy Bentham the most crucially important check on power.

Now some readers may well balk at this point, still thinking that having legal and constitutionalised limits on elected MPs, on what the legislature can do, is needed. For such readers, notice that all those legal limits have to be overseen by real life people. So in the United States they are overseen by its Supreme Court, by nine judges. And if you live in the United States (or Canada, or South Africa, or Germany, etc) what sort of limits are there that control what those nine ex-lawyers can do, that ensures

lock, needing only 50 per cent plus one of the elected legislators to be altered, but it is still locked in. Thanks to Larry Alexander for this example.

their interpretations are honest and not unconstrained? Well, there are moral limits, the attachment felt by such top judges to applying the law as written and so in accordance with their oaths of office – as opposed to just making things up at the point-of-application because some outcome or other seems morally superior to them, or preferable on other grounds. Oh, and there are political limits, as in the extent to which they can withstand criticism in the press when they go wayward. But let us say – and this is hypothetically speaking you understand – but let us say that you think that in some recent case a majority of those top judges (say five out of nine because all top courts happen to be brutally majoritarian institutions, five votes always beating four no matter the quality of the reasoning) just made something up. They pretended to be interpreting the United States Constitution when supposedly 'discovering' some implied but nowhere enumerated fundamental new right that these top judges then used to invalidate some law that had been on the statute books for ages. In other words, you think the judges lied or made it up. Are there any legal or constitutional limits on those top judges, other than political and moral limits? Of course not. In any set-up you will end up having some group of real life human beings whose actions are constrained, or not constrained, solely by morality and politics. So pick your poison. In New Zealand with its unwritten parliamentary sovereignty constitution it is the legislature that lacks legal limits.

Notice, as well, that outcomes can be locked in without a formal written constitution with its designated judicial interpreters. Take this example, which applies to every single country that still has Queen Elizabeth II as its head of state (so not just New Zealand, but also Australia, Canada, chunks of the Caribbean, a few island outposts and the United Kingdom itself).Every law student in those countries quickly learns that to pass a Bill into law it has successfully to undergo three readings in Parliament (which might be unicameral as in New Zealand or bicameral with an unelected Upper House as in Canada and the UK or bicameral with a US-style elected Senate as in Australia).After that it needs to be signed by the Queen or by her representative in that country the Governor-General. And soon those law students learn that it is a rock solid certainty that the Queen will sign all such thrice-passed Bills into law and onto the statute book. This outcome is locked in. It is more certain than most any outcome related to the US Bill of Rights and what the top judges there will say it means. Indeed, this is a locked in truth that no Kiwi or Canadian or Brit or Australian ever doubts for one moment. Yet, and here is the point, nowhere is it laid down in a written constitution or required by law that the Queen must sign these thrice-passed Bills into law. There is no formal legal recourse were she to refuse. And yet that will not happen. That the Queen (or Governor General) will sign is a core constitutional principle; more, it is an absolutely settled rule that is less likely to be broken than is just about any legally laid down provision in the Lisbon Treaty or the US Constitution with their formal authoritative interpreters in the courts.

Now surely that counts as a locked in outcome of the sort that the Alexander/Kay/Perry understanding sees as lying at the heart of constitutionalism. Just as surely it falls on the informal, rather than formal, side of the divide. Of course this example counts as a convention. In the Westminster world we think of conventions as rules that are *not* enforced in the courts. There are plenty of others. There was the near century-old convention that the legally unlimited Westminster Parliament in London would not legislate for the self-governing Dominions unless such legislation were asked for. There is the more recent convention regarding how post-devolution Scotland is treated within the United Kingdom, namely that the legally unlimited Westminster Parliament allows Scotland to control her own affairs in the devolved areas – to the point that a plausible argument can be made that there is more *de facto* federalism (in the sense of the subsidiarity principle or actual local decision-making and income taxing power) in the formally unitary UK than there is in the officially and *de jure* federal jurisdiction of Australia. There may even have grown up a convention that the Westminster Parliament will abide by the results of referenda.[97] And if you wish to determine in the

[97] See Gavin Phillipson, 'Brexit, Prerogative and the Courts: Why did Political Constitutionalists Support the Government Side in Miller?' (2017) 36 *University of Queensland Law Journal* 311 at 324. As Phillipson there points out, 'in every referendum held in the UK in the post-war period, the result has been respected' (ibid., p. 324). These include the referenda to enter the EEC (1973), to opt for devolution in Scotland (1997), Wales (1997 and 2011) and Northern Ireland (1998), to consider shifting the voting system from First-Past-the-Post to preferential or Alternative Vote

Westminster world whether there in fact exists a convention, a non-justiciable rule, Sir Ivor Jennings famously proposed[98] this tripartite test: 1) Are there precedents? 2) Do the actors believe they are bound by a rule? 3) Is there a good reason for this rule?

Let me make two further points about conventions, these rules that are not justiciable in the courts. First off, remember what Hart pointed out in his *The Concept of Law* when comparing law to the rules of a sporting game, namely that such rules can often work perfectly fine without a designated, authoritative adjudicator. For many years I regularly played pick-up basketball, and in various countries, and this worked very well indeed without any need for a referee – without the need for an authoritative interpreter and applier of the rules – despite the odd fellow competitor who (shall we say) seemed incapable of calling fouls on himself. Indeed, when there are no referees players are often pretty conscientious about not fouling and about calling fouls on themselves (the odd person excepted); they can in some ways be more rule-abiding than when a referee is present and the attitude becomes 'I can do whatever the ref lets me get away with.' Of course make the stakes high enough in sports and the need for a referee, for a Hartian Rule of Adjudication, usually becomes compelling. But the point is that rules frequently can, and do, work without referees and judges. And that is what conventions are – non-justiciable rules that are felt to be binding by the actors. Any enforcement is itself informal. It will ultimately be political, not legal.

Accept that, however, and it goes some way to giving you grounds to be careful about just what sort of temptation it is you will be giving in to when you equate informal constitutionalism with unwritten constitutionalism. That is because all forms of constitutionalism, from the most formal version of a US-style written constitution set-up all the way over to the New Zealand and (pre-1972, post-Brexit) British parliamentary

---

(2011), to decide Scottish Independence (2014) and indeed (since Parliament eventually went on to trigger Article 50, to shift to Boris Johnson as Prime Minister, and to have him and the Tories win a massive majority government fought on this issue of getting Brexit done) the one to opt for Brexit and leave the EU (2016).

[98] Sir Ivor Jennings, *The Law and the Constitution* (5th ed., London, 1959), p. 135. The last of these, number 3), is admittedly open to being gamed should the courts get involved.

sovereignty unwritten constitutions, make use of non-justiciable rules (of which conventions are the best example) and non-justiciable areas of Executive decision-making. Some countries just do so more than others. That does not change the fact that once we decide that non-justiciable rules can be included within the ambit of informal constitutionalism then it follows that all constitutional jurisdictions, to some extent at least, make use of the informal variety at least on occasion.[99]

The second point to make about conventions, and this will be obvious I suppose, is that they are not deliberately laid down. You cannot trace their genealogy back to a group of people who are treated as having the legitimate, authoritative power to make this or that rule and who then deliberately decide to do just that for future generations. Conventions are more unplanned than that; they are more Hayekian; they just grow up. And though they may have the effect of locking you in, the basis for the constraints they impose seems to me to differ somewhat from why the formal sort of constitutional rules overseen by judges (at any rate by those judges committed to a locked in view of constitutionalism rather than to living-constitutionalism) are felt to be constraining. If you are locked in by some component of informal constitutionalism, by a big ticket convention say, it is because of value judgments being made today that are focused almost exclusively on today. There is less concern for the past, and for value judgments made in the past. Or put differently, what motivates obedience to conventions has little if anything to do with 'distrust of our future politics.'

---

[99] The obverse or flip-side of that is that all forms of constitutionalism, even the most locked-in model with strong judicial review under an entrenched bill of rights, ultimately rest on acceptance today, in the present. As Larry Alexander notes, wake up tomorrow in an America that wholly rejects the Constitution of 1789 and its amendments (hence, no longer accepts what the authors did back then) and it will have gone the way of the Articles of Confederation. This is Hart's point about the Rule of Recognition, the ultimate test of legal validity, that in the final analysis it depends upon what is accepted today (for Hart by the officials in society). In other words, the difference when it comes to constitutionalism between New Zealand and the US is one of degree. It is a real and important difference to be sure. But it is simply a matter of degree.

3. Harkening back to Chapter Three and the Role of Politics in Constitutionalism

Whether or not I have managed to draw out some of the differences between informal and formal constitutionalism, I shift now to look at the role of politics in both sorts of set-ups. For the former, that role is plain. As I noted above, in New Zealand's unwritten (and so as informal as it gets) constitutional structure democratic politics – elections and voting – are the main check on power. There, politics plainly matter because in the case of parliamentary sovereignty jurisdictions it is democratic politics that resolve virtually all of the big ticket social policy issues in society. Similarly, if we move from those very few unwritten constitution jurisdictions to democracies more generally, and think about conventions (which can be seen as a circumscribed, more particular aspect of informal constitutionalism), we see that there too what ultimately enforces conventions – or every once in a while allows what they lay down to be gainsaid – is politics. The reason the Westminster parliament in London leaves the Scottish parliament free to deal with devolved areas of responsibility and is not tempted to move to repeal the devolution statute (which it is legally free to do at any time) is politics. It is an awareness of what the political repercussions would be. Likewise when the Westminster Parliament opted without request by the then Rhodesia (and indeed contrary to that government's wishes) to legislate for that country, and in direct breach of the convention to leave the self-governing Dominions to their own affairs – indeed did so knowing full well that what London enacted would be ignored and could not be enforced – this breach of convention was motivated by domestic politics, namely disgust with apartheid domestically.[100] Again, when the Queen and Canada's, Australia's and New Zealand's Governors-General always sign Bills into law they probably never for a moment consider not doing so. But if they did, they would ultimately proceed to sign anyway because of an awareness of politics and what the political repercussions would be.

Turn, though, to the role of politics in democratic jurisdictions with formal constitutional structures and of course you see differences,

---

[100] See *Madzimbamuto v Lardner-Burke* [1969] 1 AC 645 (PC).

variety and heterogeneity. But nevertheless there are trends that can be noted and generalizations that can be made. I am happy to indulge in both. And one of the first things one observes across at least the common law democratic world (though much less so in New Zealand, and a good deal less so in Australia) is the rise of judicial power. Unelected judges are becoming ever more powerful, at least outside the United States where they have been very powerful for quite some time and so had little scope to expand their influence further.[101] This trend has also been described in this way:

> …as a 'judicialisation of politics': a growing intrusion of the judiciary into realms once the preserve of the executive and legislative and a corresponding transfer of power to the courts. Policy decisions that were once the exclusive preserve of democratic institutions are now ultimately resolved by judges, often in the guise of determinations about rights. This judicialisation has expanded to include matters of the utmost political significance that define whole polities.[102]

In the context of the United Kingdom this rise of judicial power has been said to be 'a function in part of the exercise of political responsibility (notably, dubious political choices to confer new powers and responsibilities on domestic courts and to accept the jurisdiction of foreign courts) and in part of how many judges, lawyers and scholars are coming to understand the idea of judicial power itself …. [and this all] undercut[s] democratic self-government.'[103]

---

[101] This trend is noted by those who approve of it, and by those like me who disapprove.See, for just one of many writers, Ran Hirschl, 'The Judicialization of Mega-Politics and the Rise of Political Courts' (2008) 11 *Annual Review of Political Science* 93 and Ran Hirschl, 'The Judicialization of Politics' in (ed.) Robert Goodlin, *The Oxford Handbook of Political Science* (OUP, 2009). If one were looking for a five word encapsulation of the democratic world's post- World War II trends in this area, I would opt for 'the triumph of American constitutionalism' – powerful judges, sometimes gainsaying and over-ruling the elected branches, most often when claiming to be interpreting a catalogue of entitlements in the language of rights.

[102] Nicholas Aroney and Benjamin Saunders, 'On Judicial Rascals and Self-Appointed Monarchs: The Rise of Judicial Power in Australia' (2017) 36 *University of Queensland Law Journal* at 221.

[103] Richard Ekins and Graham Gee, 'Putting Judicial Power in its Place' (2017) 36 *University of Queensland Law Journal* at 375.

Let me therefore finish this chapter by considering that last claim, that many (and in some jurisdictions most) judges, lawyers and legal academics around the democratic world, and especially those in jurisdictions with formal constitutional structures including a justiciable bill of rights, have come to endorse this trend of increasing judicial power with its ratchet-up of the judicialisation of politics. This is the new orthodoxy and the legal profession embraces it. I am skeptical. I have significant, serious doubts. Of course if readers are looking for examples of this increased judicial power I could point to the Court of Justice of the European Union, the Supreme Court of Canada, the UK and US Supreme Courts, then move to uber-activist top courts in India and Israel, and still have plenty of other examples up my sleeve. But instead let me relate this ratchet-up trend back to our theme of constitutionalism, remembering that the core attraction of constitutionalism revolves around achieving predictability, certainty and locked-in outcomes. And let me say again what I foreshadowed near the start of this chapter, namely that in order for any constitutional set-up to deliver that certainty and those locked-in outcomes one needs also to suppose or believe (as I do) that written rules can convey fixed meanings – that decisions made in the past by those considered to have the legitimate authority to do so have the capacity to lock us in today. But in addition to that it also requires a certain type of interpretation at the point-of-application – one that goes some way towards locking in decisions made by constitution-makers in the past – not some ultra-flexible, living-constitution, 'politics by other means' interpretive approach. Constitutionalism, real constitutionalism as opposed to judicial power travelling under the pretence of being constitutionalism, requires everyone to be locked in to outcomes (some they will like and some they will dislike). It requires the locking in of those outcomes to cover not just the 99.99 per cent of the rest of us in society, but the top judges too. Yet what I fear this judicialisation of politics indicates is that on many top courts today, at least across the common law democratic world, that sort of 'locking us all in' constitutionalism is just smoke and mirrors.

Let me put it this way. If the choice were between ***1)*** a constitutionalism that actually would lock in certain outcomes, so that latter day judges would be delivering intended outcomes that were specified in an authoritative text written in the past, on the one hand, and ***2)*** a New Zealand-style 'anything goes' parliamentary sovereignty democracy, on the other, well I would choose the latter (as I flesh out next chapter). That choice is not the orthodox, usual, familiar one, but it would be mine. That said, it would be a close call for me and I could certainly understand the attractions of the former, for all the Alexander/Kay/Perry specified reasons. But if, instead of that choice, the first alternative were transmogrified into a ***1B)*** pseudo-constitutionalism under which unelected judges 'do politics' and when so inclined simply deliver their social policy druthers (no doubt dressed up so as to pay lip service to the now vanished ***1)*** constitutionalism) then it would no longer be a remotely close call for me. If both choices are just politics, so that really it is just a question of the size of the franchise, with one option giving all voters an equal say and input (a system otherwise known as democracy) and the other amounting to one with hefty dollops of kritarchy and aristocracy (just with the landed gentry replaced by lawyers and by unelected judges doing politics amongst themselves) that admittedly locks all the 99.99 per cent of the rest of us into what the judges often happen to think is best, then at the very least proponents of such a transmogrified pseudo-constitutionalism can expect pushback. They can expect occasional cries of illegitimacy and they can expect people to vote for political parties and politicians that will try to do something about it.

Moreover, here is another place where my doubts come to the fore because it strikes me as very plausible indeed to assert that many people (including a good many lawyers and judges) in today's Anglosphere just naturally do think that ***1B)*** is the main form of constitutionalism; indeed they take this almost for granted. It comes close to unquestioned orthodoxy. Sure, they would not put it as bluntly as I do. Still, for them the main purpose of constitutionalism is not so much entrenchment as ensuring that a lawyerly elite caste of top judges *today* have a means to check the majority and thereby ensure 'justice' and 'principle' are better advanced by people who are qualified to know what these mean (namely, them). Such people are likely to want to distinguish between 'grubby interest-pursuing politics' and 'the majestic governance of principles.' Or such is how they would want to put it. However they did put it, I would be skeptical and full of doubt as to the merits of this sort of orthodoxy, or emerging orthodoxy. Indeed we will return to this larger topic later in the book when we turn to consider constitutional interpretation.

Suffice it to finish this chapter with Steven Smith's version of that revised ***1B)*** choice, with what may follow if we go down that road:

> ...the overall result will be that the Constitution as an instrument by which 'We the People' govern ourselves will to that extent have been displaced by a sort of Rorschach constitution onto which legal elites can project policies or principles that they favour and then, under the guise of 'the Constitution,' impose those policies or principles on the rest of us.[104]

Or put differently, if written constitutionalism or formal constitutionalism collapses into little more than just judicial politics, then it seems to me that democracy will be hard to keep down over time. It will out, and will do so not just in the politicisation of how judges are selected (though we can expect that too). Put differently again, if that is the actual choice then informal constitutionalism looks a lot more appealing to me than any disguised ***1B)*** formal constitutionalism that pretends to be delivering the virtues of locked in certainty and predictability but instead only delivers whatever predictability it does to the extent that we citizens can guess the political preferences of the top judges. That is a sort of politics, no doubt. But for my tastes, given my doubts about today's orthodoxy, it is a sort that is too circumscribed, too elitist (in the bad sense), too puffed up, too lawyer-centric, and all too likely to deliver bad long term consequences.

---

[104] Steven Smith, 'The Image of Liberty,' pp.10-11 (on file with the author).

Chapter Seven

The Move from Unwritten to Written Explored

In the last chapter one thing we did was to look at what an unwritten constitution amounts to. The name says it all. 'Unwritten' as in 'no written constitution.' It is about what is missing. And what is missing is some over-arching single document – a written constitution – from which other laws obtain their legitimacy and which provides much (though not all) of a jurisdiction's Rule of Recognition. Put differently, there are no constitutionalized legal limits on the power of the elected legislature. That is the main thing to remember about an unwritten constitution. So an unwritten constitution, with parliamentary sovereignty at its heart – and, again, that just means having an elected legislature that is legally unconstrained in what it can do, though one that is of course politically constrained via the electoral process – well, that sort of New Zealand or post-Brexit British set-up leaves the last word with voters.

A common rejoinder, in any discussion of unwritten constitutionalism's pros and cons, is to point to some imagined horror that a New Zealand-style, constitutionally unconstrained legislature might indulge in – say rounding up and killing all the blue-eyed baby boys or whatever you want to slot in here. I call this 'the Mugabe objection.' 'Wouldn't it be far better,' goes this line of rebuttal, 'if there were judges standing behind a written constitution, judges who could control that legislature?.' That sort of 'we need constitutional legalized limits on the legislature' horror-hypothetical argument is deployed frequently enough. But take a second to unpack it. We are supposed to imagine an elected legislature that has gone wholly off the rails. It is not simply making calls on debatable social policy-issues such as same-sex marriage or euthanasia or what to do with those claiming to be refugees or gun control or whether convicted prisoners can vote, issues where nice reasonable people just disagree, again to paraphrase Jeremy Waldron. No, we are imagining a legislature that is indulging in Beyond the Pale brutalities. Fine. Let us imagine that. What supporters of such horror-hypotheticals never do is to stay consistent. They imagine a Mugabe-run-wild legislature but then they assume that nine judges could stop Mugabe – that the brutal Mugabe legislature will stop because a half-dozen ex-lawyer judges tells it to (remember, top courts are the most procedurally majoritarian institutions going so it would only have to be a bare majority of those judges). Give me a break! If a legislature really has run wild in some horrific way then no handful of judges will stop it. They will be replaced or killed. As H.L.A. Hart put it, in such awful scenarios it is up to all citizens to rise up, otherwise '[t]the society in which this was so might be deplorably sheeplike; the sheep might end up in the slaughterhouse.'[105]

So the Mugabe scenario will not work as an argument against unwritten constitutions. It imagines some one in ten million situation when (truth be told) a written constitution and nine judges will not help in the slightest anyway – yes it imagines that – to justify quite a massive transfer of power to the judiciary over the myriad day-to-day social policy decision-making scenarios such as who can marry, or vote, or take his or her own life, or have an abortion, or own a gun, or where the limits on free speech should be, the usual things where an ex-lawyer's moral sensibilities are no better than a plumber's or a secretary's. The Mugabe hypothetical takes supporters of orthodoxy, of written constitutionalism, nowhere.

We also saw, last chapter, what the essence or point of written constitutionalism might be. What it is promising you. What it is selling. Supporters of written constitutions give one of two answers. The more orthodox and long-standing answer, the one we looked at briefly last chapter, is that a written constitution is about locking things in. So you might lock in a division of powers, or bicameralism, or a requisite minimum age to be President, or an enumerated list or Bill of individual rights. On this 'locking things in' answer you start with a picture of New Zealand-style parliamentary sovereignty and then you take a few things

[105] H.L.A. Hart, *The Concept of Law* (Clarendon, 1961), 114.

off the elected legislature's table. And as we saw, this is the position of American legal scholars such as Larry Alexander and Rick Kay. For them, you opt for security and certainty over future flexibility and free scope for action. But you fight and argue over every word of that written constitution because you are aiming for only some things to be taken off the table. Everything else remains at the say of the elected legislature – it will retain a sort of diminished parliamentary sovereignty, but one with largely knowable (because known) boundaries. Put differently, and taking this general point from Antonin Scalia, if your written constitution does not prevent the legislature from enacting the death penalty, there is nothing that stops the voters from electing a political party that will end capital punishment. The point, according to this school of thought, is that almost all rights provisions in an entrenched bill of rights, properly understood, serve as floors, not ceilings – by which is meant a locked in floor, not some floating, ever changing, waiting for the latest judicial dispensation floor. To re-use a US example, the written constitution forbids 'cruel and unusual punishment' – you cannot go below that locked in floor. But if your elected legislature wants to rise above that, to be more generous to those convicted of criminal offences, it can get rid of capital punishment or life sentences. It can do anything but drop below the 'cruel and unusual' floor when it comes to how to punish. Same for who can marry. Same for who can have an abortion. On the 'locking things in' model or understanding the written constitution is a new floor, but in no ways a ceiling. It cuts into parliament's sovereignty, but only to a pre-determined extent. It is not a blank check to the judiciary. It is not some ever-expanding, democracy-enervating behemoth administered by a few top judges. Nor, on this understanding, is the new written constitution being sold as (nor is it meant to be) some sort of 'all good things you can imagine can henceforth be delivered by the future interpreters of this constitution.'

Until relatively recently that was pretty much the only justification given for deciding to have a written constitution, this 'let's lock a few things in' rationale. These days there is a second option, albeit that it is one that I think is only ever given after-the-fact. Here the claim is that a written constitution's value lies in expressing the country's deepest values and commitments, that sort of thing. What its future effects will be is accordingly much less definite, much less locked in. Why? Well as society's values and commitments change then those interpreting the constitution that is expressing these core social commitments need to keep updating it. They need to have their fingers on the pulse of all these changing social mores. This sort of constitutional interpretation we will consider in Part IV of this book. It goes by the name of 'living tree' interpretation in the Westminster world and by 'living constitutionalism' in the United States. It is by far the dominant school of constitutional interpretation. In the European Court of Human Rights it can seem to be the only school.

That said, you might agree with me that no one attached to this second rationale for moving to a written constitution can be too honest about it upfront. Suppose New Zealand (or any democratic jurisdiction with unwritten constitutionalism, so parliamentary sovereignty) were considering a move to a new written constitution. And suppose I asked a supporter of such a move what things were no longer going to be decided by the elected legislature Parliament but instead, in future, would be decided by the interpreters of the new written Constitution. What, in other words, will be taken off the table by this new written constitution?

It is not an attractive answer to be told: 'Well, no one honestly knows. Give it a few decades and despite the fact that none of us drafters had the slightest intention to take from Parliament such things as X, Y or Z, and despite the fact that no reading of it that paid attention to what the framers and ratifiers thought would take them away either, the truth is that in the not too distant future the top judges might well decide to say this new constitution gives them – a handful of top judges – the power to decide who can marry. Or whether euthanasia will be allowed. Or who can have an abortion. Or which prisoners, if any, can vote. Or who can and cannot own a gun. They'll take power over all those sorts of things and more. Truth be told, no one really knows what these point-of-application interpreters will announce down the road. So do you still want to sign up?.' Or do you prefer to take your chances on democracy and the elected legislature, as New Zealand does?

To repeat, then, whatever the eventual truth of how a written constitution will be interpreted, when trying to sell a written constitution proponents will always opt for the 'we're going to lock a few things in' rationale. They have to say that they have some idea of how the written document will be interpreted or who would want to sign up for it? Few, outside perhaps segments of the legal profession and of the ranks of the judiciary, are keen to hand future top judges something that can look like a blank check at times. As I said in an earlier chapter, in terms of how to interpret this new written constitution the truth may well boil down to a general choice between ancestor worship (the locked in understanding that relies on one sort of constitutional interpretive approach) or rule by judges (the expressing our deepest values understanding, that relies on a very different interpretive approach). But before we actually get to the time when the written constitution has been adopted, any salesman trying to sell it will need to assert that things not specified will stay with the elected legislature; that what we are actually locking in and so taking off the democratic table can be, and is, knowable in advance; that it will be unchanging over time (absent future constitutional amendments); that it will be bracketed and confined, at least to a very, very large extent indeed.

Put bluntly, that is what written constitutionalism is promising you; what it *has to promise you* in order to get enough support to be adopted in any democracy. My plans in the rest of this short chapter are twofold – *1)* to explain in today's world why that promissory check can never be cashed – why a written constitution that promises ancestor worship instead delivers rule by today's top judges (those two being the only choices on the table), with constitutional orthodoxy being overwhelmingly happy with that substitution or misdirection; and then *2)* to say why I believe you should think about this looking forward, not backwards.

1. So can that Promissory Check be cashed? Can you know what's being taken off the democratic table when you opt for a written constitution?

The evidence is overwhelming on this one. The clear, basically indisputable, answer is 'no.' Anyone in the developed Anglosphere common law world who tells you they know how provisions of a written constitution will be interpreted down the road is either woefully misinformed, or lying to you. Let me quote from US constitutional law scholar Richard Kay:

> We now have a long record and a voluminous literature on the topic of constitutional interpretation. One clear conclusion can be drawn from that record and literature. The limitations that courts, in fact, apply to the actions of public authorities deviate and sometimes deviate substantially from those that the designers of the written constitution contemplated at the time the rules were chosen.[106]

To be a little less circumspect, no one who is today signing up to a written constitution has any real clue how it will be interpreted and how it will be used by future judges. The limits it will impose on future elected Parliaments will be, in a sense, pretty much up to the judiciary. For majoritarian democrats like me, positioned well outside of the legal caste's orthodoxy, this is a fairly appalling admission.

Consider even a jurisdiction with a written constitution but without a bill of rights. Most everyone's examples of the expansive nature of a written constitution's coverage – of the ratchet-up effect of rights-related judicial decisions and of judges veering away from the supposedly locked in meanings and intentions at the time of the constitution's founding – come from jurisdictions that *do* have a bill of rights as part of that written constitution. This is the most fertile soil for that sort of behavior and outcome. Australia, however, while it has a written constitution does not have a national bill of rights of any sort. Sure, to today's law students in Canada and the US, and indeed in the UK and in New Zealand, that probably sounds a bit shocking. Many will struggle to imagine that a country would not want a bill of rights. At the end of the Second World War, within the lifetime of people still walking around, only two established democracies had bills of rights – the US and France, with France's being the older of the two. Still, France's was not justiciable. You could not go to court and invoke it, not until a decade ago or so. But my point is that in the last seven decades we have seen what might be

---

106 Richard Kay, 'Changing the United Kingdom Constitution: The Blind Sovereign' in Rawlings, Leyland and Young (eds) *Sovereignty and the Law: Domestic, European and International Perspectives* (OUP, 2013) at 116.

described as 'the triumph of American constitutionalism.' Virtually every democratic country everywhere has opted for a bill of rights. Of course not all jurisdictions have the common law culture of *uber* powerful judges too. But they all have bills of rights. Well, except Australia. There is no national bill of rights in Australia to this day, though it protects rights perfectly well. Yes, two of the six Australian States have an amalgam of the NZ-UK style statutory bill of rights model that covers State legislation.But that is it. There is no national bill of rights of any sort. Australia's position in this regard has gone from being the dominant orthodoxy in the democratic world to being the outlier *par excellence*.

Yet here is the question. If we were to ditch the bill of rights in our jurisdiction would that help? Could we then be more confident that our written constitution would not be inflated by latter-day judges to make unintended and 'unwanted at the time of adoption' inroads into democratic decision-making? Does the locking things in rationale better mesh with the future facts when there is no bill of rights?

And using Australia as our guide the short answer is 'yes,' things are better. But they are far from perfect. In the early 1990s the High Court of Australia 'discovered' an implied freedom of communication. This was found in the text and structure, supposedly, of the written constitution – despite the Australian drafters explicitly rejecting a US style bill of rights; despite them rejecting a 1st Amendment type free speech right; despite two failed constitutional amendment referenda where all the citizens of Australia also rejected a bill of rights, the latter taking place only four years before the top judges did this 'discovering' of this implied speech freedom. Ninety years after its founding and the country's top court, the High Court of Australia (and be clear, judges tend overwhelmingly to support bills of rights for reasons too obvious for me to have to articulate, so most were disappointed by the 1988 referendum) simply discovered or found this enervated free speech entitlement lurking 'impliedly' (but for 90 years unseen) in the written text. Wow! And I say that as one who sees himself as one of the biggest supporters of free speech going in the common law legal academic world. But one's first order preferences and values are one thing, and one's assessment of what a text honestly means is another – even if that distinction appears these days not to be one recognised by a good many US and Canadian and many other countries' top judges.

So the highest Australian court and its seven judges did not even need a bill of rights to do this. And then, just over a decade ago, that same High Court of Australia 'found' or 'discovered' or 'made up out of thin air' (pretty much how I would also describe a good few Canadian and US Supreme Court decisions), a sort of 'right to vote' to do with prisoner voting – which is no longer up to Parliament in Australia. And more recently still they did much the same thing, they invented a sort of right, applying only to non-citizen Aborigines.

I could go on. But the point is that even an Australian written constitution (which owes much to American Founder James Madison, at least before Madison was pushed into supporting a bill of rights) can be – no, it has been – used to over-ride the elected legislature in ways never remotely imagined by those framing and drafting and fighting over every word of that written constitution, as well as by those reading it when first produced and then voting on whether to adopt it. Sure, the Australian model leaves far more to the elected Parliament than the Canadian or US variants (though not as much as in New Zealand and post-Brexit Britain with their unwritten constitutions, their parliamentary sovereignty). Yet how it will be used in the future is highly uncertain.

Any promise that a new written constitution will take only some pre-determined chunk of pie off the democratic legislature's table simply can never be honored. It is a check you cannot cash. The empirical evidence on that, as Kay and many others admit, is overwhelming. Look at the US. Look at Canada. Look at South Africa, Israel or the European Court of Justice. Look at Australia even. Orthodoxy may downplay this, implicitly suggesting the locked in model of constitutionalism. Yet once in place the facts look to be otherwise.

If you prefer social policy decision-making to be made by committees of ex-lawyers, then this will not bother you at all. Indeed that preference seems to me to come close to being unspoken orthodoxy. Put differently, that sort of attachment to a modern day variant of what might unkindly be called 'aristocracy' in no sense lacks widespread appeal. It dominates the law schools of the common law world. It dominates the Bar

Councils, Bar Associations and Law Societies too. It is by far the default view of the judges. It is the assumed outlook of the lawyerly caste. It is not mine though.

2. Decide looking forwards not backwards

Last point. Once you have a written constitution it is in any practical sense impossible to go back. And once one is in place the *ex post facto* rationales all speak in the name of 'the Constitution,' not some contentious (or patently implausible) interpretation of it. Or to make the same point in different terms, judges give interpretations in the name of the Constitution, not in the name of their own names. Rhetorically this is a 'can't lose' advantage. It will trump all else. Critics of how the written document is being interpreted will be sloughed off with observations that 'everyone is unhappy with a decision here or there.'

Similarly the related distinction between ***a)*** whether one agrees with the first-order substantive outcome of a case and ***b)*** whether one believes the interpretation of the written document plausibly allowed for that outcome gets obfuscated. For many on the winning side of some social-policy dispute, only the former matters. And this can create much consternation and pessimism when you are on the losing side of some judicially-imposed outcome that you will never have a vote on and that seems simply to have been made up by the judiciary. Let me return to Steven Smith, someone who is unhappy with recent judicial gymnastics in the US, and quote from his 2015 Constitution Day address:[107]

> …many issues are again resolved not by elected legislators but rather by unelected judges based on a mere figment of connection to the Constitution. The recent imposition of same-sex marriage on the nation by judges unwilling to allow this ostensibly inevitable development to be implemented democratically is a leading case in point.
>
> … if we do not start with a commitment to arriving at a particular, presumptively desirable destination, and if instead we ask how governance truly committed to rule by "the People"

[107] Stephen Smith, 'The Image of Liberty' at pages 6, 7, 8-9, 10-11 respectively (on file with the author, publication pending).

> would work, the whole modern enterprise looks different, and much more dubious.
>
> ...if we think of our constitutional tradition as a project in self-governance, this [now dominant 'living Constitution,' just pick some supposed principle embedded in the document and go from there interpretive] approach will seem less appealing, not to mention manifestly implausible. That is because it is hard to picture political actors making a political decision to enact some "principle" whose implications they can only dimly foresee, and thus to authorize future adjudicators to enforce their own "conceptions" of what that principle entails. Legislators could do that. But they almost surely wouldn't.
>
> ...the overall result will be that the Constitution as an instrument by which "We the People" govern ourselves will to that extent have been displaced by a sort of Rorschach constitution onto which legal elites can project policies or principles that they favor and then, under the guise of "the Constitution," impose those policies or principles on the rest of us.

Read that pessimism and anger and be warned about the potential dangers of written constitutionalism, as currently administered. And take my final claim to be that any assessment of the merits of a written constitution ought to be made looking forward, before one is in place, not retrospectively once one is already in place. And from that forward-looking vantage, knowing what we know about top courts and dominant interpretive approaches in the common law world (a topic to come in future chapters), there are solid, persuasive grounds for shunning written constitutionalism in favour of the unwritten sort – not that anyone outside of New Zealand or Britain will ever be presented with that as a live choice. In other words, I have huge doubts about the orthodox legal position in favour of written constitutions, with bills of rights, interpreted under the aegis of 'living constitutionalism.' That said, if your jurisdiction has one it is there to stay. This is a one-way street. The fight then moves to ground we will cover in Part IV.

Chapter Eight

The Types of Strong Judicial Review Distinguished

As this Part III of the book aims to give readers both a sense of constitutionalism in today's democratic world, as well as of my skepticism as regards many aspects of the orthodox views, I turn now to do something that is surprisingly rarely done. In this chapter I want to distinguish between two types of strong judicial review, two grounds on which unelected top judges in various long-established democracies can and do invalidate or strike down statutes enacted by the democratically elected legislature. (It is termed 'strong' judicial review when the judges take a matter out of the hands of the elected legislature, as opposed to gainsaying some merely administrative body.) As I said, making this sort of distinction between rights-related judicial review and federalism (or division of powers) judicial review is relatively uncommon. However, as the two sorts of judicial review rely on different rationales and justifications that for different people may well have different degrees of persuasiveness, I want here to take a short chapter to disentangle them. Certainly for those comparatively few in the lawyerly caste who are like me, who might plausibly be described as majoritarian democrats, there is a big difference between rights-related and federalism strong judicial review[108] – the two differ in terms of their desirability and of one's willingness to be subjected to them. And this is true even though both are, or can be, creatures of written constitutionalism.

---

[108] And for the rest of this chapter I will assume that the sort of judicial review under consideration is strong judicial review.

Another way to make this distinction between these two types of judicial review is to ask if one is able to give a convincing account of why someone might oppose rights-related judicial review and yet accept – or not oppose – federalism judicial review. That is the challenge I want to take on in this chapter, and to take on in particular as a majoritarian democrat. It is the challenge to explain, from that majoritarian democrat's vantage, how federalism judicial review is 'qualitatively different from the judicial protection of rights (either in the nature of the discretion conferred or in its counter-majoritarian effect);'[109] to give a persuasive reason for opposing rights-based judicial review on the one hand, while accepting federalism (or call it heads of powers) judicial review on the other. So the rest of this chapter is my attempt to take up that challenge.

I will start by sketching out a scenario or hypothetical that I hope later to draw on and that I think is roughly analogous to some of the issues under consideration. Accordingly, imagine that there are three Protestant churches which have been negotiating a merger. Let us suppose that it is the Presbyterians, Methodists and Congregationalists who are planning to merge into a new church, called the Uniting Church.[110] In creating this new Uniting Church it is likely that some churchgoers and branches will balk, refusing to merge in favor of continuing on under the old denomination. However, to ensure that as many branches and individuals as possible opt to move over to the new entity, it will be designed in a way that for the next three decades allows some decisions to be made by the component or merging former denominations. So on some issues the new Uniting Church will speak for all centrally. On other issues, the former

[109] Adrienne Stone, 'Judicial Review without Rights: Some Problems for the Democratic Legitimacy of Structural Judicial Review' (2008) 28 *Oxford Journal of Legal Studies* 1 at p. 32. Stone issued that challenge in that article and I attempted to answer it in James Allan, 'Not in for a Pound – In for a Penny? Must a Majoritarian Democrat Treat All Constitutional Judicial Review as Equally Egregious?' (2010) 21 *King's Law Journal* 233-256. This chapter is based in part on my reply to Stone in that *KLJ* article.

[110] To the extent that this hypothetical is based on factual premises it is interesting to note that this is the Australian name for just that merged church. In Canada they chose the past participle – 'United Church.' Given the fact that in neither country did all individual branches or members of the component denominations agree to the merger, it is an interesting question which choice of name is the more optimistic.

Presbyterians, Methodists and Congregationalists can make their own decisions.

And let us suppose that a list of issues over which the new Uniting Church has jurisdiction is drawn up, everything not on the list staying with the component parts (until the 30 years has passed).

Finally, for the purposes of this hypothetical, let us assume that in order to achieve this merger it has been agreed that when disputes arise between the new, central Uniting Church authorities and one or all of the component merging parts, that dispute will be resolved by a single, named lawyer, Richard Dawkins QC, who is not only renowned in the law but is also a well-known atheist. He and he alone will decide whether the power to decide some contested issue (such as, say, whether to ordain women or bless same-sex marriages or how to divide up sold-off assets or what sort of prayers or hymns to have) lies with the merging component parts or with the new Uniting Church centralized entity.

And, of course, in deciding the issues that come before him Mr Dawkins will, case-by-case, build up a body of doctrines and *stare decisis* principles that will affect how he resolves future division of powers disputes that come before him.

Now, that will suffice for the moment as far as sketching out this hypothetical goes. Before moving on, though, just ponder the following three questions briefly as regards that hypothetical. Firstly, could devout religious believers in the situation of those opting for this new Uniting Church ever have grounds to hand power to a secular atheist to decide, based on an enumerated list of powers, whether a particular church-related issue is to be decided by the new central authorities or by the merging component parts? Secondly, and far more relevantly, might such a devout, religious believer be wholly opposed to allowing Mr Dawkins to himself ever decide actual substantive, first-order issues (such as who can be ordained or married by the Church, what words hymns and prayers will contain, etc), but be far more relaxed about him ruling – umpire style – on whether the whole new Uniting Church entity or one of its merging parts will decide something, given that both of those decision-making options he must choose between will themselves be comprised of devout, religious believers? Lastly, might the advantages of having an outsider choose between the two sometimes outweigh the fact that this decision-maker would never himself be favored to make any first-order substantive decisions?

1. Preliminaries, Clarifications and Framing the Argument

This challenge, as I have recast it, is directed at democracy-based opponents of constitutional rights review who are, simultaneously, quite relaxed about federalism review. So perhaps before I clarify what counts as a democracy-based objection I should remind the reader what is at stake in the sorts of decisions unelected judges regularly make when deciding rights-related constitutional issues in, say, Canada and the United States. And then I want to set out what is at stake – what the unelected judges are actually deciding – in, say, Australia (where there is no bill of rights) or Canada or the US when they are engaged in non-rights-related, federalism constitutional judicial review.

That sort of rough-and-ready comparison is in no way conclusive and determinative of whether one can meet this challenge, however lopsided the comparison might (and does) appear. But in my view neither is it irrelevant. Accordingly, for preliminary purposes only, and to remind the reader, here are the sorts of issues on which committees of ex-lawyers have the final say when deciding constitutionalized rights-related disputes.

They, the judges, decide whether democratically mandated restrictions on abortion can stand.[111] They decide the same as far as euthanasia goes.[112] They decide whether there will be same-sex marriages.[113] They overturn immigration laws by insisting that each and every refugee claimant must be given an oral hearing (at huge taxpayer expense and with security implications).[114] They decide whether democratically enacted restrictions on carrying handguns will be struck

---

[111] *Roe v Wade* 410 US 113 (1973); *R v Morgentaler* [1988] 1 SCR 30.

[112] *Washington v Glucksberg* 117 S Ct 2258 (1997); *Carter v Canada (A-G)* [2015] 1 SCR 30.

[113] *Obergefell v Hodges* 576 US __ (2015); *Halpern v Canada* (AG) [2003] OJ 2268 (Ont CA); *Reference Re Same-Sex Marriage* [2004] 3 SCR 698.

[114] *Singh v Canada (Minister of Employment and Immigration)* [1985] 1 SCR 177.

down.[115] They overturn democratic legislation aimed at restricting private health care and bolstering a public-only, socialised health care regime.[116] They strike down capital punishment laws.[117] They re-write criminal procedure laws to favor accuseds to a much greater extent and against the judgement of the electorate and their representatives.[118] And, of course, they decide the balance to be struck between health and safety concerns (including restricting tobacco advertising) and free speech (including by tobacco companies),[119] whether incarcerated prisoners must in all cases be allowed to vote[120] and even whether limits on the salaries of provincially appointed judges in the context of a civil service-wide freeze can stand.[121]

And that is just a sampling of the sorts of issues and decision-making powers that rights-related constitutional judicial review gives to the judges. Against that, and the handing to committees of ex-lawyers of a *final say* over issues such as same-sex marriage, gun control, socialized medicine, abortion, capital punishment, euthanasia, the whole array of criminal procedures, immigration laws, and more, what is the actual substantive content of decision-making that is removed from the purview

---

[115] *District of Columbia v Heller* 128 S Ct 2783 (2008).

[116] *Chaoulli v Quebec (Attorney General)* 2005 SCC 35.

[117] *Roper v Simmons* 125 S Ct 1183 (2005).

[118] In Canada, *R v Askov* (1990) 74 DLR (4th) 355, then an extra-judicial rationalisation and apology for that decision in the 26 July 1991 edition of *Lawyers Weekly* (vol 11, no 13) followed by the recanting of *Askov* in *R v Morin* (1992) 72 CCC (3d) 11 (SCC). In the US, *Miranda v Arizona* 86 S Ct 1602 (1966).

[119] *RJR MacDonald Inc v Canada* (1995) 127 DLR (4th) 1, a dozen years later modified or recanted in *Canada (Attorney General) v JTI-MacDonald Corp* 2007 SCC 30. And notice that the interpretation of the same right (not just one to free speech, but to others too) leads to varying, indeed sometimes mutually inconsistent, outcomes in differing jurisdictions. See James Allan and Grant Huscroft, 'Constitutional Rights Coming Home to Roost? Rights Internationalism in American Courts' (2006) 43 *San Diego Law Review* 1.

[120] *Sauve v Canada (Attorney General)* [1993] 2 SCR 438 and, after lengthy legislative hearings and attempts to soften or ameliorate the ban, *Sauve v Canada (Chief Electoral Officer)* [2002] 3 SCR 519. In the latter of those cases, the Chief Justice (writing for the 5-4 majority) referred obliquely to countries mentioned in the dissent that disagree with her court's narrow 5-4 ruling as 'self-proclaimed democracies' [41], those countries including Australia, the UK, the US and New Zealand, all of which have their own cases on this issue.

[121] *Reference Re Remuneration of Provincial Court Judges* [1997] 3 SCR 3.

of *all* elected legislatures under non-rights-related, federalism (or heads of powers) constitutional judicial review?

Well, it is virtually nothing. In a federal system the judges will decide plenty of heads of powers disputes; the unelected judiciary will decide whether the elected US Congress/Australian Commonwealth Parliament/Canadian Parliament *or* the elected US/Australian State or Canadian Provincial legislatures have the power to legislate on some matter. They will take a matter out of the hands of one level of elected legislature but thereby leave it in the hands of another level. The challenge I have set myself, then, when put in this preliminary, rough-and-ready way, is for majoritarian democrats like me to provide a principled reason for objecting to unelected judges having immense power when it comes to capital punishment, immigration, same-sex marriage, abortion, socialized medicine, gun control, privacy, who can say what and when, euthanasia, and a lot more such first-order issues related to what citizens can do and say and yet not object to (or object far less vociferously to) judges having immense power to decide which level of government can decide what and when. At first glance, in other words, the second sort of judicial review – heads of powers, federalism judicial review – looks qualitatively different from the first, the rights-related sort.

Moreover, whatever one ends up thinking about whether non-rights-related constitutional judicial review is qualitatively different from its rights-related cousin, notice that from the average citizen's point of view it is inarguably different when it comes to the quantity of gainsaying – to the number of issues affecting him or her which are taken out of voters' hands and put in judges' hands. Indeed, in terms of first-order issues related to what citizens can do and say, the quantitative difference between judicial input under rights-related and non-rights-related judicial review (and, arguably, the scope for ever-widening such input to the point of kritarchy) is massive. It is quantitatively huge.

Looked at from the citizen's point of view then, indeed the citizen committed to democratic decision-making, one can certainly imagine this raw differential in the amount, scope and quantity of judicial intrusions mattering. Indeed it seems quite plausible to me to go further and from that perspective to argue that rights-related constitutional judicial review deals directly with what are often the most important and controversial issues of personal and political morality, something that cannot remotely as frequently be claimed as regards non-rights-related, federalism constitutional review. Before agreeing to some proposed new federal Constitution in the 1780s or 1860s or 1890s such a citizen may think, 'I will bargain away my democratic input over A and B in order to be part of a new federal state, but not over A through Z.' Likewise, someone born long after that Constitution has come into effect but similarly democratically inclined might think 'this system of mine with only non-rights-related judicial review is far superior to others which have rights-related judicial review too, and it is superior in no small part because of the quantitatively much reduced scope for judicial intrusions into last-word decision-making.'

That is the preliminary point. I think it is a fairly telling and powerful one. The clarifications relate to the making of democratic objections to strong judicial review. Such objections rest on at least three claims, namely: (1) that there will inevitably be reasonable disagreement over the outcomes dictated by moral concepts (like rights); (2) that abstract, amorphously articulated concepts (like rights) inevitably confer discretion on the point-of-application interpreting judges; and (3) that those same judges have no obvious expertise over such moral issues.[122]

Now someone like Adrienne Stone who was inclined to issue the challenge we are considering[123] – the challenge to try to explain, from that majoritarian democrat's vantage, how federalism judicial review is qualitatively different from the judicial protection of rights (either in the nature of the discretion conferred or in its counter-majoritarian effect) – might at this point come back with this retort. She might note that if you are someone worried about discretion – and more specifically discretion when it comes to making moral judgements over which the maker has no obvious expertise – then you should worry too about non-rights-related constitutional judicial review. In that sphere, too, interpretation of those

---

[122] This, in substance, is the way the democracy clarification is set out by Adrienne Stone in 'Judicial Review without Rights: Some Problems for the Democratic Legitimacy of Structural Judicial Review' (2008) 28 *Oxford Journal of Legal Studies* at pp. 6-8. See footnote 109 above.

[123] See fn. 109 above.

constitutional provisions requires similar evaluative judgements 'over matters on which there is reasonable and intractable disagreement.'[124]

Let me therefore pause here and make three comments. First off, in any comparison between A and B – where both exhibit some disapproved of quality X, but A has more of that quality than B – there is no entailment from a rejection of A to a necessary rejection of B. The amount of X might be relevant, even determinative. Consistency does not foreclose a disliker of X from saying that she cannot live with A but can live with B, where A contains more of X than B. Of course that fact in no way requires her to accept B either. It is just that the opposition to A carries no necessary grounds for opposing B, given the differential size or quantities of X. The final decision on whether to oppose B may depend on the viability and attractiveness of other alternatives and on whether these alternatives also contain X. In down-to-earth terms, one can be virulently opposed to having to accept 200 overnight visits per year from one's in-laws (due to some disliked quality X), and yet feel perfectly resigned, even happy, to accept eight or nine such overnight visits per year – for all sorts of counter-balancing consequentialist reasons.

Secondly but relatedly, discretion, even where it is caused by having to make normative judgements due to the amorphousness, indeterminacy and the moral-ladenness of terms, is not an all-or-nothing, one-size-only quality. As H.L.A. Hart made clear, all rules (however fanatically detailed they be) will have a 'core of settled meaning'[125] and a 'penumbra of doubt.'[126] But the relative penumbras of different rules can vary extensively. In other words, not all discretion, or wide discretion, is equivalent. Two activities can both involve wide discretion 'to make evaluative judgements over matters on which there is reasonable and

---

124 Adrienne Stone, 'Judicial Review without Rights: Some Problems for the Democratic Legitimacy of Structural Judicial Review' (2008) 28 *Oxford Journal of Legal Studies* at p.12.

125 HLA Hart, *The Concept of Law* (Clarendon, 1961) 140.

126 *Ibid.*, 119 *inter alia.*

intractable disagreement'[127] and yet have quite differently sized penumbras of doubt.

My third comment is this. Opposition to rights-related judicial review is premised on the fact that there is (to majoritarian democrats) an obvious alternative on offer that is superior, namely leaving rights-related line-drawing exercises to the elected legislature. When we turn to the other side of the ledger, to heads of powers, federalism judicial review that some (such as Stone) try to suggest ought to be just as fervently opposed by majoritarian democrats, we need to know what the alternative to having the unelected judges decide supposedly is. Is that alternative a democratic one or not? Is there an element of not being a judge in your own cause type objection to handing such federalism umpiring decisions either to a State legislature or to the country's central legislature? An umpire known to favour the States (which would give the obvious appearance, and probably the reality, of bias when having State legislatures decide federalism disputes) is not really much, if any, of an improvement on one known to favour the center – as, likewise, would handing these calls over to Congress or the Commonwealth Parliament in Australia. No, the aim is to have an impartial or disinterested umpire ruling on such disputes, an aim that may impel the devout members of the newly merged Uniting Church in my hypothetical above to accept Mr Dawkins – as the least bad option going – to be the umpire of such disputes for them, despite his sharing few of their first-order moral positions.

Another clarificatory point to make involves the 'is/ought' distinction and the precise nature of this challenge to majoritarian democrats. On one level it is clear that the challenge being laid down lies on the 'ought' plane. It amounts to asserting that majoritarian democrats ought to oppose heads of powers, federalism judicial review too, or at least they ought to provide a principled reason for distinguishing it from rights-based review. But there is often an implicit 'is' judgement lurking about when laying down this challenge, namely that most majoritarian democrats (as a matter of empirical fact) do *not* oppose heads of powers

[127] Adrienne Stone, 'Judicial Review without Rights: Some Problems for the Democratic Legitimacy of Structural Judicial Review' (2008) 28 *Oxford Journal of Legal Studies* 12.

judicial review as vociferously as rights-based review, if they oppose them at all. For what it is worth, I think that implicit empirical claim is correct. I myself am a happy federalist. Or rather, I am a happy one when the top court does not lean massively too much to the center, as it does in Australia.[128]

Related to that point is this. In looking at rights-related judicial review and heads of powers review are we, or are we not, to confine ourselves to what top judges happen to be doing, in fact, right now? Certainly much attention needs to be paid to the way judges are, at present, actually doing their jobs when it comes to constitutional judicial review. That said, one should be slightly uneasy about limiting the scope of consideration to the way things happen to be, at the moment. At the level of trifles, that 'here and now' sort of focus might allow an anti-federalist majoritarian democrat in Australia to answer part of Stone's challenge simply by saying 'the Australian High Court in division of powers cases almost always sides with the Commonwealth Parliament and upholds its legislation[129] which is as democratic an outcome as anyone could desire. So there is no need to answer your challenge there.' I happen to think that this sort of an answer, alone, will not do as section ***2.*** of this chapter below aims to show. But this pointing to this or that jurisdiction as it stands at present, by way of refutation of the larger challenge, is a danger of any single-minded focus on the here-and-now 'is' realm.

More serious, however, is this worry. It is the worry that the dominant method of interpretation really matters when it comes to constitutional judicial review,[130] and over middling to longish periods of time – based on experience – we can expect that dominant approach to change. For example, I suspect that a good many of the majoritarian democrats opposed to rights-based judicial review would soften their criticisms (and some drop them altogether) if the main approach to interpretation were not a 'living Constitution' or 'progressive' or

---

[128] I make that case with my colleague in James Allan and Nicholas Aroney, 'An Uncommon Court: How the High Court of Australia has undermined Australian Federalism' (2008) 30 *Sydney Law Review* 245.

[129] See *ibid.* for arguments that this is broadly an accurate statement.

[130] I certainly think the method of constitutional interpretation matters greatly. Indeed, Part IV of this book focuses just on that topic.

'Dworkinian' or 'moral reading' approach but instead some version of originalism that saw the enumerated rights as locking in a floor-level, stable set of protections above which the legislature was sovereign and could decide – say, as regards same-sex marriage or abortion entitlements or removing capital punishment – via the democratic process whether to extend rights and entitlements, or not. But the fact of the matter is that as things stand at present the 'living Constitution' or 'living tree' approach is arguably still dominant in the United States (and pretty much the only game in town in Canada and before the European Court of Justice and many other top courts). That 'is' fact, however, ought not to foreclose us from recognizing that Stone's challenge, and attempts to meet that challenge, can vary and shift as the facts, and especially the facts related to how judges are interpreting, change.

My final clarification, and in some ways the most important one, has to do with vantage and timing. When we come to consider whether the majoritarian democrat ought to oppose heads of powers judicial review are we to assess that at the time before the written constitution has been adopted but is being seriously considered (when, perhaps, the live alternative is some version of British (before or after the EU) or New Zealand-style parliamentary sovereignty) or at the present day, when as a matter of 'is'-based fact we have zero chance of moving to parliamentary sovereignty? Put more bluntly, the preferred time of assessment can matter to the answer one gives.

Similarly, are we to attempt to answer this challenge from the vantage of the concerned citizen attached to democratic majoritarianism, or from the vantage of the judge with that same attachment, or from some other vantage? In my view that too may affect our response.

2. Constitutional Judicial Review of the Heads of Powers Federalism Type

With those preliminaries and clarifications behind us we can see the gist of a very powerful response to this challenge to distinguish federalism judicial review from the rights-related sort. In essence, it is that with federalism judicial review judges clearly have the role of division of powers arbiters, so that while no single parliament can be said to be supreme or sovereign, it is also true that one of the legislatures (the particular State legislature or the central Parliament or Congress) has the judicially unrestrained power to do whatever is attempting to be done. And it is also true that with heads of powers federalism-related judicial review the unelected judges are simply choosing between which of two democratically elected legislatures can do precisely what some statute is attempting to do. It is true, put differently, that the judges are not putting this precise attempt beyond the reach of all democratic politics, state or national (as happens with rights-related judicial review).

Well, one reply (one that Adrienne Stone gives) might be to note that from that sort of response of mine 'it does not follow that [heads of powers] federal judicial review has no counter-majoritarian effect.'[131] Rather, or so goes this reply, the significance of leading heads of powers federalism decisions by a top court 'lies as much in its effect on the shape of … federalism'[132] as on its effect on the issues directly being litigated and contested by the two levels of federal government in any particular case.

However, that is no very good reply to my response. The fact that a court, in deciding the heads of powers federalism cases that come before it, builds up a body of doctrines and *stare decisis* principles that will affect how it resolves future heads of powers disputes – that will make more likely the center's or the State's prevailing in some future dispute – goes no distance at all towards changing the fact that in all those future heads of powers cases one of the two elected legislatures will be ruled to have the judicially unrestrained power to do whatever is attempting to be done. And that remains true whether the built-up doctrines and principles tend (on average, over time) to favour the elected national legislature (as in Australia and the United States), or whether they tend to favour the state or provincial legislatures.

No amount of pointing to the accretions of sophisticated principles that will guide future such disputes alters the reality that in these sorts of

---

[131] Adrienne Stone, 'Judicial Review without Rights: Some Problems for the Democratic Legitimacy of Structural Judicial Review' (2008) 28 *Oxford Journal of Legal Studies* (n 3) p. 22.

[132] *Ibid.*, 22.

cases the unelected judges act as umpires, choosing between two democratically elected decision-makers. In this type of judicial review, then, the unelected judges cannot take anything off the table as far as what majoritarian politics can enact. They merely distribute specific legislative endeavours between the two tables.

Stone asserts that 'the critical matter to appreciate [with heads of powers federalism related judicial review] is that the Court's decisions in this respect are within the Court's control and not subject to revision by any Parliament.'[133] But there is nothing critical about that at all as regards the challenge she has issued to majoritarian democrats. Sure, an Australian or American or Canadian federal system will bring with it heads of powers disputes where the unelected judges will have the power to choose which elected legislature will win. And that power to choose will itself stand outside democratic politics. It will not be 'subject to revision by any Parliament.'[134]

Nevertheless, a 'cannot be gainsaid' power to choose between two or more majoritarian decision-makers is a different (and I would assert a less objectionable to majoritarian democrats) power than a 'cannot be gainsaid' power to choose oneself as the point-of-application interpreter.

Go back to my hypothetical. The devout and religious member of the newly established Uniting Church might have a number of principled grounds for preferring Mr Dawkins (with all his accompanying atheist baggage) as umpire deciding these heads of powers disputes, and for preferring him not just over the leadership of the new Uniting Church but also over any sub-set of Uniting Church members (or at least any sub-set on which her views did not regularly and obviously prevail).

First off, she may think Mr Dawkins has less of a dog in the fight, that he will be more disinterested and more focused on honest interpretation rather than *ex post facto* rationalisations of his own first-order policy preference outcomes. Such a calculation is by no means a certainty. We can well imagine a secular, atheist, *Guardian*-reading lawyer coming to the conclusion that same-sex marriages ought to be performed or women ordained by some church, and then having the mental

133 *Ibid.*, (n 3) 22.

134 *Ibid.*, 22.

acuity to argue for those very outcomes surreptitiously, in terms of what the heads of powers list and what a theory of interpretation dictate (with not a mention of what the two competing levels of decision-makers are likely to do on those issues, though this be at the front of his mind when allocating the power here rather than there). But that is to assume dishonest interpretation – an assumption that might apply to any alternative umpire to Mr Dawkins as well. And worse, those alternatives may well involve decision-makers more likely to be swayed by their first-order moral positions, as might happen if other devout and religious people were asked to decide these umpiring issues.

Accordingly, my hypothetical points towards two possible grounds for preferring heads of powers judicial review to be done by the unelected judges, namely the likelihood of greater disinterestedness and the paucity of any attractive alternatives. Both, I think, constitute principled grounds for choosing the judges – on a least-bad option available basis – though any such consequentialist calculation will depend on context and other institutional facts.

And notice how difficult it is to offer an alternative to the judges when it comes to heads of powers adjudication. When we look around for some alternative perhaps the best we can find is today's United Kingdom. The UK is not in form or in theory a federal jurisdiction. Nevertheless, in practice, it more and more today operates as one; it operates as a *de facto* federation of sorts. So when it comes to Scotland and Wales there are powers or areas of jurisdiction that fall to them, rather than to the Westminster Parliament in London. Now unlike in Canada or the United States or Australia there is of course no written constitution in the UK. The delegation of powers to Scotland and Wales is found in an ordinary statute of the Westminster Parliament (*i.e.*, the center's legislature). In theory these could be taken back by a new statute or by repealing the earlier one. But in practice, due to political realities, that would never happen without some referendum in Scotland or Wales indicating the approval of the majority of people there. What you observe in the UK today, then, looks like a sort of federalism – it is just not locked in by some written constitution that is considerably harder to amend than is a normal statute. But even in the United Kingdom any jurisdictional disputes – any questions about which level of government has jurisdiction over any border line calls that fall within the penumbra of doubt of the rules that allocate the powers to Scotland and Wales – will be decided by judges. We can no doubt dream up some alternative to handing the resolution of these issues over to the judiciary. But none of such dreamt up alternatives is attractive.

Here is something else that needs stating plainly. No majoritarian democrat would oppose giving power to judges whatever the circumstances and whatever the likely alternatives on offer. Indeed, I know of no such majoritarian democrats who think that. Way back when I lived in pre-handover Hong Kong and wrote about that jurisdiction's bill of rights I always said (not quite in so many words) that only a fool would prefer the Chinese Politburo to the unelected Hong Kong judges.[135] And so the simple fact that one can dream up alternatives to handing heads of powers disputes to judges does not somehow mean a majoritarian democrat must here too be opposed to federalism strong judicial review – say, to remain consistent in one's wariness of the judges and one's desire to limit their power. In a world where all the alternatives on offer to federalism judicial review appear likely either to undermine federalism (by giving the umpiring power to an interested party, say the constituent State legislatures or the central legislature) or to be just as undemocratic as the judges, one is free to come to the conclusion that the benefits of federalism (and they are many) outweigh any costs that flow from the discretion this will inevitably put in the hands of the judges doing the heads of powers umpiring.

In blunter terms, the handing of second-order powers to unelected judges (to decide if this elected legislature or that one can legislate in some area) is nowhere near as egregious to majoritarian democrats as handing first-order powers to those same judges (to decide what any elected legislature can, and cannot, do). Take up the vantage of someone living in a country with one of the world's oldest democracies where alternatives to the judges deciding federalism, heads of powers disputes are hard to

[135] See James Allan, 'Rights Without Anchors – Hong Kong Adrift' in R Wacks (ed), *Hong Kong, China and 1997: Essays in Legal Theory* (Hong Kong University Press, 1993) 41.

imagine, nowhere successfully being practiced, and in all likelihood alternatives that would be destructive of federalism as a working method of government. In such a world, our world, it seems to me to be false to claim that the majoritarian democrat would, or should, have to reject federalism judicial review or need to call for some unspecified constitutional reform in preference to the unelected judges. After all, we live in a world where one chooses between least-bad alternatives all the time – that, in fact, was the core basis of my defence of democracy and democratic decision-making in chapter four above.

To be clear, I am certainly someone who is not afraid of the parliamentary sovereignty model of New Zealand, but in the context of Australia, the United States and Canada that option simply is not on the table in the year 2022. And nothing in the majoritarian democrat's core principles and beliefs requires him or her to tilt at windmills, or ignore the democratic credentials of likely alternatives, or have to forsake heads of powers federalism especially if that is the only route to nation building.

My claim, then, is that heads of powers judicial review is qualitatively different from rights-related judicial review. The former deals in deciding which of two democratic bodies will decide some issue. The latter deals in deciding whether *any democratic body* will be allowed to do so. Add to that qualitative difference the dearth of any plausible alternative that will either be any more democratic than the judges or that will not involve handing the power to a legislature or elected body with an interest in the dispute (to say nothing of having virtually no chance of coming to pass) and you have strong grounds for thinking that I have met the challenge I laid down to start this chapter. Hence, yes, I have been able to give a convincing account of why someone might oppose rights-related judicial review and yet accept – or not oppose – federalism judicial review.

I suppose there is one last ditch argument that might be directed at the majoritarian democrat who, at core, has a trust in 'letting the numbers count' decision-making as the least-bad option going. This last ditch gambit would involve suggesting that if parliaments can be trusted to approach rights questions in good faith and as competently as courts – the gist of the majoritarian democrat's position – then perhaps we should also expect parliaments to take heads of powers commitments seriously.

The gambit here amounts to alleging that distrust is distrust. Or put the other way round, if you trust parliament then you trust parliament; you cannot pick and choose when to bestow trust.

However, although superficially alluring, that last ditch gambit is almost certainly false on both the empirical plane and the normative one.

Firstly, there is nothing whatsoever inconsistent in saying both of the following: (1) 'When it comes to first-order moral and political issues such as how to deal with refugees, same-sex marriage, abortion, and all the rest, the least-bad approach – the one with the best consequences all things considered – is to count everyone equally and vote to choose people to resolve them. Call that being trusting of the legislature if you wish.' And at the same time saying (2) 'When it comes to an agreed list of powers, according to which some decisions will be made by this elected legislature and some by that one, the least-bad approach is to hand them over to some third-party (and even some unelected third party) decider. Call that not being trusting of the legislature if you wish.'

As I have tried to show in this chapter, the decision-makers in (1) and (2) are being asked to do very different things. So already we might have grounds for least-bad trust in an elected legislature when it comes to (1), but not (2). After all, the trust in (1) is directed at making a substantive first-order moral or political decision. By contrast, the trust in (2) would be directed at hoping that the decision-maker does not favor itself when it comes to resolving which of two elected bodies gets what powers. Again, the two tasks are qualitatively different.

Moving back to what we see today in Canada or the United States, in (1) the judges are deciding the substantive issue themselves. In (2) they are deciding if big or small majoritarian bodies will decide. Distrust of unelected committees of ex-lawyers in (1), in no obvious or self-evident way transfers over to a distrust of them in (2). Likewise, not trusting Mr Dawkins to decide the substantive issue himself can be perfectly compatible with trusting him more than anyone else to decide which level of democratic legislature (or Uniting Church body) will be given the responsibility to decide. Hence, when it comes to heads of powers federalism-related judicial review, even that last ditch argument fails to convince. The majoritarian democrat can very persuasively provide principled grounds for why this differs from rights-related judicial review – why it is qualitatively a different undertaking and hence might be entrusted to the judiciary without inconsistency.

Of course this is not to deny that federalism judicial review can be characterized as having a counter-majoritarian effect. That characterization can be trotted out every time a decision is made by the judges to allocate a decision-making power to Tasmania's legislature, or Ontario's, or New York's, rather than to the national legislature just as it can be trotted out when talking of bicameralism with an upper House based on equal numbers of senators from each state. Both can be said to have that effect – though with federalism one might just as easily argue that the local forum is in a sense more democratic insofar as it is closer to the voters whose preferences the system is trying to reflect. In fact, I suppose one could even structure an argument that majoritarian democrats ought only to prefer a unicameral, unitary set-up as in New Zealand. But nothing about the case for majoritarian democracy – even when structured on a Waldronian strong rights or non-consequentialist basis of the sort already discussed in chapter one and elsewhere – requires that no other values be given any weight or that compromises and trade-offs be wholly shunned. The case is a comparative one between elected legislatures and unelected ex-lawyers and is by far at its strongest when it comes to the making of first-order moral and political decisions about highly contestable issues over which smart, nice, reasonable people disagree, indeed decisions that cannot be gainsaid by the voters without involving the machinery of constitutional amendment.[136] That a full and convincing account can be given of why the majoritarian democrat would oppose rights-related judicial review and yet accept non-rights-related federalism judicial review should now be obvious. This chapter is just such an account.

---

[136] A point buttressed by the related observation that rights-related judicial review seems to carry with it an in-built opportunity for what might be thought of as a ratchet-up effect – use the enumerated rights to discover some further right (say, to privacy) and then use that to discover a further right still (say, to abortion). It is hardly contentious to claim that such a ratchet-up effect occurs across jurisdictions with bills of rights, and occurs not infrequently.

Chapter Nine

A Last Word on the Latest Constitutional Innovation

Part III of this short book has considered the general theme of constitutionalism and has canvassed my doubts as regards various aspects of today's constitutional orthodoxy. Put simply, I have tried to make the skeptical outsider's case against much of today's supposed conventional wisdom. This chapter will conclude this Part of the book. It will do so by looking at the latest constitutional innovation in the English-speaking common law world, the statutory bill of rights. Again, where many see these instruments as delivering the best of both worlds (namely, dollops of judicial input on rights-related social policy issues that somehow leaves the elected legislature supreme), I do not. I am immensely skeptical both as to the stability of this claimed halfway house status as well as to the overall desirability of such instruments. As much as I dislike entrenched, constitutionalized US and Canadian style bills of rights that hand an invalidating or striking-down power to the judiciary, there is at least a sort of honesty about the fact that last-word power rests with the unelected judges. In trying to have it both ways – giving lots of input to judges but trying to keep the nominal last word with the elected legislature – statutory bills of rights risk giving us the reality of the Canadian or US position (ie judges have the last word on these rights-related social policy disputes) but masking that reality from the average citizen. In big picture terms, then, this brief chapter will sketch my doubts and skepticism about this latest constitutional innovation, the statutory bill of rights.

Let us begin by admitting that the merits and demerits of 'strong form' or entrenched and constitutionalized bills of rights have been debated at length. I do not intend to re-enter that debate in this short chapter, other than to repeat my long-held view that US-style striking down of primary legislation powers in the hands of unelected judges cannot be justified on superior moral expertise grounds, on ersatz Upper House grounds, on achieving better consequentialist outcomes grounds, and plainly not on its being a more legitimate decision-making process grounds.

A good many bill of rights supporters will disagree with that view. Actually, let us be honest – near on *all* of the lawyerly caste in the common law world will disagree with me on this point, as will a solid majority of politicians and of the public. But some will not. These doubters will agree with me that constitutionalized bills of rights with their strong form judicial review hand too much power to unelected judges. A very real temptation, then, is for these doubters to think that what is needed is a 'weak form' of judicial review of legislation, some sort of statutory bill of rights that preserves parliamentary sovereignty. Carefully frame the debate in those terms, as being about a statutory bill of rights that will ensure that the elected legislature retains last-word sovereignty, and the attraction of this constitutional innovation to those who doubt the wisdom of 'strong form' judicial review becomes plain. In the rest of this chapter I will aim to give such doubters grounds for resisting this temptation, for thinking statutory bills of rights are in fact no better, potentially worse, than their older constitutionalized cousins. In other words, my goal here is to show that the hoped-for middle ground desired by some bill of rights proponents is elusive.

The most well-known and influential statutory bill of rights in the anglosphere is Britain's, legislated into existence as the *Human Rights Act 1998*. Now New Zealand's statutory bill of rights is older, at least in the more modern incarnations of these statutory instruments,[137] and was the model for Britain's version. But as this is to be a short chapter, aiming to raise general doubts about this constitutional innovation, I will largely limit my focus to the far more influential British variant. My argument will come in three segments. In the first I will consider the reading down provision, one of the two core operative provisions that makes these

[137] Meaning I am not including Canada's over half-century old Bill of Rights Act, which quickly became toothless and largely otiose.

statutory bills of rights work and gives them their oomph. In the next segment I will look at the other main way in which statutory bills of rights empower judges at the expense of the elected legislature, the declarations power. Lastly, I will briefly digress, confronting head on a possible rejoinder from supporters of statutory bills of rights.

1. The Reading Down Provision in a Statutory Bill of Rights

The main tool for increasing the power of the judiciary under a statutory bill of rights is the reading down provision. No provision has more potential to transmogrify the powers available under statutory versions into something approaching those under constitutionalized versions. Indeed (and here is what proponents downplay back when they are pushing for the enactment of a statutory bill of rights), if judges take such reading down provisions to be Spike Lee-like licenses 'to do the right thing,' then these provisions leave open the possibility of affording judges scope to do what the disinterested observer would characterize as an out-and-out rewriting or redrafting of other statutes.

Consider the reading down provision in the *Human Rights Act 1998* which is section 3 (New Zealand's is similar) and reads to start:

> So far as it is possible to do so, primary legislation and subordinate legislation must be read and given effect in a way which is compatible with Convention rights.

The danger with these sort of reading down provisions – these directions to give the words of other statutes a meaning that you, the point-of-application interpreter, happen to think is more moral and more in keeping with your own sense of the demands of fundamental human rights – is that just about any statutory language (however clear in wording and intent) might possibly be given some other meaning or reading in the quest to make it rights-respecting (according to you, the judge).

Here is how I framed the danger, the scope for abuse, of these provisions in an article I wrote a decade and a half ago:

> Put differently, reading down provisions such as these throw open the possibility of 'Alice in Wonderland' judicial interpretations; they confer an 'interpretation on steroids'

> power on the unelected judges. So although there is no power to invalidate or strike down legislation, the judges can potentially accomplish just as much by rewriting it, by saying that seen through the prism (that is, their own prism) of human rights, 'near black' means 'near white' or 'interim order becomes a final order' means 'interim order does not become a final order.' They can make bill of rights sceptics half long for the honesty of judges (under constitutionalised bills of rights) who strike down legislation rather than gut it of the meaning everyone knows it was intended to have (rule of law values notwithstanding).[138]

Whether that characterization would prove to be alarmist or not, indeed how different the judicial approach to interpreting other statutes would end up being, was a question of fact. In the United Kingdom it would depend upon how the top judges in the House of Lords (and, from October 2009, the UK Supreme Court which on that date replaced the Appellate Committee of the House Lords) – judges who a few decades ago were widely considered to be the most interpretively conservative judges in the Anglo-American common law world – would use the section 3 reading down provision to alter their former approach to interpretation.

And so let us turn to the leading case of *Ghaidan* in which the UK's top court, back in 2004, said this about the s.3 reading down provision:

> It is now generally accepted that the application of s. 3 [the reading down provision in the United Kingdom's Human Rights Act] does not depend upon the presence of ambiguity in the legislation being interpreted. Even if, construed according to the ordinary principles of interpretation, the meaning admits of no doubt, s. 3 may none the less require the court to ... depart from the intention of the Parliament which enacted the legislation ... It is also apt to require a court to read in words which change the meaning of the enacted legislation, so as to make it convention-compliant, [meaning bill of rights compliant].[139]

---

[138] James Allan, "The Victorian Charter of Human Rights and Responsibilities: Exegesis and Criticism" (2006) 30 *Melbourne University Law Review* 906 at 909-910.

[139] *Ghaidan v Godin-Mendoza* [2004] 3 All ER 411; 2 A.C. 557 (hereinafter '*Ghaidan*') at paragraphs [29], [30] and [32] per Lord Nicholls. All the other Lordships, even Lord Millett in dissent, broadly agreed on the question of this new

This is so remarkable, what these top judges were prepared openly and explicitly to admit they believed they could now do with the section 3 reading down provision in place, that some of their claims bear repeating. They said that when interpreting all other statutes they could 'depart from the intention of … Parliament.'[140] They could do so when 'the meaning admits of no doubt.'[141] They could 'read in words which change the meaning of the enacted legislation.'[142] They could assert that '[t]he word "possible" in s. 3(1) is used in a different and much stronger sense.'[143] They could imply that anything short of outright 'judicial vandalism' is now within their purview at the point-of-application.[144] They could even use this new interpretive power to overrule one of their own House of Lords authorities – a case on the meaning of exactly the same statutory provision, an authority under four years old, and one that had held the meaning of that same statute to be clear.[145]

I could go on. I could note again that this *Ghaidan* approach to using the reading down provision is no outlier and continues to be affirmed

interpretive approach. See my "Portia, Bassanio or Dick the Butcher? Constraining Judges in the Twenty-First Century" (2006) 17 *King's College Law Journal* 1 for a fuller discussion of this case. And note that *Ghaidan*'s interpretive approach has been affirmed again and again, including in *National Westminster Bank v Spectrum Plus* [2005] UKHL 41; *Secretary of State for Work and Pensions v M* [2006] UKHL 11; *Countryside Alliance and others v Attorney General* [2007] UKHL 52; P & Ors, Re (Northern Ireland) [2008] UKHL 38, and so on and so forth. That said, there have been a few hints, but only hints, of seeming uncertainty. See, for example, Lord Bingham in *Secretary of State for the Home Department v MB* [2007] UKHL 46 at para [44] and Lord Hope in *Doherty & Ors v Birmingham City Council* [2008] UKHL 57.

140 *Ghaidan*, para [30], per Lord Nicholls. And could do so despite a total lack of ambiguity. Para [29].

141 *Ghaidan*, para [29], per Lord Nicholls.

142 *Ghaidan*, para [32], per Lord Nicholls. The judges did not claim, though an after-the-fact defender might try, that there should be a difference between pre- and post-1998 legislation. On this attempted defense the claim is that the former have been indirectly amended via some sort of delegation to future judges to use their point-of-application judgement to make those pre-1998 statutes more rights-respecting. Some sort of defense like that. Yet any sort of delegation to future judges of that sort that was done openly and plainly would, in my view, never have had a chance of being passed through Parliament.

143 *Ghaidan* AC p.573, per Lord Steyn.

144 *Ghaidan*, paras [111]-[112] per Lord Rodger.

145 *Fitzpatrick v Sterling Housing Association* [2001] AC 27.

and affirmed and that the top judges now see themselves operating under 'a new legal order'[146] – one in which their views on a host of political and moral line-drawing exercises became significantly more influential after the statutory bill of rights than they had been before. I could explore the Rule of Law implications of this new *Ghaidan* approach to interpretation – how citizens' knowledge of what any statute means becomes wholly and inextricably linked to judges' views of the scope, range, content and reasonable limits on human rights, all of which are contentious and debatable and give rise to reasonable disagreement amongst smart, well-informed and even nice people. Put bluntly, this new *Ghaidan* approach to interpretation, whatever other sins it might have, most assuredly magnifies uncertainty from the citizen's vantage and hence lessens the ability of all non-judges to know what the law demands of them and to be able to shape their conduct and expectations accordingly. I could even look at the historical evidence to determine the extent to which those enacting this statutory bill of rights, and British voters more generally, were made aware of the possibility or probability of this revolutionary ('new legal order') approach to statutory interpretation that in fact followed in the wake of its passage. There would even be plenty of scope to argue that what the *Ghaidan*-take on the reading down provision gives us is not really interpretation at all, but rather a form of after-the-fact, *ex post facto* creation or construction of deemed meaning at the point-of-application, one that will prevail until latter day judges reconsider the issue and change their minds sometime in the future.

Instead, let me leave it at this. No provision in a statutory bill of rights is more potent – and does more to transmogrify the powers available under statutory versions into something approaching those under constitutionalized versions – than reading down provisions. As I said near the start of this chapter, if judges take such reading down provisions (with their injunctions to make all other statutes as rights-respecting as the interpreting judge thinks possible) to be licenses 'to do justice' then this operative provision comes very close to allowing the judiciary to do what

---

[146] 'The Human Rights Act 1998 [incorporating the European Convention on Human Rights – the United Kingdom's bill of rights] created a new legal order.' *Jackson v Attorney-General* [2006] 1 AC 262 at para [102] per Lord Steyn.

the disinterested observer would characterize as the redrafting of judicially disfavoured statutes. True, they *do not* afford judges any striking down or invalidating power. Also true, they *do* afford judges the power to claim a statute says what no lawmaker ever thought it said or intended it to say but only what a majority of top judges now assert it should say. Whether that sort of rewriting power is less potent than a striking down power is no doubt debatable. My own view is that used aggressively, as I would say it has been by Britain's judges,[147] a reading down provision is almost as potent as an invalidating power. Indeed, it may be even more so as it need not be confined to 'negative lawmaking' since it gives scope to judges to create new affirmative regulations. Meanwhile it is more opaque, yes. Less open and honest, yes. While potentially at least as potent. It allows or empowers or fails to stop (according to your outlook) judges (up to some unspecified point on the spectrum denominated by them, and them alone, as 'judicial vandalism') to redraft and rewrite legislation by reading words in, ignoring clear intentions, trumping the otherwise plain meaning, and not requiring the least ambiguity before doing so. Once engaged in that redrafting or refashioning task the legislation under consideration is not in any straightforward sense being interpreted. It is being rewritten. The most that can be said is that the reading down provision has itself been interpreted,[148] and it has been interpreted as granting judges a license to rewrite (short of some indeterminate point termed 'vandalism') all other legislation. And that is an extremely unattractive set-up not just for majoritarian democrats like me, but for a good many others. Only in an incredibly formalistic and legalistic sense can a jurisdiction with judges openly and explicitly engaged in this sort of UK-style reading down hanky

[147] I also agree with Mark Tushnet that these sort of statutory bills of rights are unstable. Over time they might ratchet-up into a US or Canadian-style 'strong' from of judicial review. This is what I would say has happened in Britain. Or they might collapse into a much weaker, not-terribly-noticeable 'weak' form handbrake on parliamentary sovereignty. New Zealand's judiciary has used its broadly similar statutory bill of rights much less vigorously than has Britain's judiciary, which I suppose would not be hard. Although not 'weak form' judicial review it is much less virulent in New Zealand than in Britain.

[148] I would say the judges have not read the s.3 reading down provision the way it was intended to work; they have given it far more oomph than was intended.

panky be said to be performing 'weak form' judicial review that leaves parliamentary sovereignty in place.

2. The Declaration Provision in a Statutory Bill of Rights

If the above discussed reading down provision were the only means by which statutory bills of rights were able to increase the power of the unelected judges at the expense of the elected branches of government, that would be bad enough – albeit more than sufficient grounds in my view for seeking repeal of the *Human Rights Act*. However, it is not the only means; just the most egregious.

Let me in this chapter's second segment detail the other main means by which the United Kingdom's statutory bill of rights increases the decision-making powers of the point-of-application judges. I will be relatively brief.

This is the Declaration of Incompatibility power. Section 4(2) of the *Human Rights Act* reads:

> If the court is satisfied that the [under consideration statutory] provision is incompatible with a Convention right [ie one of the listed substantive rights], it may make a declaration of that incompatibility.

Now notice carefully that wording – if the court is satisfied that the provision is incompatible. And notice what that wording implies, namely that the judges' decisions about rights are to be treated as somehow the correct or right or indisputable and certainly the authoritative ones. The implication, then, – an incorrect and inaccurate one in my view – is that when the judges issue one of these Declarations of Incompatibility the elected Parliament's legislation is at that point definitely and without doubt at odds with some individual's enumerated human rights and so if the legislation stands, rights will be infringed. As I put it in that earlier article of mine from a decade and a half ago, these Declarations of Incompatibility:

> can convey the impression that the unelected judges have some authoritative, definitive (and to me, mysterious) ability to know and to declare precisely where to draw all the highly contestable

> and disputed lines (including knowing just what amounts to a reasonable limit and what does not). So if the judges say that statutory provision X breaches rights, then the wording of the declaration section implies (wrongly, but for some persuasively all the same) that their view is incontestably correct.[149]

The point is that this section 4 Declaration of Incompatibility provision is worded in a way that is both factually incorrect as regards what is often in dispute and that makes it extremely difficult for the elected Parliament to stand up to, and gainsay, the unelected judges.

Take the second point first. It is a remarkable and relevant fact that since the enactment of the *Human Rights Act* the United Kingdom Parliament has only ever once stood up to the judges when a Declaration of Incompatibility has been issued – just once, on the issue of prisoner voting! There have been dozens and dozens of Declarations and in every case where remedial action had not been taken before the judicial declaration was made, the government responded by repealing, amending or committing to repeal or amend, the relevant provision. Every single time, but once.

One is tempted to remark that the distance between that and some US-style striking down power is somewhat less than a million miles.

One reason for this reticence, in my view, is that the Declaration power is structured implicitly to hand power to judges to declare what are and are not our fundamental rights in the whole cross-section of line-drawing calls that bills of rights ask judges to make (including what limits on them are and are not reasonable), and then Parliament is left with the power to say 'We're going to take your rights away.' The empirical evidence says that that sort of Parliamentary response is only a usable power *in extremis.*[150]

---

[149] See footnote 138 above, p. 914. For an excellent discussion of the related issue of dialogue theory, and in particular its shortcomings, see Grant Huscroft, "Rationalizing Judicial Power: The Mischief of Dialogue Theory" in (Kelly and Manfredi, eds) *Contested Constitutionalism* (2009).

[150] This issue about the biased wording of Declarations of Incompatibility repeats a similar point made about Canada's section 33 notwithstanding clause. See, for example, Jeffrey Goldsworthy, 'Judicial Review, Legislative Override, and Democracy' in Campbell, Goldsworthy and Stone, eds., *Protecting Human Rights: Instruments and Institutions* (2003); Grant Huscroft, 'Rights, Bills of Rights, and the

Think of it this way. Suppose there were a marriage and in that marriage decision-making was divided up in the following manner. The wife, and only the wife, gets to write down what the couple will do: who is allowed in their home; what their daughter can wear to school; whom their son can marry; everything. She writes it down, not the husband.

The husband, however, is given a *Ghaidan*-like power of interpretation. He can read all of his wife's directives to be in accord with *his* view of what is in keeping with everyone else's fundamental rights and say, definitively, that that is their meaning. And so we might well expect that husband to treat the section 3 'is it possible?' test as one that can surprisingly often be answered in the affirmative. 'Yes it is possible,' thinks this sort of husband, 'for me to read a whole host of my wife's provisions and directives (however lacking in ambiguity and however clear her intentions) in a new, different manner compared to how I could before this *Ghaidan* directive was offered up to me. There is now lots of scope for me to read them in a way I happen to think is a better, more rights-respecting way.'

But that is not all. For those leftover cases where the husband constrains himself and feels he has reached the point of vandalism and so in this case he cannot take his wife's directives and read words in, ignore her clear intentions, and override a meaning of hers that admits of no doubt, he can nevertheless declare that his wife is taking away people's fundamental rights. His wife is then left with the option of prevailing by saying 'yes, I will override my husband and breach your [timeless, fundamental, pick your favourite adjective] rights.'

Those who sell statutory bills of rights such as the *Human Rights Act* as being a 'weak form' of judicial review and as retaining

---

Role of Courts and Legislatures' in Huscroft and Rishworth, eds., *Litigating Rights* (2002); and Jeremy Waldron, 'Some Models of Dialogue between Judges and Legislators' in (Huscroft and Brodie, eds) *Constitutionalism in the Charter Era* ((2004) 7, who make a similar point. Indeed, Waldron goes on to assert that, as an empirical matter, 'one could never get a Canadian enthusiast for the Charter to accept a "notwithstanding" clause that involved an honest acknowledgment that rights might be disputable or … that a … legislature might have a view of rights that was, though controversial, no less reasonable than the view arrived at by the judiciary' (*ibid.*, pp 38-39). On both points see James Allan, "The Travails of Justice Waldron" in Huscroft, ed., *Expounding the Constitution* (2008).

parliamentary sovereignty in some real sense, want you to believe that the wife has the last word power in this hypothetical marriage and that being forced into the position of saying 'I will breach people's rights' is somehow a regularly-usable live option for the wife. Put differently, statutory bill of rights proponents need, at a bare minimum, to convince you that the wife is in the preferable position in this marriage, not the husband (not to mention giving you some grounds for thinking husbands have better rights intuitions than wives). Yet that claim is only remotely plausible where the elected legislature, the wife, is left in a position in which it/she feels able, on occasion at least, to disagree with and overrule the judges/husband. And there is precious little evidence of that being the case.

And this takes us back to the first point I made about section 4 Declarations of Incompatibility above, that the wording is factually incorrect as regards what is often in dispute between the judiciary and the legislature. In many, many instances the elected legislature and the unelected judiciary (or, rather, a majority of the former and a majority of the latter) simply disagree over a highly contestable decision about how best to respect rights and about what limits on them are reasonable. Put differently, it is grossly misleading in terms of a characterization of what is in fact happening and in dispute to portray the legislature (and indeed to force them to portray themselves) as wanting to take people's rights away. They are, in fact, disagreeing about the scope, reach and limits of rights in a way that happens every day, all the time, amongst smart, well-informed, reasonable people. Moreover, absent some implicit assumption that committees of ex-lawyers have better moral antennae than elected legislators, there is no reason for preferring judges' moral and political rights-related views just because they are judges. The recognition and acceptance of that fact are key factors for those who find Canadian and US-style strong judicial review unpalatable. And yet so-called weak form judicial review under a statutory bill of rights can go a long, long way towards also delivering these same debatable, contestable social issues over to the lawyerly caste from which top judges are chosen, just as strong form review does. It can be much of a muchness.

3. A Brief Digression to Confront a Possible Rejoinder

There is a rejoinder that defenders of statutory bills of rights might be tempted to make at this point. In fact, few such bill of rights proponents resist this temptation. It involves shifting the focus away from after-enactment outcomes and forcing it onto the process that led to the statutory bill of rights becoming law.

Now it is true that many proponents of statutory bills of rights claim that, once in place, such instruments will in fact leave majoritarian decision-making largely untrammelled. They claim that parliamentary sovereignty will continue. My arguments thus far in this chapter have been directed at convincing you that such a line of defence is unconvincing – because of the rewriting scope that reading down provisions in statutory bills of rights such as the *Human Rights Act* afford to judges, because of the way judges' decisions about rights are explicitly and implicitly treated as somehow the correct or right or indisputable (and certainly the authoritative) ones, and because the accumulated evidence thus far is that elected politicians almost always defer to (or cave in to) judges' declarations of incompatibility.

In the face of such arguments directed at the effects of a statutory bill of rights – at how so-called weak form judicial review can ratchet up (and in Britain has ratcheted up) into strong form review, enervating parliamentary sovereignty in all but the most formalistic and, yes, lawyerly senses – one theoretical rejoinder is to look instead at the process by which a statutory bill of rights became law. If that pre-enactment process appears to have complied with some defensible version of majoritarianism, of 'letting the numbers count,' then this rejoinder suggests that the post-enactment grievances are significantly enervated, perhaps even wholly negated, especially as a similar process can be used to repeal the statutory bill of rights at any time.

I spent much of chapter five arguing why that rejoinder fails. To remind readers, it is not just because of the trite point that from the fact **A.** that a democratic majority might vote henceforth to live under a dictatorship or aristocracy it in no way follows **B.** that the legitimacy and desirability of the process used to make that initial decision (distinguishing process from outcome here) entails that what it delivers is itself legitimate or desirable. Good 'how made' credentials do not guarantee good 'here's what we've now got' credentials. Not even the fact that the majority could at some future point pull back from aristocracy or dictatorship will do that, will make more palatable the decision-making process *now being used* until some unspecified future day arrives when it is ditched.

That is a brief reminder of the argument I made in chapter five and the basis for my saying that this sort of rejoinder often offered up by defenders of statutory bills of rights ought to be rejected. The temptation ought to be resisted.

Part IV

And Lastly on to Constitutional Interpretation

Chapter Ten

Laying the Groundwork

In this final Part IV of the book I will move from the big picture stuff of constitutionalism writ large down to the day-to-day world of constitutional interpretation. As I noted in the introduction, this is what really matters in jurisdictions such as my native Canada and in the United States and in the Australia where I have lived and worked the past decade and a half. How ought judges to interpret the words in the constitution? And why? I have argued in Part III that with written constitutionalism all regular citizen voters are always locked in. That is the point of written constitutionalism. The choice boils down to being locked in by constitution makers (however long ago they were doing that making) or by those doing some sort of 'not constrained by the makers' interpreting today. To repeat myself, the average voter will inevitably be locked in by one of those two groups under written constitutionalism in a democracy. Remember, either the top judges are themselves locked in. Or they are not locked in. Whichever it is, the rest of us – the 99.999 per cent of us who are just regular voters and not top judges – will be locked in either way.

Today's constitutional orthodoxy amounts to a preference *against* what is sometimes unkindly described as ancestor worship, the preferences and intentions of the long dead constitution makers. Instead, it is a preference *for* being locked in by the beliefs, sentiments, judgements, druthers, and policy preferences of today's lawyerly caste from which is taken the small handful of top judges in the country (over, or rather than, the preferences of some long dead constitution makers). But a choice has to be made. 'Pick your poison,' as it were. I pick the rather unfashionable choice of going with the views of those way back when who were given the legitimate authority to frame and ratify the constitution in play. I pick being locked in by them, not by the druthers of today's top judges. If you don't like what the constitution makers gave us, amend it. Amend it openly and in accord with the laid down amending formula. Again, mine is the minority or skeptic's position, the one that doubts today's constitutional orthodoxy.

In this chapter I want again to look forwards, not backwards. I want to lay the groundwork for this Part's consideration of constitutional interpretation by tracing out a hypothetical trip in three stops. To start, let us once more imagine that we live in a jurisdiction (this time call it 'Allania') that currently operates as a parliamentary sovereignty system. And in that system there is a good deal of confidence in, and support for, democratic decision-making to resolve the inevitable social disagreements that flow from differing moral outlooks and political frameworks. Smart, well-informed, even nice people simply can be seen to disagree across a wide range of issues in this jurisdiction. There is obvious moral dissensus. And to overcome those disagreements and that dissensus and to arrive at a set of legal rules that applies to everyone, a legally unchecked legislature (or parliamentary sovereignty) has up until now operated.

As I noted, that pre-supposes at least a significant degree of support for democratic decision-making and 'letting the numbers count' processes to resolve social disagreements, including disagreements over issues related to (or articulated in the language of) rights. So that is our starting point. And now we are going to leave it. In deference to the tide of post-World War II constitutional history, which might as I said earlier in this book be summed up as 'the triumph of American constitutionalism' or at least as the scramble to adopt a written constitution, Allania is going to jettison its parliamentary sovereignty arrangements in favor of a written constitution. In the course of Allania's trip that sees it change the main aspect of its Rule of Recognition from whatever the elected legislature enacts to whatever the new written constitution allows (as interpreted by the top judges), there will be some stops along the way where we all need to disembark briefly to clarify why something has happened or what the motivations or intentions were. After each stop we can restart the trip, one that will conclude when Allania has a written constitution. Once that is the case, with the trip ended and the new constitution adopted and approved, the crucial question of how this new constitution ought to be interpreted will arise and will be of great practical importance.

At that point I want to make some initial arguments about the least bad approach to interpreting it. My claim will be – at least for Americans and Canadians – that some version or other of originalism[151] will be that least bad (and in that sense most attractive) approach to interpreting it. Put the other way round, I want to elaborate on what set of assumptions are needed to make some alternative to originalism seem better or preferable. And at that point I want to argue that those very same assumptions – the ones that would prevent or disincline or deter a judge from opting for some version of originalism *after* the Constitution's adoption – would have made completing the trip to written constitutionalism extremely unlikely. Had the assumptions of those after-the-fact interpreters favoring 'living Constitution' or 'living tree' or 'most moral' or 'Dworkinian best-fit' or 'progressivist' interpretations been made explicit at the start of the trip towards written constitutionalism, few citizens would have favored the move to a written constitution. There would have been next to no chance of adopting the new Constitution had these assumptions been made explicit and widely publicized.

Whether that matters when it comes to interpreting the new Constitution, after the fact of its adoption, will also be discussed.

1. Stop One

We need to be abundantly clear that the written constitution Allania will have is not being imposed on it from outside. This will not be some African-type situation where the departing colonial power leaves in its wake a written constitution to govern the newly independent country. Likewise, it will not be a Japan-like situation where defeat in a large scale war is followed by the victorious powers (or at least the Americans) imposing a new written constitution on the losers.

---

[151] In the next chapter I will flesh out what I mean by originalism and originalist constitutional interpretation. For now it suffices to think of it very generally in terms of meaning being stable and unchanging, locked in (directly or indirectly) by the intentions of those who had the legitimate authority originally to make the law.

If it be true that the issue of ***a)*** *how to interpret a constitution* cannot (or rather should not) be wholly separated from ***b)*** *what one takes the purpose of a constitution to be*, then we need first to ask or consider whether anyone post-adoption of that constitution cares much, or in the slightest, what the constitution makers and approvers were trying to do. That is another way of asking whether the constitution to be interpreted has legitimacy (or how much legitimacy). Some might answer issue ***b)*** above in terms of the 'locking things in' response I defended in Part III of the book — that the very point of adopting a written constitution is to lock in certain divisions of powers, say, or rules related to how members of the legislature (and executive) are to be chosen, or maybe some embedded set of rights. And these provisions will be, are meant to be, procedurally harder to alter and change than the regular procedure used to enact statutes. And what motivates that desire to lock certain provisions in is the calculation that society is better off 'risking rigidity rather than risking security.' That said, others might answer issue ***b)*** above in very different terms. Their response would forswear any emphasis on a constitution aiming to 'lock things in' in favor of understanding it as 'a statement of our most important values and the vehicle through which these values are created and crystallized.'[152] That is how they will want to understand the new constitution's purpose, whatever the later truth of how much parliamentary sovereignty regular voters will themselves have forsaken. Yet neither of these responses to issue ***b)*** matters much – or at the very least neither will perform any constraining function on what post-adoption of the constitution interpreters feel they can and cannot do – unless the way that constitution was adopted is later on – after adoption – generally perceived to have been legitimate.

Now as I think one can certainly say that about the written constitutions of Canada and the United States,[153] I want this first stop of

---

[152] Frederick Schauer, "Judicial Supremacy and the Modest Constitution" (2004) 92 *California Law Review* 1045 at p. 1045. (Schauer is not endorsing this view, just enumerating it.)

[153] Admittedly recent events in the US make this claim less widespread than it was only a decade or so ago. But support for the US Constitution's legitimacy is still the view of the vast preponderance of citizens. Perhaps not always for their lawmakers, nor for their Constitution's interpreters. But for the Constitution itself.

ours to make it clear that Allania's new written constitution will be the product of a process overwhelmingly perceived to be legitimate. Let us assume that before the new written constitution is approved and adopted all the voters (both nationally and, if a federation, then in each State) must approve it in a referendum. Indeed we will stipulate that the voters in these referenda were eligible to vote on the basis of a universal adult franchise (so that Allania's constitution-making procedures are even less vulnerable to attacks on the basis of legitimacy than those of Canada or the United States).

We leave stop one, then, knowing that the process used to shift Allania from a parliamentary sovereignty to a jurisdiction with a written constitution (one that judges will need to interpret post-adoption) did not involve outside imposition. It did not follow catastrophic defeat in war or a departing bequest by the former colonial master. It was opted for by a clear majority – indeed some sort of super-majority – of adult Allanians then alive.

2. Stop Two

Our journey has barely re-started when we need to make another stop. When the journey ends we will have a written constitution that requires interpreting at the point-of-application, most obviously by the top judges in the jurisdiction. But we need to know what will be in that new written constitution that will require interpreting. More specifically, in order to focus on essentials, we need to know if there will be a federalist division of powers between the centre and states (or provinces) as well as whether there will be an enumerated list of embedded rights (rights overwhelmingly articulated in vague, amorphous terms laying down what on any account are moral abstractions).

In moving from a parliamentary sovereignty to a jurisdiction with a written constitution Allania might opt to put a federalist division of powers into that constitution, but forswear any bill of rights. (That is the choice Australia made, copying much from the United States but explicitly rejecting a bill of rights.) Alternatively, Allania might opt for a bill of rights, but not federalism (as France did). Or it could opt for both (as both the United States and Canada have done).

Why do we need to know this? Because it is possible – both on theoretical grounds and as a matter of empirical outcomes – that our post-adoption top judges might adopt different interpretive approaches as regards heads of powers federalism disputes versus rights-based disputes. This is especially likely in view of my argument in chapter eight that these two sorts of strong judicial review are structurally different and make quite distinct inroads on democratic decision-making and parliamentary sovereignty.

Start with federalism issues. The main interpretive alternatives to some version or other of originalism — say 'living Constitution' or 'living tree' approaches, or 'moral readings,' or 'progressivist' approaches — are hard to apply to division of powers disputes. As we saw in chapter eight, these sort of federalism disputes will more or less leave parliamentary sovereignty intact. If some State statute is struck down for being outside its power, then the federal or central legislature will have that power and could enact the same statute, should it so decide. Conversely, if some legislative initiative is held to be outside or beyond the power of the center, then the States could enact it, should they so decide. As we saw, opting for a written constitution that embeds a federalist division of powers but no bill of rights leaves parliamentary sovereignty largely (not completely, but largely once we assume the judges engage in honest interpretation) in place.

So on straight federalism heads of powers disputes one might expect originalism (any version) to be attractive to some people who would shun it for rights-based disputes. Indeed, that may well be an accurate description of Canada.[154]Consider what your alternative outcomes are in such heads of powers federalism disputes. Neither option (State wins or central government wins) is more progressive or more moral or more in keeping with the demands of changing social values – or rather neither is in and of itself; you need a further prop to your argument, namely some sort of empirical basis for thinking one level of elected legislature is more likely to pass such progressive, or socially aware, legislation. But

[154] See Justice Ian Binnie 'Constitutional Interpretation and Original Intent' in G. Huscroft and I. Brodie (eds) *Constitutionalism in the Charter Era* (LexisNexis, 2004), pp. 345-382.

that is not a 'progressivist' or 'more moral' or 'living tree' interpretation of the words used (eg. 'trade and commerce'), so much as an underlying preference for one of the two federal levels of government. (Moreover it is a preference that can shift over time as first the Center and then later some of the States become perceived to be the more progressive levels of government.)

My point is that some methods of interpretation that are available for interpreting rights – where a potential outcome is that no level of government can legislate in the way desired, not merely that the power to so legislate vests here rather than there – are not easily available in federalism disputes. Indeed some may say it is not even clear what a 'progressivist' or 'living document' approach means in this context. The same may apply to interpretive approaches that direct the words to be given their most moral understanding (whether that is earlier founded on a belief this was the framers' or approvers' intention, or not). After all, for that to be possible it is arguable that the words used have to be morally pregnant or morally imbued words. And division of powers provisions (eg. 'navy,' 'inter-state trade') may make that highly artificial.

A more likely alternative to originalism in heads of powers disputes is some version of textual literalism. That is the approach that has largely been taken by Australia's highest court in a century of division of powers disputes.[155] The effect of that approach however, given Australia's US-style 'one list' version of federalism and where the words of each head of power are read individually and separately and given their widest ambit, has been an ever expanding list of approved fields for legislating for the center and an ever shrinking playing field for the States. Meanwhile interpretation based on framers' intentions, or on the original understandings of those approving the constitution in the various referenda, or what a well-informed person at the time would have taken them to be, would have produced outcomes considerably less friendly to the center. More to the point of this chapter, though, that sort of originalist interpretation would have put more constraints on the point-of-application

---

[155] See James Allan and Nicholas Aroney, 'An Uncommon Court: How the High Court of Australia Has Undermined Australian Federalism' (2008) 30 *Sydney Law Review* 245.

interpreters; it would have left the judges with fewer plausible or 'penumbra of doubt' options than textual literalism leaves them.

Whether you agree with me on that, or not, put it aside. Likewise put aside my empirical claim that some variant or other of originalist interpretation is likely to have more adherents for heads of powers disputes than when it comes to how to interpret guarantees or protections afforded in the language of rights. Instead, here at stop two, consider the decision those in Allania will have to make as regards whether to opt for a federation or a unitary state. One factor that will bear on their decision is the most likely answer to the 'how will the new written constitution be interpreted?' question, not least because they will want to know how much decision-making power will be left with their pre-federation colony or province. Of course no one can see into the future and know for sure. But the likely or most plausible answer to this question will affect whether some people support this new constitution.

And that is even more the case, I suspect, as regards whether this new constitution ought to contain a bill of rights. Hence let us assume Allania is mooting the inclusion of a bill of rights (á la Canada and the United States) in its new written constitution. As we have seen, this will clearly involve a greater inroad, a much greater inroad, into parliamentary sovereignty than does federalism and heads of powers disputes between the centre and the States (or Provinces). And because that inroad is so much more pronounced, the interpretive issue of how the rights-articulated moral abstractions are likely to be interpreted becomes correspondingly more crucial.

Let me put that point slightly more directly. We can assume that one of the big debates in Allania, as it ponders leaving behind parliamentary sovereignty in favor of written constitutionalism, is just this question of whether to include an enumerated list of embedded rights. There will be opponents. They might prevail, as they did in Australia. Similarly there will be supporters. And they might prevail, as they did in the United States and (from 1982) in Canada.

Of course I have stipulated that at present Allania is a parliamentary sovereignty where there is a good deal of confidence in, and support for, democratic decision-making to resolve inevitable social disagreements. This support, we are assuming, will not be enough to prevent the adoption of a new written constitution with an entrenched bill of rights. But by the same token it is unlikely that there will be some sort of Damascene conversion-type move in Allania over to thinking 'letting the numbers count,' as a procedure for resolving disputes, has no value independent of the moral worth of the decisions it produces. And that means support for this new constitutionalized bill of rights – or rather the ability to attract sufficient support to get it approved, adopted and entrenched – will be influenced by how people in Allania think, or assume, it will be interpreted by latter day unelected judges. Indeed, given the far greater inroads into parliamentary sovereignty this bill of rights will make, its likely interpretation may well matter a good deal more than how the federalist heads of powers are likely to be interpreted.

3. Stop Three

One short stop remains. It is largely for clarificatory purposes. At this third stop we alight briefly to ensure Allania's citizens realize that the rights in their mooted bill of rights are not self-interpreting or self-enforcing. In Australia, where the debate over whether to have a bill of rights is even today a live one, proponents often seem to argue as though the listed moral abstractions articulated in the language of rights can define themselves when it comes to how they will play out in any specific line-drawing question that will reach the courts. That is to say, these instruments are sometimes sold on the unspoken premise that there will be no need for human judgement in deciding whether, say, the right to free speech or to be free from unreasonable search and seizure does or does not result in some statute of the elected legislature being struck down or read down. The technique here is not one of finessing disagreement by focusing on the Olympian heights of moral abstractions rather than down in the quagmire of day-to-day contentious line-drawing exercises; it is not quite even the related ploy of leaving the listener blithely to assume that what those vague, amorphous rights will require in specific cases will correspond in some 1:1 way with his or her own beliefs or sentiments (though both those are used too).

No, at this third stop we simply are making sure that Allania's citizens are clear that *some* interpretation will be necessary. And the sort of interpretive approach applied will affect the extent to which any traces of parliamentary sovereignty remain. If the rights are interpreted as a broad and generous grant to later-in-time unelected judges to use *their own moral judgments or sentiments*, a grant that has at least some scope to grow and expand in line with the growth of a metaphorical living tree or constitution or in keeping with a progressive view of changing social values, then very big inroads will be made into parliamentary sovereignty. On the other hand, if the rights are interpreted as extending no further than the extent intended by the framers and ratifiers – or the extent understood by some well-informed Allanian at the time – then these bill of rights' rights will serve as a floor-level set of guarantees, above which parliamentary sovereignty will remain and so 'progressive outcomes' there will have to receive democratic support.[156] More to our point here, that latter approach might attract considerably more Allanians over to supporting this mooted written constitution with its bill of rights; and that is because knowing in advance that not all social policy disputes are potentially being handed over to future judges to resolve is likely to find more support in Allania.

Put more bluntly, and as I have argued in earlier chapters, not all interpretive approaches will be equal in so far as their effects on parliamentary sovereignty. Of course by opting for a bill of rights – any bill of rights — some inroads will be made. Allania will be putting less faith in its democratically elected legislature and a good deal more in its unelected, point-of-application interpreting judges. But the extent of that abjuring of faith will vary, and vary significantly, depending upon the approach to interpreting the bill of rights that is ultimately adopted. And for those Allanians who think originalist modes of interpretation impose more constraints on the point-of-application interpreter – that a search for historical or past facts limits the answers some changing-through-time group of judges (with individually differing moral sentiments and beliefs)

---

[156] See my "Portia, Bassanio and Dick the Butcher" (2006) 17 *King's College Law Journal* 1. Justice Antonin Scalia makes the same point in a far more entertaining way in "Romancing the Constitution: Interpretation as Invention" in G. Huscroft and I. Brodie (eds) in *Constitutionalism in the Charter Era* (LexisNexis, 2004), 337.

can honestly give more than does a quest to discover the ‘most moral’ or ‘most progressive’ or ‘most in keeping with civilization and changing social values’ answer those same judges can give – then how future judges are likely to do their interpretive jobs will matter. For some it will matter a lot and determine whether they agree to this new, mooted written constitution. It will affect whether the framers and ratifiers of the constitution would conceivably have included and approved certain provisions, including any bill of rights.

At an extremely bare minimum then, we can end this third stop on our trip confident that before adopting or approving this bill of rights, the framers, approvers and ratifiers in Allania will care about how it is likely to be interpreted.

At Trip’s End

With our three disembarkations behind us we can now say Allania’s journey has come to an end. It now has a new written constitution with a federal division of powers and an embedded bill of rights. How to interpret that new Constitution will soon become a highly important question, important in the practical sense that it will affect the lives of many of Allania’s citizens. Hence let us consider what Allania’s hypothetical trip from parliamentary sovereignty to written constitutionalism has shown us about the later interpreting of that finished constitutional product. Let us spell out the assumptions needed to make some alternative to originalism appear more attractive. And let us focus on interpreting the bill of rights, because (to paraphrase the Frank Sinatra song) if you’re an originalist there, you’re an originalist everywhere when it comes to constitutional interpretation.

A first, and obvious, ground for rejecting originalist interpretation is that the founding events are, from today’s vantage point looking back on them, widely or universally seen to be illegitimate. Where a written constitution is imposed from the outside, by a departing colonial master or by a vanquishing military foe, that will very often be the case. But we explicitly ruled that out as regards Allania, not least because it did not happen in the case of the United States or (in a meaningful way) in Canada.

Even where the written constitution is home-grown, of course, its legitimacy can be questioned or attacked. In our hypothetical, Allania's new Constitution was stipulated to have passed the staunchest of universal suffrage hurdles, though of course one need not (and some do not) accept majoritarianism as an indicator of legitimacy. Yet even conceding that, it is also true that most people do look for that sort of legitimacy as far as their own written Constitution is concerned, even people who in other contexts (perhaps ironically) look far less favorably on full adult franchise majoritarianism. Turning from our hypothetical to the United States and Canada, though, leaves more room to attack the legitimacy of the founding events – think of slavery, and no franchise for women, and proceeding without the agreement of Quebec (or indeed without any plebiscite or election specifically on point and so with no notice to the electorate). Having mooted those lines of possible attack, my own sense is that in both countries the founding events are overwhelmingly seen to be legitimate. If so, one of the most obvious bases for rejecting originalism disappears.

A second ground for rejecting originalism is equally straightforward. Here you just come out of the closet and admit that democratic decision-making is not that important to you. And let me be clear what I mean. As noted at stop three of our hypothetical journey, any move to a written constitution will involve a sacrifice of self-government in favour of judicial oversight. Here I am referring to the extra sacrifice involved in foregoing originalist interpretation in favor of, say, what is believed to be the most moral reading or the most progressive reading. It is that extra degree of foregone or forsworn self-government that might be accepted with a simple 'other things matter to me more' reply.

But not in Allania. Allanians are prepared to move to a written constitution, but not at any cost. They will write a check to the judiciary, but not a blank check. Originalist interpretation of the rights in the bill of rights treats those rights as more or less determinate floor-level guarantees, above which parliamentary sovereignty operates. Other approaches enlarge the range of plausible outcomes, some significantly. Given the posited lack of fear in Allania of a legally unconstrained legislature, the interpretive approach that leaves the greatest residue of parliamentary sovereignty is likely to be most people's preferred approach.

Nor will reciting slogans about originalist interpretive approaches amounting to 'ancestor worship' be overly effective in Allania. If citizens there wished not to be locked in by the new constitution, and by the original intentions or understandings of its reach and scope, they could have remained a parliamentary sovereignty. I make that point in chapters six, seven and eight. In a straight out choice where 'ancestor worship' is wholly shunned and hence either ***a)*** the elected legislators or ***b)*** the unelected judges are left free to update and keep pace with civilization according to their particular moral consciences' views of what is best, few Allanians would opt for the judges.

Someone like Antonin Scalia would assert the same is true of Americans.[157] I agree (though, with much regret, I have to concede that I am not completely confident the same is true in my native Canada). Of course that assumes that it is made clear to people – as we stipulated at stop three – that the bill of rights and the rest of the written constitution are not self-interpreting. So let us assume that. Let us make it crystal clear to people. Then it seems to me that any upfront and open spelling out in advance of what the effects of non-originalist interpretive approaches will be vis-à-vis judicial power would make it extremely difficult, if not impossible, to get sufficient support to adopt or approve the new constitution at all – if these non-originalist options be the interpretive approaches on offer. (And for what it is worth I can say that proponents of a bill of rights in Australia never spell out the likely effects of the non-originalist interpretive approaches most of them favor.)

Notice, too, this. If the framers and approvers and ratifiers of a constitution wanted and intended latter day judges to interpret it (or at least the bill of rights portion of it) simply by bringing their later-in-time judicial moral antennae to bear on the disputed issue and deciding based on what they in future think is most moral, they really could not say so openly. If in fact the constitution-makers had that sort of 'you future judges interpret based on what you think is most moral' intention, they could never explicitly spell it out. Spell that out bluntly and openly, along with

[157] See Justice Antonin Scalia, 'Romancing the Constitution: Interpretation as Invention' in (eds. G. Huscroft and I. Brodie) *Constitutionalism in the Charter Era* (LexisNexis, 2004).

the implications it would have vis-à-vis later-in-time judicial power, and those proposing this new written constitution could not garner sufficient support to have it and its bill of rights approved and adopted. That is my belief and is certainly true of Australia today.

A third ground for rejecting originalist interpretation involves a refusal to accept that anything other than the post-adoption perspective matters. What brought the Constitution (and these particular words in this form) into being, in other words, becomes irrelevant. Now in one sense that is simply to assert that originalist interpretation is defective or sub-optimal, a sort of tautological claim. But it can be taken in a different way, as suggesting that the text of the Constitution ought to be treated as a brute fact. 'Here it is. How it got here should not influence what you interpret it to mean.' For citizens of Allania that is unlikely to hold much allure, given the highly participatory and democratic input that went into its creation. And in terms of national cohesion and the benefits thought to flow from recognizing a shared history (whether partly based in myth, or not), this is a non-starter. Worse, the brute-fact approach glosses over a key question for those who see constitutions as being about locking things in. If it turns out that a constitution is just going to be treated as a brute fact – 'words on paper' – whose history is irrelevant, and hence one that will be interpreted either in some sort of 'living document' way or in some textualist 'mindless law' way, then is that outcome more attractive than parliamentary sovereignty? Is it more attractive for those who value the benefits and virtues of locking things in – of a hefty degree of certainty and security at the expense of flexibility? I think some of them would have to admit they would prefer parliamentary sovereignty (as Scalia implies he would). And related to that is the fact that these sorts of interpretive approaches, if spelt out, would likely have made the framers jettison the bill of rights (though perhaps not heads of powers federalism). Does that matter?

A fourth ground for rejecting originalist interpretation takes a quite different tack. Here one goes right back to an earlier claim – that in the context of interpreting a written constitution originalism imposes more external constraints on the point-of-application judge than any other interpretive approach – and one rejects it. This would involve asserting that the search for historical fact (when honestly pursued) is less (or no more) constraining than the attempt to 'find' or 'discover' the most moral answer or the Dworkinian best-fit answer or the most progressive answer or some other alternative (when honestly pursued). I think such assertions are implausible, though I suppose if the historical record happened to be sparse enough, and so the 'penumbra of doubt' large enough, this could conceivably be half-true. In the case of the United States, though, and even more so of Australia, I think it is not true.

If, like me, none of those four grounds strike you as persuasive, our hypothetical trip has given you at least *prima facie* grounds for being attracted by some variant or other of originalist interpretation. In the remaining two chapters we will look more closely at originalism. But be warned. If you favor the sort of originalism I will be elaborating there, you will be rejecting today's orthodox view of interpreting a constitution.

Chapter Eleven

Why Doubters Like Me Like Originalism

1. Introductory Remarks

This chapter shifts vantage to look at the task of interpretation itself after a written constitution is in place. From there it also aims to show why people like me – majoritarian democrats with more than a few doubts about how easy it is to provide solid foundations for non-legal human rights claims – ought to be particularly attracted to originalism as an approach to constitutional (and statutory) interpretation. A good few others with quite different core commitments will also find originalism attractive. But doubters like me will have as strong grounds as any.

At core, originalists believe that meaning is locked in at the time of enactment or promulgation. There are two main camps. One, the older variant most associated with Richard Kay, Larry Alexander and Stanley Fish (and the one I find most persuasive), looks to the real-life author's (or authors') intentions, and this camp is variously described as 'original intended meaning originalism,' or the 'OIM camp,' or 'Old Originalism' or 'subjective intentionalism.' It is the minority variant. The newer, these days more widely subscribed to variant looks to what a well-informed person at the time of enactment or promulgation would have taken the words to mean. This camp is known as 'original public meaning,' or 'OPM originalism,' or 'New Originalism' or 'objective intentionalism.' Here, amongst many others and in various iterations, you have Larry Solum, Jeff Goldsworthy and, in a basic version, Antonin Scalia. But notice that both camps think meaning is fixed and stable. It does not change over time. The OIM camp believe it is fixed by the actual intentions of the authors. The OPM camp believe it is fixed by what the well-informed person, at the time, took the words used to mean at that time — so real-life lawmakers' intentions matter here, too; it is just that they are filtered through a hypothetical well-informed person at the time — most plausibly (in my view) for Rule-of-Law reasons (although perhaps also to avoid the difficulties involved in determining a group's intention, the more-than-one difficulty). Now, as we shall see I think there are good grounds for preferring the OIM variant, but in practice (as virtually all originalists across the spectrum agree) there is not much in it. Overwhelmingly the two approaches will deliver the same results, not least because normally lawmakers — as opposed to, say, James Joyce or those sending coded messages to Occupied France in World War II — will use words in their standard, conventional sense. The two variants only diverge where the author's intended meaning is one thing, and what a well-informed reader of the words at the time takes the meaning to be is another. And that will be rare — often, perhaps, because of incompetence on the part of the law-maker.

To repeat, then, on either version of originalism meaning is fixed. It is stable. It does not vary with changing social values, or with the shifting views of the point-of-application interpreter, or due to newly perceived moral truths by judges or legal academics. And here readers will notice that on top of linguistic philosophy arguments about what meaning just is, there are also important legitimacy arguments in favor of originalism of the sort sketched out in the last chapter. If we give authoritative lawmaking power to a certain group of people — if they are the legitimate lawmakers — then it is *their* intentions that matter, directly for the OIMs and indirectly for the OPMs. What is not vested with anywhere near that level of legitimacy are the views, intentions and druthers of the lawyerly caste from which a handful of top judges are chosen. What those judges happen to believe to be best, or most reasonable, or proportional, or in keeping with today's values, has nowhere near the same level of legitimacy — whatever you think of the merits of the competing substantive views. And that claim goes up in orders of magnitude in a democracy.

None of that is to deny that any particular citizen might come to the conclusion that his or her jurisdiction's constitutional arrangements are in fact illegitimate. He or she might badly want them to change. And then the choice might come down to revolution, working for democratic change, or quietly cheering on the unelected judges to remake what is not liked. But if it is the last of these, then notice again that it cannot be done openly, as admitted constitutional updating and remaking at the point-of-application. It will have to be dressed up as honest interpretation, whether that claim is believed or not by the remakers or anyone else. Done openly and honestly, as 'we top judges are hereby changing these constitutional arrangements because we know better than those given the task of creating the Constitution,' and you would have riots in the streets.[158]So no approach to constitutional interpretation ever admits to doing that (though a judge here or there might hint at this in extra-judicial writings).

And now I can, for present generalised purposes, lump all non-originalist interpretive approaches onto the other side of the ledger. Be it 'moral readings' of the Constitution, Dworkin's 'best fit' Herculean approach, 'living Constitution or living tree' approaches, natural-law-type attempts to discern timeless (or even not always timeless) moral truths undergirding and giving life to the Constitution or anything else, meaning for these people is not locked in. And that means some group of real-life people has to do the updating. Judges. Top judges, who as it happens resolve their own disputes (whether they be originalist or non-originalists) by voting.[159]Five votes beat four, regardless of any substantive merits or moral persuasiveness to any of the opinions or judgments.

However, what if circumstances have changed substantially since the time of the constitution's writing? In that case, is it not a good idea or perhaps even necessary for interpreters to take account of those changes in order faithfully to render what might be thought of as the authors' true intended meaning? Well, not so fast. It depends. If the authors intended to set down standards that in effect were delegations to latter-day judges to use their first-order moral and political judgement, then fine. And the reason that would be fine is that the authors intended to abdicate this power

[158] Richard Kay makes this same point in blunt and unequivocal terms in 'Democracy, Mixed Government and Judicial Review' in (eds. Crawford, Emerton and Smith) *Law Under a Democratic Constitution* (Hart, 2019), 199 at 221 *inter alia*.

[159] And who, as Larry Alexander points out, always expect you to read *their* opinions and judgments in originalist terms, even their group decisions. These judges assume they will be read in line with their intended meanings. See Larry Alexander, 'Simple-Minded Originalism,' in (eds. G. Huscroft and B. Miller) *The Challenge of Originalism* (2011) at p.93, fn.15.

to future beings. But if the authors intended to lay down a rule, then it is not fine at all. Then they – the law-makers – would intend their views to be determinative, subject to use of the amending formula that they also provided (and which was used in the US 'to keep pace with changing social values' by, say, passing the 19th Amendment to extend the franchise to women). This distinction is often side-stepped. When that happens it brushes from sight the raw historical or empirical truth that virtually no group of real-life constitution-makers did, do or ever would intend to hand over these key substantive judgements to unnamed members of the lawyerly caste of the future.

Here is a variation on that non-originalist 'things have changed' gambit. This one traces out the assertion that 'a contemporary interpreter … must [go on to] ask whether the intentions of the framers, whatever they may have been at the time, would be different if they were here today.'[160] Here the text's meaning is supposed to change over time as the imagined intentions of the constitution makers are thought also to be changing. Or something like that. To be clear, my position (and I daresay that of all originalists) is that a text's meaning does *not* change over time. But this gambit argues that it does, albeit in a way that requires the interpreter to 'ask what [the framers] would take [the provision in dispute] to mean if they were around now,'[161] and so with a link to the law-makers' intentions – just not to any intentions they really, actually had back when drafting and ratifying the constitutional text. And that makes this a very unattractive gambit. It is much the same as wanting to bring Jane Austen back to life to dole out dating advice between men and women. Sure, on that sort of intellectual lark the imaginary Austen would give different answers in the1820s than in 1940s, than in the 1960s, than today. But that is because the fictional Jane Austen would be doing virtually none of the work. The interpreter summoning her back from the dead would simply be infusing the fictional hypothetical being with his or her own first-order beliefs, preferences and druthers. Likewise imagining what the framers and ratifiers would have intended today had they been alive. The range of

---

[160] A clear expression of this gambit can be found in Jonathan Crowe, 'Constitutional Text, Authorial Intentions and Implied Rights' (2021) 49 *Federal Law Review* 149.

[161] *Ibid.*, 152.

possible (and indeed reasonable) answers to that sort of question is simply not constrained. It is arbitrary. Or worse, you get out what you put in. As David Hume (perhaps apocryphally) said about social contract theories, 'they aren't worth the paper they weren't written on.'

Or put differently, it is one thing to seek the intentions of real-life people at the time they lived and wrote. That may be hard, and the evidence sometimes exiguous, but there will often be external constraints on what can plausibly be claimed to be the answer to their meaning when they wrote and spoke. Other times, it will be obvious and uncontestable. But hypothetically bringing them back to the future is nonsensical, with all due respect.

And so to two quick clarifications. Firstly, making the meaning of a legal text a joint enterprise of writer and reader is to make the reader a collaborator in the creation of meaning, and that is to abandon the very notion of a usable rule, with all the benefits that H.L.A. Hart makes clear rules bring with them.[162] Secondly, and I will come back to this, the meaning or sense of constitutional (or any) text never changes — only those things to which the text refers. So we have to be careful not to conflate two different notions: (1) that the enactors intended a category or class, the contents of which may change over time; and (2) that the enactors, if they were alive today, might intend something different than they intended. Now (1) in the realm of the external, causal world — think inventing new things like planes or telephones — is surely true. Indeed, this is relevant to legal interpretation, although as I will argue next chapter I would not extend it to normative categories. In those normative cases — unlike when it is factual categories about the external, causal world, where things like gravity are imposed on us and are mind-independent — separating meaning and expected application will not work in my view because the meaning and the expected application are too tightly wrapped up in each other. As for (2), clearly the endeavor is highly speculative. Often such claims may be very likely or plausible. But one struggles in vain to think of a plausible justification for making the results of this sort of speculation in (2) the basis for declaring what our current law is. I cannot see why anyone would pledge allegiance to the outcome of such

[162] In his magisterial *The Concept of Law* (Clarendon, 1961).

speculations. Where is the underlying legitimacy of such speculations? Of course, cynics might wonder if such speculations merely mask all the first-order beliefs, sentiments, judgements and druthers of the point-of-application interpreter. It is not the hypothetical and reincarnated Jane Austen. It is the interpreter claiming to perform this bit of reincarnation.

2. The Simple-Minded Larry Alexander

Let us turn to a more detailed account of originalism. The versions I find most persuasive have been offered by Rick Kay and by Larry Alexander. Here I will outline the latter's position though in reality I do not think there are any substantive differences between Kay's and Alexander's versions of originalism. None at all.

As a self-described 'simple-minded originalist'[163] Alexander embraces his position firstly as a thesis about how language is used, secondly as one about the nature of all interpretation and thirdly in normative terms about why in interpreting we should defer to the intended meanings of the authors of legal texts – so it is all three for Alexander, semantic, pragmatic and normative. In fact, in an end-of-book reply[164] to critics and commentators of his position Alexander lays out an abbreviated step-by-step account of his position, one which I am here further condensing:

> 1. A text ... is a set of symbols ... that is meant by its producer – the author(s) – to communicate a message to the intended audience....
>
> 2. If there is no author – no person who produced the marks, sounds, etc. in order to convey a message – we do not have a text. [The marks] may be a sign of something, much as smoke is a sign of fire .... Marks that might look like symbols, when we understand they are not – think of cloud formations that

[163] Larry Alexander, 'Simple-Minded Originalism' in (eds. G. Huscroft and B. Miller) *The Challenge of Originalism* (2011), p. 87 *inter alia.*

[164] The book grew out of a celebratory conference or *Festschrift* to honor Alexander's achievements. The book consists of 22 contributors' chapters, some (not all) on the topic of originalism. See Heidi Hurd (ed.) *Moral Puzzles and Legal Perplexities: Essays on the Influence of Larry Alexander* (CUP, 2019). The reply runs from page 407 to page 439.

resemble the letters C-A-T – render certain questions nonsensical that would make sense were there an author....

3. Texts are individuated by the messages their authors are intending to convey thereby. That is why the text of the US Constitution in Spanish can be the same as its text in English ....

4. When our interest is in the actual authors of a text and the message they intended to convey thereby, we are acting as 'originalists.'...

5. The 'conventional meanings' of words – what meaning the dictionaries would assign them – are merely the meanings most people at a particular time and in a particular locale would intend to convey by those words. These meanings are therefore time and place bound, and can and do change over time and from place to place. But authors may, and often do, employ unconventional meanings....If their intended audience understands [what the authors are unconventionally doing] then the authors can be successful in conveying their message to their intended audience....

6. Authors rely on implicatures and implicitures in conveying their intended messages. They often mean more, and sometimes less, than they actually say ....

7. [Turning now explicitly to interpreting legal texts:] In whomever the authority to enact legal norms resides ... then, when they decide which norms to enact and attempt to communicate those norms through a written or oral text, the job of the intended audience is to figure out what norms the authors enacted and intended to communicate. If the audience chooses legal norms that differ from those the authors chose to enact and communicate, the authority of the authors is undermined. Only originalism is authority-preserving.

8. Any departure from originalism either transfers authority from the authors to someone else – for example, to judges – or to some mindless process, such as the process by which the meanings of words change over time ....

9. ....[N]onoriginalist interpretation really represents a transfer of authority ... from one body or person to another or to some mindless (nonplanning) process ....

> 10. Interpretation of texts is an empirical, not a normative, endeavor. The interpreter wants to know what norm the authorities intended to communicate through their text. It is often quite difficult to answer the interpreter's question. The authorities may have expressed their intended norm poorly. Or the text may be old or ambiguous, and the context of its promulgation unclear or unknown. But, however difficult interpretation may be, it is unavoidable if the norms we are to be governed by are the norms those with authority to govern us intended.
>
> 11. Finally, interpretation must deal with the fact that some legal authorities are multimember bodies, and sometimes bicameral multimember bodies, and can enact legal norms only with the concurrence of majorities or supermajorities. What is the intended meaning of a legal text when the members who voted to enact it did not intend to convey the same meanings and, hence, the same norms by it? This is the aggregation problem. In my view it cannot be avoided. And when there is no shared meaning that the requisite number of norm enactors endorse, then the text they enact is legal gibberish....Perhaps that unfortunate result is rare. Perhaps it can be avoided by having those who vote for the text accept the meaning intended by some person or committee without having that meaning in mind themselves. I see no way, however, to make the aggregation problem disappear without at the same time undermining the authority of those who are supposed to possess it.

That, at its core, is the strand of originalism often dubbed, as I noted above, 'Original Intended Meaning' or 'OIM' or 'subjective intentionalism' originalism. In blunter terms, its basic position is that the meaning of the legal (or indeed any) text is what the authors intended to communicate to their chosen audience; what they intended that audience to take the authors to have meant. That is, therefore, a question of empirical fact, however difficult it may sometimes be for limited biological creatures such as humans to unearth those facts. Notice, too, that on top of that sort of semantic claim there is also a normative one. We vest certain people with legitimate authority to make the law. It follows that it is *their* views that matter, not some latter day point-of-application judges' views. So it is what the lawmakers intended that we must try to find if we are to uphold the law's authority – namely undertake an empirical search for the authors' subjective intentions. Again, Larry Alexander along with Richard Kay and (the later) Stanley Fish are probably its best-known and most insightful proponents. At any rate this OIM or 'old originalist' camp is a small one, certainly much smaller than the other main strand of originalism which most often travels under the moniker 'Original Public Meaning' or 'OPM' or 'objective intentionalism' or even 'new originalism.' Before we look at that strand let us consider one of its close cousins, conventional meaning textualism.

Start that consideration this way, by asking what you take the core function of law to be. The most plausible answer to that – in a world of well-meaning people who unavoidably have reasonable moral and political disagreements amongst themselves – is that law's core function is to deliver a settlement of those disagreements, a sort of second-best solution in a world where that is as good as can ever be on offer. Flowing from that premise one can wonder whether the best way to settle such disagreements is *A)* to go with the conventional meaning of the words used (disconnected from the intended meanings, when the two infrequently differ) and forget about intended meaning. Or, when the two conflict, *B)* to go with intended meaning. As Alexander sees it, and I think he is correct, the problem with going with the legal text's conventional meaning in order to achieve this desirable settlement function is that you are throwing your lot in with what amounts to 'mindless law.' No living being intended it. Now in a world of picking your poisons, or choosing between least bad outcomes, that might be a cost worth paying. Fred Schauer thinks it is. 'Or, to put it bluntly, conventional meaning textualism might suck, but at some times and in some places and on some subjects it might suck less than original intent originalism.'[165] The Alexander reply is that 'mindless law should be an anathema. The vision it conjures is of lawmakers choosing symbols but then some mindless process determining what they shall mean… [like] consulting the entrails of an ox, or the oracle of Delphi. For all the many imperfections of human lawmakers and of those seeking to glean the lawmakers' intended meanings, I think we

[165] See Fred Schauer, 'Intentions in Tension' in (H. Hurd ed.) *Moral Puzzles and Legal Perplexities: Essays on the Influence of Larry Alexander* (CUP, 2019) 206 at p. 219.

should prefer them to the mindlessness of non-existent[166] conventional meanings.'[167]

I side with Alexander on this issue of whether conventional meaning interpretation ought to act as the settlement function; it should not. And I side with Alexander not just for the reasons he gives above, which boil down to the persuasive claim that a locked in commitment to doing one's best to find intended meaning will suck a lot less – on average, over time – than just applying dictionary definitions (or however it is you think conventional meaning can be cashed out), even when you know for certain no one intended them. I also suspect that Schauer-type defences of conventional meaning textualism, whether intended to do so or not, can function as a sort of disguised vehicle for handing more power to those at the point-of-application of laws, the judges. Conventional meanings absent actual human intentions, at the very least, will deliver a lot more uncertainty which some living being today will have to reduce, remove or resolve. Likewise this textualism will force answers we know to be wrong. (When Snoop Dog describes something as 'bad' are we really going to insist, everywhere and always, that the evaluation is an unfavorable one?) Likewise again, when conventional meanings suck more than answers delivered by some other approach do we not suspect, all of us, that the judges will abandon conventional textualism? And, anyway, what sucks for one of today's judges might not suck for one of today's voters – so who made the judge the effective lawgiver, which he or she by default becomes when imposing the mindless law? And why should I as that voter feel there is any legitimacy to such judge-made or made-by-no-one law, to the extent of obeying it? At any rate, that is the gist of why I think a focus on intended meaning is more palatable and more desirable when interpreting than some version of conventional meaning textualism.

That brings us back to the other main strand of originalism which I have said most often travels under the moniker 'Original Public

---

166 They are 'non-existent' given Alexander's point 2 above, his denial that marks on paper have any meaning, conventional or otherwise, in the absence of the assumption of some author who means something by them. (See p. 175 above).

167 See Larry Alexander, 'Conclusion: Appreciation and Responses' in (H. Hurd ed.) *Moral Puzzles and Legal Perplexities: Essays on the Influence of Larry Alexander* (CUP, 2019) 206 at p. 425.

Meaning' or 'OPM' or 'objective intentionalism' or even 'new originalism.' Here, the basic position is slightly, but only slightly, different from OIM's. For OPM adherents the meaning of a legal text is what the intended audience was likely to have taken the authors to have meant; in other words we are still to look for the author's intended meaning, we just have to do so by restricting ourselves to the publicly available evidence and what a well-informed person at the time of promulgation would have taken the meaning to be. Now a moment's thought will show you that these two approaches to interpretation – subjective intentionalism and objective intentionalism or OIM and OPM – are very close cousins indeed. In effect, we have moved into the terrain of intra-family debates, where the OPM positions are in agreement with the OIM ones vastly more often than not and where the former, new originalism approach will overwhelmingly deliver the same outcomes as Alexander's and Kay's old originalism or subjective intentionalism strand. We are talking about disagreements at the outer margins of the known originalist solar system, in other words. To flesh out those differences let us take Larry Solum, who may well be America's leading OPM originalist, certainly he is one of them, and Jeffrey Goldsworthy, who is Australia's best known originalist bar none. Start with Solum, who helpfully situates OIM within the wider originalist family[168] after having noted that '[i]ntentions are essential for meaning, but this does not entail the conclusion that the meaning of a text must be the meaning the author intended to communicate.'[169] When I come to Goldsworthy in a moment I will come back to this question of the meaning of 'meaning,' but Solum's idea is that a text can mean more than what its author(s) intended – as the 'existence of conventional semantic meanings is entirely consistent with the notion that intentions play a role in the production of meaning.'[170] In other words, (*contra* Schauer) conventional

---

[168] Lawrence Solum, 'Simple-Minded Originalism? Simply Wrong!' in (H. Hurd ed.) *Moral Puzzles and Legal Perplexities: Essays on the Influence of Larry Alexander* (CUP, 2019) 189 at p. 191.

[169] *Ibid.*, p. 190.

[170] *Ibid.*, p. 196. It is worth remarking that some OPM proponents, at times, come close to suggesting that actual intentions are irrelevant in originalist interpretation. In my view, that sort of straight textualism, undergirded by appeal to nothing much more that conventional meanings, is a very weak and unconvincing position.

meanings are best understood as a function of intended meanings, which is why Solum's OPM strand of originalism, and Alexander's OIM strand, 'are likely to produce identical [interpretive] results except in cases where there was a failure of constitutional communication.'[171] Authors' intentions are crucial to both, it is just that Solum wants to stake out the position, in contrast to Alexander, that 'conventional semantic meanings are not identical with or reducible to individual communicative intentions, nor are they supervenient on such meanings'[172] .... so that the 'public meaning of a constitutional provision is the meaning that the provision had for the public at the time the provision was framed and ratified.'[173] Hence under the Solum OPM framework you potentially have public meaning as well as author's meaning, and while 'author's meaning and public meaning may differ, there are good reasons to believe that they will converge most (or almost all) of the time.'[174] Still, 'there are situations where the two meanings can diverge.'[175] When they do, says Solum, 'a choice must be made'[176] with the moniker OPM being a big clue as to how he thinks you should choose. Leave aside one or two exceedingly minor quibbles between Solum and Alexander and that is the core dispute, and what lies at the heart of the back and forth debate, between them and between OPM and OIM.

That said, I want to take up this debate between OIM and OPM originalists, not least because I am one of the rare few who has changed his mind in the unusual direction and moved away from OPM to thinking OIM is the more persuasive branch. And I want to do so by focussing here on Goldsworthy's views, though truth be told readers will struggle to put a piece of paper between the core Solum and Goldsworthy positions. I think I just find Goldsworthy's terminology easier to use for the non-afficianado as Goldsworthy talks in terms of subjective intentionalism ('SI'), objective intentionalism ('OI'), and public meaning originalism

---

171 *Ibid.*, p. 192.
172 *Ibid.*, p. 197.
173 *Ibid.*, p. 199.
174 *Ibid.*
175 *Ibid.*
176 *Ibid.*, p. 200.

('PMO') – while noting that 'PMO is often a version of OI.'[177] Accordingly, the debate that interests Goldsworthy is between OIs like him, and SIs like Alexander (and, full disclosure one more time, like me). It is, as I said, an intra-familial dispute and Goldsworthy sees it as one where 'SI maintains that judges should seek the lawmaker's actual subjective intentions, whereas OI holds that those intentions are relevant only insofar as they were publicly manifested, in that sufficient evidence of them was made readily available to the public or at least to legal advisers.'[178]

Remember, both SI and OI put much weight on authors' intentions. Indeed both camps agree that non-originalist interpretive approaches, from 'living Constitutionalism' to 'moral readings' on to 'Dworkinian best-fit approaches' transfer authority from the author to the point-of-application interpreter (or to some mindless process). And recall that Alexander and his fellow SI types think that intended meaning is the uptake an author wants to produce in his or her audience, which OI does not seem to dispute. Or put differently, texts are the messages authors intend to convey.

Accordingly, the nub of the theoretical disagreement between OIs and SIs centers on situations in which an author or authors fail to communicate the meaning he, she or they intend to communicate. There is misunderstanding. There is miscommunication. Suppose, for instance, that in uttering a statement you intend to communicate to your chosen audience message X but most or all of that audience (based on the publicly available evidence) understands Y. Now one can at this point ask the theoretical question of whether the meaning of the statement was X or Y. And that depends, as it were, on the meaning of 'meaning' – is it ***a)*** what you as author intended them to take you to have meant by your statement or is it ***b)*** what your audience is likely to take you to have meant by your statement? Goldsworthy says, and I think Solum concurs, that it is ***b)***.

---

[177] Jeffrey Goldsworthy, 'Subjective versus Objective Intentionalism in Legal Interpretation' in (H. Hurd ed.) *Moral Puzzles and Legal Perplexities: Essays on the Influence of Larry Alexander* (CUP, 2019) 170 at p. 182 – with Goldsworthy earlier stating explicitly that in his view 'Larry Solum's public meaning originalism [is] a version of the latter [i.e. OI] position.' (p. 170)

[178] *Ibid.*, p. 175.

'[W]hen your utterance fails to communicate your meaning to your intended audience (through your fault not theirs), but communicates some other meaning to them instead, that other meaning – and not your meaning – must be the meaning of your utterance.'[179]

But to my mind there is no 'must' about it. Alexander's reply to Goldsworthy is that Goldsworthy 'seems to me [i.e. to Larry] to trade on a confusion between what is said and what is meant. Or to put it in terms that I think are more apt, Goldsworthy's distinction is between what your audience is likely to take you to have meant by your statement and what you intended them to take you to have meant by it.'[180] I would put it this way: this debate about the best or preferable understanding of 'meaning' is not a dictionary dispute; it is not a definitional matter. Just as H.L.A. Hart makes clear in chapter nine of *The Concept of Law*[181] when urging readers to adopt a wider rather than a narrower understanding of 'law' (i.e., one that includes the morally egregious), this is not an 'is' matter but an 'ought' one. How should we understand law? And Hart gives a list of utilitarian reasons for adopting the wider understanding.

Likewise here. The debate between OIs and SIs is on the 'ought' level; how should we understand what counts as the meaning of a text. Because it seems clear to me that a person could, if he or she wished, specify or announce or designate that the dictionary understanding of 'meaning' from henceforth onwards would be either ***a)*** or ***b)*** above. Similarly, pointing to what courts presently do (as Goldsworthy does[182] to buttress his side of the argument) is on the 'is' plane. At most it tells us what judges today treat as falling within the aegis of 'meaning.' But that is not a conclusive answer on the theoretical plane of how 'meaning' should be understood. There, on that theoretical plane, the question is which understanding is preferable. Hence here are some of my own grounds for siding with Alexander and Kay (and in a way with that well-known SI Humpty Dumpty) and saying it is ***a)*** – that meaning *should* be understood as being what you the author intended it to be; it *should not* be

---

[179] *Ibid.*, p. 178 (italics mine).
[180] Larry Alexander, fn. 167 above, p. 420.
[181] H.L.A. Hart, *The Concept of Law* (Clarendon, 1961), 181-207.
[182] Jeffrey Goldsworthy, fn. 177 above, pp. 171-172.

understood as being what the audience took it to be, however justified in doing so that audience may have been.

1. Alexander's SI view makes 'meaning' an empirical question. Goldsworthy's makes it in part a normative or value-laden (or added value-laden) question. Goldsworthy seemingly concedes that his 'meaning is what the audience understands' view entails the fact that there can be different meanings for different audience members.[183] 'If this is a bullet ... then OI must bite it'[184] concedes Goldsworthy, with his proviso that SI can lead to the same utterance having different meanings for different listeners as well, if that is what the author intends – think of coded messages to spies in occupied Europe, say. But that proviso is weak. The author's meaning for the Gestapo should they come upon the message is intended by the author to be X and for the French Resistance it is intended to be Y, and for the same marks on the same paper. For SIs, the search for meaning is empirical, what was intended by real life humans. For OI adherents, author's intentions are not always ultimately determinative, by their theory's stipulation in fact. So sometimes meaning depends, for Goldsworthy, on identifying a representative member of the intended audience. And at that point I further agree with Alexander and Kay that such an identifying task is an unavoidably arbitrary process, despite Goldsworthy's claim that '[t]his seems to [him] an exaggeration.'[185] Actually, it is arbitrary in one sense and in another we know before we start the 'let's identify some representative member of the audience' task that it is a process that is overwhelmingly likely to deliver up a 'representative audience member' who, when uncertainties arise, will look a lot like the interpreter who went in search of him or her in the first place – a lot like Scalia or Solum or Goldsworthy or whomever it is that happens to be doing the interpreting through the prism of the 'representative member of the audience.'

2. Goldsworthy, as just noted, thinks the force of this 'arbitrary' point is over-stated. We should ask 'what a well-informed, intelligent and competent lawyer at the time of enactment would have understood the law

---

[183] *Ibid.*, p. 185.
[184] *Ibid.*
[185] *Ibid.*

to communicate.'[186] Presumably Goldsworthy believes that will get rid of most of the range of possible 'OI meanings.' But I think Goldsworthy is wrong. For instance, take any of the handful of statutory bills of rights at the State level in my country of Australia. Off the cuff I can immediately think of a law professor (in favor of such instruments where I am not) who would disagree with me about big chunks of any of those statutes, about what they mean. So either one of us is not competent, intelligent or well-informed, or one of us is not basing his or her views on the publicly available evidence of legislative intent. Or – my position – the views and beliefs and value-judgements and even sentiments of the interpreter, even one who is a 'well-informed, intelligent and competent lawyer,'[187] matter. Sometimes they matter a lot. There is a range or spectrum of people who fall under the aegis of being reasonable, smart, competent and well-informed and picking between them is, well, arbitrary. (Nor would that fact surprise a Humean non-cognitivist like me.) Moreover, we see this all the time even with judges who disagree with other judges, even with judges who claim to be originalists. So I think both the arbitrary point and the 'too many alternative possible meanings' point are persuasive factors in deciding how we should understand what meaning is. They push you towards thinking SI is preferable to OI.

3. Here is another difficulty for Goldsworthy and the OI position. I refer to the notion of 'fault.' You see as Goldsworthy makes clear, OI is only supposed to kick in when the miscommunication is the fault of the author, not when it is the fault of the listener or listeners.[188] I take it that if the miscommunication is the fault of the intended audience, then for Goldsworthy the statement means what the author intended it to mean. Hence, for OI adherents only if it is the author's fault does the miscommunication result in the statement meaning something other than what the author intended. But this fault-based divide is obviously a problematic distinction. Imagine a 99 person audience. The author intends his message to mean X. Fifty take it to mean X. Forty-nine take it to mean

---

186 *Ibid.*

187 *Ibid.*

188 Goldworthy makes this explicit as I have said: he says 'through your fault not theirs' (fn. 177 above, p. 178). 'Your' refers to the maker of the utterance and 'theirs' to the intended audience.

Y. All base their choice on publicly available evidence. So the OI meaning is X, and by numerical luck that happens to line up with the SI meaning. Of course if it were 49-50 the other way, then the meaning would not be what the author intended for Goldsworthy and the OIs. It would be what fifty out of ninety-nine understood it to be based on the publicly available information. For Alexander, Kay and the SIs the meaning would still be X but the author should have done a better job communicating. Put differently, the meaning would be stable for Alexander and me even if one audience member changes her mind about what the author was trying to convey. What can vary for SI adherents is whether the author's intended meaning was in fact successfully communicated, not the meaning itself.

Or go back to our ninety-nine person audience where this time fifty of ninety-nine misunderstand the author and think Y rather than the intended X. And now assume in my above scenario that the audience's median (or indeed any single person's) IQ was 120 and then start lowering it one IQ point a minute. Just when, precisely, does the meaning of the author's utterance change? – because as you lower the median IQ or a single person's IQ at some point the miscommunication will become the fault of the audience, at which point we are to suppose that the meaning reverts to the SI one of author's intended meaning. Meaning, in other words, becomes hostage to the intelligence of the audience, or at least to the author's ability to discover that intelligence and craft his method of communicating his intended meaning accordingly. Or, we could cut through all of this and just say 'meaning' is stable, and whether an author is able to communicate it successfully is variable and dependent upon a host of factors.

At any rate, those are some of the grounds for why on the theoretical plane I some time ago moved over to agree with Alexander and Kay and prefer SI to OI. Or, if you would like to think of it this way, the SI/OI difference comes down to there being, in rare situations, a serious problem for each position. In cases where the difference matters (which Alexander, Goldsworthy, Kay, Solum and most other originalists all agree is seldom) – i.e., when there has been a mistaken communication – once the mistake has been convincingly discovered SI calls for the enforcement of the 'until recently inaccessible' law that we now believe was intended (subject to compensating reliance interests, of course, and not doing so if the costs would now be catastrophic). OI avoids this problem, but at the price of wanting to continue to enforce a law that no lawmaker ever adopted or intended or legitimately brought into being. So it is a kind of pick-your-poison situation. I am with Alexander and Kay and Fish and a few others in the SI camp rather than with Goldsworthy, Solum and the more numerous OI/OPM strand of originalism. That said, I also agree that in practice, on the plane of real life interpreting, there is virtually nothing in it. The two approaches overwhelmingly deliver the same outcomes because both look to what authors intend to convey.

Of course one can understand what is bothering many OIs in terms of rule of law values. Alexander hints at this himself when he gives this caveat: 'Let me also put aside the possibility that a legal system might have rules limiting legal interpretation to only certain types of evidence.'[189] If there were such rules they would flow from having done a cost-benefit analysis of when the benefits of restricting the search for authors' intended meaning outweighed the costs. That, as I just said, is what seems to be motivating the qualms Goldsworthy (and others) are feeling in the legal realm about legislators' subjective intentions. And that is all perfectly understandable. Yet, in my view, it remains a mistake to say that because of such concerns, and in some ineffable way, the 'meaning' of the legal text is not what the authors' intended. I think what is a better characterization is to be blunt and just say that for rule of law and other policy reasons in law (and as regards legal interpretation) one might choose to lay down a rule (or rules) that sometimes restricts the search for evidence of authors' intentions. Alexander himself does not deny that such a step might be defensible. Indeed, back in 2004 he and Saikrishna Prakash made plain that in their view the only two plausible games in town – and I am talking now specifically about legal interpretation – are **i)** interpreters use all the evidence there is of authors' intentions, and **ii)** we restrict some of the evidence that can be sought for various policy-based reasons (of the

[189] Larry Alexander, fn. 167 above, p. 422.

sort Goldsworthy focuses upon).[190] Moreover, you can make that choice between **i)** and **ii)** without undergoing some partial, limited Damascene conversion that shifts your allegiance from SI to OI in the legal realm. Rather, you just concede that other things matter too, not just a law's meaning, especially (or perhaps, only) where the lawmaker has plenty of scope to try again and this time be clearer. Yes, there will be a cost in terms of authority and why people should obey not the law but instead this cost/benefit rule that once in a blue moon gives us something different from the intended law. But there will be rule of law benefits too. And no doubt different people would, and do, strike different bargains between **i)** and **ii)**. At any rate, that is how I would characterize what is going on and where the competing trade-offs lie.[191]

And that is why this doubter of much of today's constitutional law orthodoxy likes originalism – why I think that interpretation at the point-of-application ought to be constrained by the search for the legitimate law-makers' intended meanings.

---

[190] See Larry Alexander and Saikrishna Prakesh, '"Is that English You're Speaking?" Some Arguments for the Primacy of Intent in Interpretation' (2004) 41 *San Diego Law Review* 967.

[191] And in line with that characterization of mine, I argued back in 2000 (in an article that seems to have convinced absolutely no one) that there are solid grounds for making different cost-benefit analyses as regards statutory interpretation and constitutional interpretation. In other words, I would be more open to restrictions vis-à-vis statutory interpretation than constitutional interpretation because the comparative costs of the lawmaker responding to the interpreter (of over-riding the authoritative and legitimate source of law based on some policy-related search-restricting rule) are so much lower with statutes. Put differently, we should be much more open to restrictions as regards statutes because there is much, much more scope for the legislature to respond and say 'you got our meaning wrong by using these rule of law enhancing presumptions so we have passed a new, clearer statute.' With constitutional interpretation, by contrast, you basically can never do that; we know going in, indeed the top judges doing the constitutional interpreting know going in, that constitutional amendments correcting an erroneous imputed 'meaning' that results from some policy-related interpretive rule will not happen, or virtually never will happen. Hence the costs of using a 'let's advance rule of law or keep costs contained' rule will be considerably higher in constitutional interpretation while biting much less into the authority of law as regards statutes, where there is a realistic chance the legislature will and can reply. See James Allan, "Constitutional Interpretation v Statutory Interpretation: Understanding the Attractions of 'Original Intent,'" (2000) 6 *Legal Theory* 109.

Chapter Twelve

Some Last Words on Constitutional Interpretation

I finish Part IV and the substantive part of this book with three short sections that flesh out my doubts about much of the orthodoxy as regards constitutional interpretation in today's democratic world. The first considers, and rejects, an objection to the sort of intended meaning originalism I defended last chapter. The second looks at an approach to constitutional interpretation that is not really interpretation at all; not really concerned with the constitutional text at all; where judges are seen as a sort of modern day aristocracy there to rein in the worst instincts of the elected branches. Here, lip-service is assuredly paid to the supposed task of interpreting the constitutional text but in fact the judges are simply a third legislative house, injecting their first order substantive views into the mix. It is tricameralism if you will. And it is not just countenanced but celebrated. It is advocates for that sort of view of the judicial job, even half-hearted ones who offer it up in despair, that I will try to counter or rebut in section two. And then lastly, in this chapter's third section and in keeping with the second, I will have a little to say about proportionality. Not much, because much has already been said by many others. But just enough to indicate my deep skepticism about this sort of approach to constitutional interpretation.

1. The Hurd Objection to OIM Intentionalist Interpretation

Heidi Hurd is very much against interpreting a constitutional text according to the intentions of those who framed and ratified it. Indeed she attacks or contests this approach from the vantage of a non-originalist or 'living constitution' adherent. So let us consider the gist of Hurd's thesis, her attack on OIM/old/(or what she calls 'strong') originalism. You see I think Hurd has it wrong as regards what she claims is the big fault in OIM originalism. I think she also has it wrong in her concomitant suggestion that OPM or new originalism is unstable – that it is not a middle way between non-originalism and OIM originalism that can prevent itself from collapsing into one or other of those two alternatives. And thirdly, she is wrong in her core or deep-seated view that originalist interpretive theories are normatively unattractive because they give the dead power over the living – at least I say that in so far as Hurd's core view is understood as a comparative claim.

Hurd's claim about the big fault in OIM originalism relates to what she describes as 'the intentional states [of mind] to which strong originalists might be referring.'[192] Hurd then sets out five ways an OIM intentionalist might derive the relevant intention – (i) by treating the words used as exemplars; (ii) by going with conventional meaning of the words; (iii) by their hypothetical meaning; (iv) by some believed reference; (v) by the larger purposes of lawmakers. All these fail she says. Hence, '[t]hat strong originalists do not have a clear and clearly defensible theory of the nature of the subjective intentions that fix the meaning of legal terms is, thus, a reason to doubt the coherence and practicality of strong originalism.'[193] However, to the best of my knowledge no OIM/subjective intentionalist/strong originalist actually subscribes to *any* of the five methods Hurd describes. Certainly Larry Alexander does not. Nor does Richard Kay. Nor, for that matter, do I. On top of that, not a single strong originalist/OIM adherent is cited by Hurd as falling into any of the five possibilities she lays out. These five mooted options for how a subjective intentionalist or OIM/strong originalist might derive the relevant mind-independent interpretive constraints are therefore, not all that surprisingly – and remembering, again, that no real life person seems to hold any of

---

[192] See Heidi Hurd, 'The Moral Motivations for Moderate Originalism' in (L. Burton Crawford, P. Emerton and D. Smith eds.) *Law Under a Democratic Constitution: Essays in Honour of Jeffrey Goldsworthy* (Hart Publishing, 2019) 113 at p. 117.
[193] *Ibid.*, p. 120.

them – pretty poor possibilities. Hurd herself notes Alexander's 'rejection of all [Hurd's] preferred candidates.'[194]

To be blunt then, Hurd's five are by no means the only games in town; indeed hers are part of a game no known originalist is actually playing. Nor is it that hard to sketch out a better possibility than any raised by Hurd. What I take the Alexanders and Kays to think on this question of the intentional state of the lawmaker's mind that the interpreting judge ought to be seeking (and what I certainly think) would be something along these lines: The enactors in promulgating a law or constitutional provision set out a category of actions. They have an intended sense of the terms they use. (And that sense will differ from exemplars, conventional meaning, hypothetical meaning, believed reference or purpose.) That sense can be inferred based on all the historical evidence available – the language used, the good or mischief with which the authors seemed to be concerned, everything. The first step will often be to decide, based on the empirical evidence, whether or not the lawmaker intended to delegate some sort of moral judgement to later in time point-of-application judges. If so, this will in effect mean the provision being considered works as a standard, not as a rule. Put differently, if I am a lawmaker and I intend simply to delegate to later-in-time Judge X, then that is my intention and the judge makes the normative call. Of course (and Rick Kay is better on this point than anyone), these sort of cases of 'I intend to delegate to a future point-of-application interpreter to use his or her moral druthers' are exceptionally rare. Think about it. As I made clear in chapter ten, how would you ever sell that to ratifiers at the time when some constitution was being mooted? You would have to say, were you opting for honesty, 'look our intention is to take some things off the democratic table; we can't specify what those things are; we don't even know ourselves; we're just going to delegate such calls to the lawyerly caste from which judges in the future will be chosen.' As I argued earlier, I suspect that would have zero chance of getting past the ratifying voters. Nor would many framers of a Constitution be inclined to want to make that sort of delegation anyway. One may well believe, in some unique set of circumstances, that he or she is part of a privileged group that is well-placed to be a constitution maker,

[194] *Ibid.*

to lock-in certain constitutional provisions that will be harder to change going forward than ordinary statutes. But as that sort of constitution maker it is near certain that you will also think it is *your group's views and your own views* that should be determinative. Moreover, the historical evidence basically never backs up those who claim otherwise, who contend that the lawmaking authors intended to make a standard-like 'we want you future judges to use your own moral druthers on this one' delegation. Remember, this is a question of historical fact, full stop. Yes, yes, yes more than a few commentators – not least Ronald Dworkin – claim this sort of 'they intended latter day judges to use their latter day moral sensibilities and judgement to decide.' But Dworkin and the rest cannot offer even halfway convincing proofs or arguments that real life constitution ratifiers and framers actually did intend this. Sure, they might rip some quotes from *The Federalist* out of context or point to the choice of broad language. But that is about it[195] and as evidence goes it is clearly outweighed by what points the other way.

As for the massively more likely scenario whereby the evidence shows that the constitutional lawmaker did not intend to delegate big moral judgements to future judges – did *not* intend to delegate via a standard of some sort – the interpreter's focus should be on the constitution or law maker's intention as regards the relevant provision (which will usually not be a standard). In other words, what was the author's intended sense of the terms used? That, and nothing hypothetical or more complicated, is the intentional state the interpreter seeks. And here we will be bound by that subjective intention. Will the lawmaker have thought of every possible item that might fall inside the sense of the terms used? Of course not. Will there be grey areas and debateable penumbral cases? Yes. But where we have known intentions as regards something, and do our best to apply them to the facts at hand, we are done.

At this point a subtlety arises, one that I alluded to in section ***1.*** of the last chapter. These authorial senses of the terms used can, you see,

---

[195] Richard Kay responds to that sort of weak argument very powerfully in 'Adherence to Original Intentions in Constitutional Adjudication: Three Objections and Responses' (1988) 82 *Northwestern University Law Review* 226 at 259-284, and especially 281-284.

cover references the author did not anticipate. But this will most always relate to unforeseen facts (in the external, causal world) not to values. It is one thing to point to the category of 'fish' and say that the authors intended all creatures in this category and that some of them wrongly would have included 'whales' back then had you asked them but we know now that whales are not fish. Or likewise when extending a federal head of power over the 'army and navy' to include an 'air force,' this being just different factual weapons as it were. It is quite another matter, however, to take the notion of 'cruel and unusual punishment' and to say 'we know that virtually none of the ratifiers and framers intended capital punishment to fall into that category but we are all the same going to over-rule the authors on this intention of theirs based, implicitly if not explicitly, on the premise that we today have better moral values and insights.' Leave aside that with moral values there is no obvious mind-independent external causal world that can adjudicate on contested facts,[196] to tell us in simplistic terms such things as whether gravity exists. No, worse, the pronoun 'we' two sentences above would be referring only to nine top judges today. They would, in effect, have scope to take this issue off the democratic table today, or if not today then when their – the judges' – moral views (or views of what they believe are others' moral views) shift sometime in the future. By contrast, lock yourself in to the intended moral views of the authors, their sense of 'cruel and unusual,' and what is taken off the democratic table does not shift or ratchet-up. Hence, taking capital punishment as an example, everything not within the ratifiers' sense of 'cruel and unusual' stays on the democratic table. If the evidence says the authors clearly did not intend capital punishment to fall within the aegis of the sense of that phrase – and I have made this point already in this book – it in no way follows that society is stuck with capital punishment. It just remains an issue up for resolution in the cut and thrust of democratic politics – not for resolution by some shifting judicial sense of what today is cruel or unusual. And that is far more preferable if you found Parts II and III of this book persuasive.

---

[196] I expand on this point in James Allan, 'Jeremy Waldron and the Philosopher's Stone' (2008) 45 *San Diego Law Review* No.1, 133-162.

Why, though, distinguish between facts and values? Because it is clear that most any constitution makers would have intended that. 'Sure, we are happy to be updated at the margins on fact-based stuff we did not foresee. But forsaking New Zealand-style parliamentary sovereignty in favor of a written constitution that locks in certain outcomes is a big step, taking certain things off the democratic table as it does, and that means that buying a written constitution means you are buying only our unchanging, unexpanding, bracketed, intended-by-us normative calls on those sort of issues – and you are only buying those until society's views have shifted enough to amend the Constitution. (Remember, too, that these normative calls are overwhelmingly floors, not ceilings, so the elected legislature whenever it wishes can enact laws forbidding capital punishment or extending marriage; it is just that the written constitution cannot be used by the judges to do so.) Hence we authors, unsurprisingly, have no intention at all of handing these above-the-floor moral calls over to a future committee of unelected ex-lawyers in some shifting, expanding way and if we ever did want that, any constitution with that sort of concomitant intended interpretive approach, would never, ever be ratified.'

We can now see why Hurd is also wrong in suggesting that Solum or Goldsworthy style OPM originalism must collapse into 'living constitutionalism' or into OIM originalism. The OPM or new version of originalism is just as committed to the lawmakers' intentions as the old, OIM variant is. As explained last chapter, the difference revolves around what both will do when there looks to have been a miscommunication. Either go with intended, miscommunicated meaning (while no doubt compensating reliance interests) once we find out about the miscommunication or stay with what we now realise is the intended-by-no-one sense, to be blunt the mindless law, that was likely to have been understood that way at the time because of the miscommunication. Both choices have costs and benefits and you pick your poison. As I made clear last chapter, I think on balance and as a 'should' matter that we ought to prefer the OIM/subjective intentionalism originalism of Alexander and Kay to the Solum and Goldsworthy OPM/objective intentionalism strand. But in no way at all is the OPM position an unstable one or one that somehow will inevitably collapse over time into either 'living constitutionalism' or into the OIM strand that Hurd labels 'strong originalism.'

I think, too, that by now in this book I have also made clear why I disagree with Hurd's suggestion that originalist interpretive theories are normatively less attractive than non-originalist 'living constitution' ones. Sure, originalism presupposes being locked in by the intentions of long dead people, by the dead hand of the past. But as I have made clear again and again 'living constitutionalism' involves being locked in by the moral (or other) judgements of nine top current day judges. The 99.999 per cent of us who are just non-judge voters are locked in either way. Whichever interpretive school is chosen to interpret the written constitution – a version of originalism or non-originalism – we will not be living in a New Zealand-style parliamentary sovereignty. We voters will not get to make the call. And so for powerful normative reasons most obviously related to self-government concerns I think Hurd is wrong and that originalism is normatively the more attractive of the only two options in play. This is so not least because originalism does not promote a 'living' constitution whose prohibitions on what the elected legislature can do are able continuously to expand and ratchet up over time as the normative, moral and other sentiments, judgements and druthers of nine top judges alter and shift over time – and whose own judicial differences are always resolved, as Jeremy Waldron regularly points out, on a wholly majoritarian procedural basis of 5 votes beat 4 regardless of the moral, political or aesthetic quality of the respective majority and minority judicial opinions or judgments.

2. The Kay Gambit

Let us assume you are like me and that you believe that originalist interpretation of the OIM or intended meaning variety is the only game in town if one purports to be interpreting the Constitution. Sure, you can live with the OPM or new originalism approach because it so seldom veers from what you take to be the proper approach to constitutional interpretation. And assume, too, that you believe that when judges in a liberal democracy opt to employ some other, non-originalist mode of constitutional interpretation they are in fact, case-by-case, altering that jurisdiction's ultimate test of legal validity or Rule of Recognition[197] (however minisculely that might happen to be). They are forswearing constitutionalism, to put it bluntly and in keeping with the account of constitutionalism I have provided in this book. Put even more bluntly, we are assuming that you, like me, believe that such non-originalist judges have effected a small revolution by not being faithful to the intended meaning of the written constitution. Take away the empirical search for finding the meaning of what some (considered-to-be) legitimate and authoritative law-making body in the past laid down as pre-established legal rules and what you are left with are judges who are engaged in a law-making exercise. At the constitutional level that amounts to a judicial exercise in changing some component of the jurisdiction's Rule of Recognition. It delivers you some degree or other of juristocracy or kritarchy.

So we are assuming that you agree with all that. We have an assumed consensus. But what happens if the world we live in does not happen to look much like one where our top judges are *in fact* doing what constitutionalism (and what we say is proper interpretation) demand that they do – they are not upholding the intended locked in meaning some authoritative and legitimate law-maker in the past laid down but instead are treating the document as a 'living Constitution' or are affording it a moral reading or a Dworkinian best fit one or using it as vehicle to keep pace with their view of changing social values? What then? And that is an important 'what then?' question because there are strong grounds for believing that that 'judges are not doing constitutionalism' world is in fact (to a large extent) our world. Take Rick Kay, who as I have said is one of the best known OIM originalists going and who sees constitutionalism and proper interpretation in precisely the assumed terms I have just set out. Yet Kay also believes, as a matter of empirical fact, that as regards today's United States (and indeed Canada and elsewhere) judges are far more often than not doing something other than what constitutionalism demands. In a recent publication Kay has made this abundantly and unequivocally clear.

---

[197] That term being coined by H.L.A. Hart in his magisterial *The Concept of Law* (Clarendon, 1st edtn 1961, now in its third printing).

> [A] fair examination of actual constitutional judgments is unlikely to convince many observers that those decisions closely match up with the rules in the constitutional text.[198]

And I agree with Kay. Gaze around the common law world and, as he says, top judges look largely (nay, overwhelmingly) to be doing something very different to what OIM constitutionalists like Kay (and Alexander and I) – or even what the more numerous OPM constitutionalists – say honest interpretation demands.

At this point, perhaps out of despair or in the spirit of a least-bad option, Kay offers up what I am calling a justificatory gambit. You see if you accept that the preponderance of top judges are doing something that looks nothing like what both Kay and I think they should be doing as honest interpreters working in a jurisdiction with constitutionalism at its core, you might ask a different question. You might ask whether this new task the top judges are performing can be justified and defended. Kay's gambit is to say that it can, that we can understand and then endorse this sort of 'living Constitution' judiciary as a sort of Super Senate, tricameralism-type check and balance. The Kay gambit asks us to 'reconceptualiz[e] constitutional courts as discretionary decision-makers in a mixed government'[199] and then to endorse them in that role. As I shall argue I think Kay's gambit fails to convince. It should be declined.

However, first things first, let me quickly sketch the gist of Kay's argument in a recently published chapter of his[200] and then afterwards say why I find it unpalatable and unpersuasive. In effect, Kay's argument is that democracy is not all that it is generally cracked up to be.So in the first part of that chapter Kay (as he puts it) 'raise[s] some difficulties associated

---

[198] See Richard Kay, 'Democracy, Mixed Government and Judicial Review' in (L. Burton Crawford, P. Emerton and D. Smith eds.) *Law Under a Democratic Constitution: Essays in Honour of Jeffrey Goldsworthy* (Hart Publishing, 2019) 199 at p.212. See too *id.* at p. 213: 'In a significant number of cases, the courts act not on the basis of pre-existing rules but according to their own evaluation of public welfare. This is implicit in the historical experience of many jurisdictions and is explicit in much of the academic commentary including the extrajudicial writing of constitutional judges.'

[199] *Ibid.*, p. 221.

[200] Kay sets it out in his 'Democracy, Mixed Government and Judicial Review' chapter, fn. 198 above.

with the decision-making competence of voters, difficulties which may have been exacerbated in recent decades.'[201] He reminds readers of the distrust the American founders had for unconstrained democracy, their worry that for many people passion would over-ride reason,[202] not to mention just how limited the franchise was back at the time of the adoption of the US Constitution.[203] He wonders about voter ignorance and incompetence. If not quite offering a paean of praise to the role of experts and expert opinion in modern life, Kay certainly comes down on the side of giving them and it a big role. He even finishes this first part of his chapter by reminding readers that Winston Churchill's famous quote – 'that democracy is the worst form of Government except all those other forms that have been tried from time to time' – was spoken by the great man *in opposition to* a Bill that 'would have reduced the power of the [wholly unelected] House of Lords to delay legislation passed by the [wholly elected House of] Commons.'[204] Then, in the second part of that chapter, Kay offers up his defence of strong judicial review where it takes place *not* as part of the traditional understanding of OIM (or even OPM) judging that underlies constitutional government but rather one with what I would call an aristocratic element with that role now being filled by the top judges.[205] Kay sees this sort of strong judicial review as resembling a form of 'mixed government' with the judges playing the role of some sort of Super Senate or tricameralism-type check and balance, and he prefers that to raw, 'no strong judicial review at all,' New Zealand-style democracy. Then, in Part III of the chapter, Kay makes clear that for him this 'mixed government' type role for judges is a second best form of judicial review – not as good as a constitutional state (and indeed, probably not as good as a properly constituted 'mixed government' arrangement either).[206]

That is a rough and ready account of what I am dubbing the Kay gambit. You start with a hefty dollop of skepticism as regards the value of

---

201 *Ibid.*, p. 200.
202 *Ibid.*, p. 202.
203 *Ibid.*, p. 207.
204 *Ibid.*, p. 211 (internal quotation marks and citations omitted).
205 *Ibid.*
206 *Ibid.*, pp. 199, 211, 212-213, 219.

majoritarian democracy, leaven that by pointing to similar such concerns amongst America's Founding Fathers, and then opt for giving a sort of overseeing role to the lawyerly caste from which judges are chosen rather than opting to try to rein in the judges and veer towards a more vigorous majoritarian or New Zealand-style parliamentary sovereignty path (which, once the OIM/OPM constitutional state is forsaken, are really the only two choices left on the table).

Here is my brief response to the Kay gambit. First off, the whole 'voters are ignorant' grievance against voters is to my mind far less telling than Kay pre-supposes, as I made clear already in chapter four. That Ilya Somin-type grievance or argument against democratic decision-making,[207] I argued, is ultimately unconvincing. To remind readers, the main weaknesses with these 'assertions about the ignorance and incompetence of the [voting] population'[208] inspired attacks on democracy include: (i) the overblown trust in experts such arguments exhibit, without much if any empirical support for that trust; (ii) the flaws inherent in trying to pigeonhole social policy differences in society into mere questions of 'fact' rather than ones where people come to the particular debate with different underlying sentiments or values or preferences – thereby simply assuming away Humean-type claims that we humans live in a fact/value dichotomy world and hence implicitly elevating the importance of expertise when it comes to the sort of issues that reach a top US-style written constitution and bill of rights common law court (issues like who can marry, when life should be understood as beginning, how to treat those claiming to be refugees, the most desirable scope for protecting speech, what limits to put on gun ownership, how best to draw district or electoral boundaries, the list going on and on into the distance);[209] and (iii) the

---

[207] See Ilya Somin, *Democracy and Political Ignorance: Why Smaller Government is Smarter* (2d ed. 2016) (making the 'central argument . . . that widespread political ignorance . . . should lower our confidence in the effectiveness of the modern democratic state as a tool for making important policy decisions' p. 224). And see chapter four above, in particular pp 58-60.

[208] Kay, 'Democracy, Mixed Government and Judicial Review' chapter, fn. 198 above, at p. 202.

[209] And it is not just the assumption that differences of opinion in society are overwhelmingly 'fact-based' rather than 'value-based' (contra David Hume-type thinking); also seemingly at work here is a needed implicit acceptance that Kant's

insouciance about accountability concerns displayed by such attacks on democracy, remembering that one of the core virtues of democracy is that it lets us 'throw the bums out' while in a Benthamite way (again, as we saw in chapter four) going some small distance towards aligning the interests of the elected politicians (who, to keep their jobs, need the votes of more than half of those who go to the polls) with those of the voters – an imperfect alignment, no doubt, but perhaps a least-bad one and better than just trusting judges (or anyone else) who cannot be removed from office.[210]

Secondly, any defence of what amounts to an aristocratic element

---

account of human reason is preferable to Hume's. I much prefer Hume's account. See my *A Sceptical Theory of Morality and Law* (Peter Lang, NY, 1998).

[210] Which, after all, is the sentiment that lay behind Churchill's famous quote that 'democracy is the worst form of Government except all those other forms that have been tried from time to time.' Kay, 'Mixed Government and Judicial Review' fn. 204 above, mentions this Churchillian quote and then reminds the reader that it was spoken in opposition to a Bill that 'would have reduced the power of the [wholly unelected] House of Lords to delay legislation passed by the [wholly elected House of] Commons.' But to put that in further context still, the Parliament Act 1911 had limited the unelected House of Lords' power to delay Money Bills to only one month and non-Money Bills to two years (assuming passage by the House of Commons in three successive sessions). The Parliament Act 1949 reduced the latter of those delaying powers in the hands of the unelected House of Lords down to one year (assuming passage by the House of Commons in two successive sessions). Now Churchill made his quote about democracy as the least-bad system, as Kay says, in the context of opposing the shrinking of the Upper House's delaying power by one year. My response would be that in the context of a British system under which the Prime Minister can at any time threaten to have (and if pushed actually have) the Monarch appoint as many new Lords as needed to enable passage of a Bill being blocked by the Lords – as, in fact, was exactly what Prime Minister Asquith did threaten to do to force through passage of the Parliament Act 1911 itself and which was recently mooted be done if the Lords became difficult over Brexit legislation – and Churchill's support for keeping the Lords' delaying power at a maximum of two years rather than just one year hardly looks in any way like support for a 'mixed government,' strong judicial review set-up under which unelected ex-lawyer judges can and do regularly gainsay the elected branches on a vast array of matters and there is nothing the latter can do in response. Put differently, I do not think that Kay can plausibly call in aid Mr. Churchill, even in the most enervated way, as some sort of implicit supporter of his 'mixed government' gambit. For my discussion of a leading British constitutional case that centred on the Parliament Acts of 1911 and 1949 see James Allan, 'The Paradox of Sovereignty: Jackson and the Hunt for a New Rule of Recognition?' (2007) 18 *King's Law Journal* 1.

in one's constitutional arrangements (and be clear that on Kay's 'mixed government,' tricameralism-like defence of strong judicial review that will be precisely the role that top judges play) always looks better – or so say I – when one is himself part of that aristocracy. Take away the widespread view that the judges are interpreting and enforcing rules that have been legitimately locked in and laid down in the past and my bet is that the vast preponderance of citizens (the ones not part of this lawyerly caste that will be deciding based solely on what they happen to think best) will find this a rather unappetizing prospect. Former US Supreme Court judge Antonin Scalia certainly agreed with me on this point.

> The people are not stupid. When the primary function of the Supreme Court was thought to be interpretation of text and identification of legal tradition, the people were content to have justices selected primarily on the basis of legal ability. But they know that Harvard Law School, Stanford Law School – yea, even Yale Law School – do not make a man or woman any more qualified to determine whether there ought to be a right to abortion, or to homosexual conduct, or to suicide, than Joe Six-Pack.[211]

Robert Nagel does too.[212]

This leads to a third problem for Kay's 'mixed government,' tricameralism-like defence of strong judicial review. You could never sell it to people upfront and openly. Kay more or less concedes as much when he says:

> If constitutional courts were to respond to this problem [i.e., 'the disjunction between what these courts say they are doing and what they actually do'] by candidly aligning their rhetoric with their practice, a different problem would arise. Such an

---

[211] Antonin Scalia, 'Romancing the Constitution: Interpretation as Invention' in (eds. G. Huscroft and I. Brodie) *Constitutionalism in the Charter Era* (LexisNexis, 2004), 343. See too p.340.

[212] See Robert Nagel, *Constitutional Cultures: The Mentality and Consequences of Judicial Review* (University of California Press, 1989), especially chapter two. In an e-mail to me Nagel also wondered why anyone would expect those trained to find uncertainty and loopholes in rules to be good at upholding constitutionalism's 'locked-in' values. That is an excellent point rarely heard or raised.

> approach would subvert the legitimacy that these institutions enjoy in the eyes of the public.[213]

Hence Kay sees his 'reconceptualization of constitutional courts as discretionary decision-makers in a mixed government [as] a post hoc explanation.'[214] In more straight-forward terms, the Kay gambit requires the public to be kept in the dark. If you put such a role for the judiciary to all of us voters in a referendum or at some sort of constitutional convention it would be defeated, and be defeated badly. Of course I concede that in theory best consequences can diverge from the path of honesty and of openness and of any realistic ability to sell the proposal to one's fellow citizens. But having conceded that, I also think most of us would be more than a little skeptical of the worth of constitutional arrangements that can never honestly be revealed to one's countrymen. For me there is just too much whiff of 'elitism piled on aristocracy' about such arrangements. It smacks to me of the worst aspects of the European Union and much of the (to me inevitable) voter backlash flowing from the paucity of democratic credentials of that supranational body's institutional arrangements.[215]

So that is my response to the Kay gambit and why I think it fails to convince.

3. Even Bigger Doubts about Proportionality

In this chapter's task of fleshing out my doubts about much of the orthodoxy as regards constitutional interpretation in today's democratic world I was tempted just to pass over in silence any mention of proportionality. Or abridging. Or balancing. Or asking about what are reasonable and justifiable limits on rights. Certainly plenty has been written about this topic. In Europe, and indeed Canada, these are the fundamental queries top judges ask themselves when holding up some impugned legislative provision against some enumerated rights guarantee – Is the law proportional? Despite being rights-limiting or rights-infringing, is the law nevertheless reasonable and justifiable in a free and

---

[213] Kay, 'Mixed Government and Judicial Review' fn. 198 above, at p. 221.

[214] *Ibid.*

[215] I detail some of this in James Allan, 'Democracy, Liberalism and Brexit' (2018) 39 *Cardozo Law Review* 879.

democratic society? And that is not all. Heading down this rabbit hole these sort of questions then get broken down into sub-questions. In Canada,[216] this determination of a law's proportionality or reasonableness is sub-divided into four sub-queries. These are: **1)** Whether the law's objective or aim is deemed to pass muster. Is it a legitimate one? Think of national security, say, or public order concerns. The top judges in Canada look to see if this aim or objective is pressing. Elsewhere it might be asked in terms of its being 'proper.'[217] **2)** Whether the law has an appropriate or suitable or rational connection to the identified aim or objective. Does the design of this law pass muster vis-à-vis achieving the above aim? **3)** Whether the law delivers its aim with as few inroads on the right or rights in play as possible. In the current jargon, has there been minimal impairment of the right? Is this the least impinging road that could have been taken? That sort of sub-query. **4)** Whether the law's rights-infringing effects are balanced out by – are proportional to – the important objective being pursued. Is there an overall balance or proportionality at work with this law or provision? That sort of thing, with new cases arguably tending to make the applicable test ever more complicated and thereby affording more opportunities to manipulate it.

Simply setting out these queries and sub-queries is enough to show readers that this sort of proportionality analysis involves rather massive dollops of discretionary judicial decision-making. I would say that it amounts to subjective evaluation piled on subjective evaluation. In a highly skeptical and excellent overview of the proportionality judicial task, Gregoire Webber goes into detail as to where all the discretionary judicial calls or opinions lurk when performing this sort of analysis.[218] For a small sample, how abstractly ought sub-query **1)** to be framed? And what are the criteria for deciding what is and is not pressing? As regards sub-

---

[216] The case giving the leading or best-known articulation or formulation is *R v Oakes* [1986] 1 SCR 103, paragraphs [69] and [70] in particular.

[217] That is the language of the former President of the Supreme Court of Israel, Aharon Barak. See his *Proportionality: Constitutional Rights and Their Limitations* (CUP, 2012).

[218] It is one I recommend to readers. See Gregoire Webber, 'Proportionality and Limitations on Free Speech' in (A. Stone and F. Schauer, eds) *The Oxford Handbook of Freedom of Speech* (2021, OUP), 173-192.

query **2)**, ought judges to look at the law's policy design or its likely effectiveness? And sub-query **3)** throws up all sorts of uncertainty. How do top judges decide what would count as an alternative law that might be less rights-infringing? Is it a moral or technical test? How does one decide whether a mooted alternative pursues the same objective (re-raising the 'how abstractly to frame this' problem above)? And if it pursues it to some degree, but not as well, does that suffice? Sub-query **4)**, the overall balancing or proportionality test, is no better. Cash this out in US terms, of the 1950s and 1960s First Amendment cases involving a balancing of interests,[219] and there is no agreement as to what interests are to be balanced – nor the number in play, how to characterize them, formulate them, balance them, what to do if they do not seem comparable, and so on and so forth. 'Cometh the judge, cometh the favored interests,' in other words. And beyond US shores 'interests' are abandoned in favour of instead balancing – or purporting to balance – values, benefits, effects, burdens, principles, costs, gains, the list goes on and on. That shift is not one that eliminates any of the subjectivity or arbitrariness.

On all this Webber is excellent and his skepticism convincing. Indeed, it is arguable that all these factors are incommensurable except when describing each one with a well-chosen, 'does-the-work-for-you' adjective – 'this vital interest of X as against that mere improvement of Y,' or some such phrasing. Whether that be the case or not, what you end up with when you go down this Canadian and European proportionality road is not so much rights interpretation, and the interpretation of the intended scope of protection of some enumerated right, but rather judges deciding what they do and do not happen to consider to be reasonable on the part of the elected legislature. On this model, 'what you have by virtue of having a … right is a right against disproportionate'[220] infringement. Or more accurately put, you have a right to be protected against *what top judges consider to be disproportionate and unreasonable* inroads. You have what Thomas Poole scathingly considers to be a malleable and discretion-enhancing exercise in the hands of the judiciary, not least

---

219 See *ibid.*, pp. 172-175 in particular.

220 Stephen Gardbaum, 'The Structure of a Free Speech Right,' chapter 12 in fn. 218 above (after fn. 70 in main text).

because 'proportionality is plastic and can in principle be applied almost infinitely forcefully or infinitely cautiously, producing an area of discretionary judgment that can be massively broad or incredibly narrow – and anything else between.'[221]

It is extremely difficult to see this judicial task as compatible with constitutionalism as I set it out in this chapter and elsewhere in this book. These proportionality-mandated tests (calling for evaluations of compatibility, degree of burdensomeness, balancing, proportionality, suitability, minimal impairment, necessity and so on and so forth) amount to value judgement piled upon value judgement. And for at least some of these prescribed value judgements – looking as they do much more like the sort of line-drawing calls involved in legislating in a democracy – it is far from clear what a law degree, years of working as a lawyer, and great experience as a judge contribute (or could contribute) to making them more expertly. Or less subjectively. Or somehow divorced from the core political and moral outlooks the evaluator happens to bring to the table.

Yet this seems so undeniable and obvious that, as I said, I was tempted to pass over it in silence. I resisted that temptation because this European and Canadian approach is so extremely unappetizing that I thought it worth a small section at the end of this Part IV making plain my doubts about this area of constitutional orthodoxy (or at least non-American orthodoxy).[222] But I kept it short and I finished this chapter with it.

---

[221] Thomas Poole, 'The Reformation of English Administrative Law' (2009) 68(1) *Cambridge Law Journal* 142 at p. 146.

[222] It has even been picked up, in a small way, in Australia where I have lived and worked these past sixteen years. In Canada and Europe there are abridging provisions (a global one and right-specific ones, respectively) related to the rights enumerated in the entrenched bills of rights, and so some small excuse for this. In Australia, to my great appreciation, there is no national bill of rights of any sort. And yet the top Australian judges have managed to 'discover' (I would say 'make up out of whole cloth') 'an implied freedom of political communication' and they use this sort of proportionality analysis in that limited domain. In that sense, the unelected Australian judges have simply given themselves the task of asking if the elected legislature's statutes are reasonable, justifiable, legitimate, balanced, appropriate, suitable, proportional, or however you prefer to articulate it. For more detail of my claims as to the deep-seated illegitimacy of what the Australian judges have done see, *inter alia*, James Allan, 'Constitutional Interpretation Wholly Unmoored from Constitutional Text: Can the HCA Fix its own Mess?' (2020) 48 *Federal Law Review* 30-45.

Last Remarks

This has been an outsider's take on much of current constitutional orthodoxy in the common law democratic world. It is an outsider's take that will mostly appeal to other outsiders. I hope, however, that it has been thought-provoking enough that even insiders might be moved to reconsider one or two of their strongly held views. This is a book by someone unafraid of majoritarian democracy who is also skeptical of the foundations on which much of today's constitutional orthodoxy sits – including the offered groundings for the human rights claims that underlie the rights thinking and rights-respecting demands of much constitutional law. I have taken readers on a doubt-filled wander (remember, this is a journey-free book) across much of today's constitutional landscape. I have offered doubts about the prevailing approaches to constitutional interpretation, in all their 'living constitution' manifestations; doubts about how constitutionalism itself is sometimes understood; doubts about fat, substantive understandings of democracy that undercut its 'letting the numbers count' appeal; doubts about those who doubt majoritarianism; doubts about the latest fad, statutory bills of rights; doubts about those who wish to anaesthetize law from politics and top judges from democratic input; doubts about proportionality analyses; doubts about pushing the line that 'living constitution' interpretation somehow locks in all of us voters less than originalist modes of interpretation; and more.

This book has been my attempt to give readers the reasons for my skepticism and doubts about the modern constitutional law settlement or orthodoxy. Nothing more. Unfashionable, perhaps, but with any luck an interesting take. This has been a doubter's guide to constitutionalism in a modern democracy. And not a mention of a 'journey,' 'conversation' or 'discourse' in the entire book.

Indicative Bibliography

Alexander, Larry, 'The Search for Legislative Intent' (2014) 33 *University of Queensland Law Journal* 397

Alexander, Larry, 'Constitutional Theories: A Taxonomy and (Implicit) Critique' (2014) 51 *San Diego Law Review* 623

Alexander, Larry and Sherwin, Emily, *Demystifying Legal Reasoning* (Cambridge University Press, 2008)

Alexander, Larry, 'What's the Problem of Judicial Review?' (2006) 31 *Australian Journal of Legal Philosophy* 1

Alexander, Larry and Prakesh, Saikrishna, '"Is that English You're Speaking?" Some Arguments for the Primacy of Intent in Interpretation' (2004) 41 *San Diego Law Review* 967

Alexander, Larry (ed), *Constitutionalism: Philosophical Foundations* (Cambridge University Press, 1998)

Bentham, Jeremy, *An Introduction to the Principles of Morals and Legislation* (Clarendon Press, 1907 – first published in 1780)

Bietz, Charles, *The Idea of Human Rights* (Oxford University Press, 2009)

Campbell, Tom and Bourne, Kylie (eds), *Political and Legal Approaches to Human Rights* (Routledge, 2018)

Campbell, Tom, Ewing, Keith and Tomkins, Adam (eds), *The Legal Protection of Human Rights: Sceptical Essays* (Oxford University Press, 2011)

Campbell, Tom, Goldsworthy, Jeffrey and Stone, Adrienne (eds), *Protecting Human Rights: Instruments and Institutions* (Oxford University Press, 2003)

Crawford, Lisa, Emerton, Patrick and Smith, Dale (eds), *Law Under a Democratic Constitution: Essays in Honour of Jeffrey Goldsworthy* (Hart Publishing, 2019)

Dworkin, Ronald, *A Bill of Rights for Britain* (Chatto & Winders, 1990)

Dworkin, Ronald, *Law's Empire* (Harvard University Press, 1988)

Dworkin, Ronald, *Taking Rights Seriously* (Duckworth, 1977)

Ekins, Richard, *The Nature of Legislative Intent* (Oxford University Press, 2012)

Finnis, John, *Natural Law and Natural Rights* (Oxford University Press, 2nd ed, 2011)

Goldsworthy, Jeffrey, *The Sovereignty of Parliament: History and Philosophy* (Oxford University Press, 1999)

Harel, Alon, *Why Law Matters* (Oxford University Press, 2014)

Hart, H.L.A., 'Bentham and the United States of American' (1976) 19 *Journal of Law & Economics* 547

Hart, H.L.A., *The Concept of Law* (Clarendon Press, 1961 – this first edition specifically, not the later editions)

Hurd, Heidi (ed), *Moral Puzzles and Legal Perplexities: Essays on the Influence of Larry Alexander* (Cambridge University Press, 2019)

Huscroft, Grant, Miller, Bradley and Webber, Gregoire (eds), *Proportionality and the Rule of Law: Rights, Justification, Reasoning* (Cambridge University Press, 2014)

Huscroft, Grant and Miller, Bradley (eds), *The Challenge of Originalism: Theories of Constitutional Interpretation* (Cambridge University Press, 2011)

Huscroft, Grant (ed), *Expounding the Constitution: Essays in Constitutional Theory* (Cambridge University Press, 2008)

Kay, Richard, 'Adherence to Original Intentions in Constitutional Adjudication: Three Objections and Responses' (1988) 82 *Northwestern University Law Review* 226

Lawson, Gary, 'What is "United" about the United States?' (2021) 101 *Boston University Law Review* (forthcoming)

MacIntyre, Alisdair, *After Virtue: A Study in Moral Theory* (University of Notre Dame Press, 3rd ed, 1987)

Mackie, J.L., *Ethics: Inventing Right and Wrong* (Penguin, 1977)

Mackie, J.L., 'The Third Theory of Law' (1977) 7 *Philosophy and Public Affairs* 3

Murray, Douglas, *The Madness of Crowds* (Regnery, 2019)

Nagel, Robert, *Unrestrained: Judicial Excess and the Mind of the American Lawyer* (Transaction Publishers, 2008)

Nagel, Robert, *Constitutional Cultures: The Mentality and Consequences of Judicial Review* (University of California Press, 1989)

Poole, Thomas, 'The Reformation of English Administrative Law' (2009) 68 *Cambridge Law Journal* 142

Scalia, Antonin, 'Romancing the Constitution: Interpretation as Invention' in (Huscroft, Grant and Brodie, Ian, eds) *Constitutionalism in the Charter Era* (LexisNexis, 2004)

Scalia, Antonin, *A Matter of Interpretation* (Princeton University Press, 1997)

Schauer, Frederick, 'Rights, Constitutions, and the Perils of Panglossianism' (2018) 38 *Oxford Journal of Legal Studies* 635

Schauer, Frederick, 'Judicial Supremacy and the Modest Constitution' (2004) 92 *California Law Review* 1045

Schwarzschild, Maimon, 'Reply – and Gentle Dissent – to Michael Blake's "Democracy and Deference"' (2019) 56 *San Diego Law Review* 929

Schwarzschild, Maimon, 'Complicated – But Not Too Complicated: Sunset of EU Law in the UK After Brexit' (2018) 39 *Cardozo Law Review* 905

Smith, Steven D., *Fictions, Lies, and the Authority of Law* (University of Notre Dame Press, 2021)

Smith, Steven D., *Law's Quandary* (Harvard University Press, 2007)

Somin, Ilya, *Democracy and Political Ignorance: Why Smaller Government is Smarter* (Stanford University Press, 2nd ed, 2016)

Tasioulas, John, 'Towards a Philosophy of Human Rights' (2012) 65 *Current Legal Problems* 1

Waldron, Jeremy, 'The Core of the Case Against Judicial Review' (2006) 115 *Yale Law Journal* 1346

Waldron, Jeremy, *The Dignity of Legislation* (Cambridge University Press, 1999)

Waldron, Jeremy, *Law and Disagreement* (Oxford University Press, 1999)

West, Robin, 'Rationality, Hedonism, and the Case for Paternalistic Intervention' (1997) 3 *Legal Theory* 125

Index

www.ingramcontent.com/pod-product-compliance
Lightning Source LLC
LaVergne TN
LVHW010718210926
848485LV00008B/1447/J